CW01334756

Praise for Daaji and
Spiritual Anatomy

"Exceptional... *Spiritual Anatomy* blends the wisdom of yogic philosophy with practical techniques to unlock your infinite potential."

—**Deepak Chopra**, *New York Times* **bestselling author of** *Quantum Body*

"The challenge for so many of us is how to achieve our purpose in the face of modern life. Through *Spiritual Anatomy*, Daaji offers us the path to take our fragmented lives and integrate them to achieve our highest potential. He also reminds us that the path to elevated consciousness is always through the heart."

—**James R. Doty, MD, Professor of Neurosurgery at Stanford University School of Medicine, and bestselling author of** *Into the Magic Shop*

"Using awareness and meditation as tools for health, Daaji's work brings a most valuable heart into the field of healing science. Daaji gifts readers an important resource for traversing personal transformation."

—**Sharon Salzberg**, *New York Times* **bestselling author of** *Lovingkindness* **and** *Real Life*

"Daaji offers a profound road map and guide, as *Spiritual Anatomy* reveals our opportunity to actively engage the chakras in our spiritual journey."

—**Lisa Miller, PhD, Columbia professor, and** *New York Times* **bestselling author of** ***The Spiritual Child* and *The Awakened Brain***

SPIRITUAL ANATOMY

SPIRITUAL ANATOMY

Meditation,
Chakras,
and
the Journey
to the Center

DAAJI
KAMLESH D. PATEL

HarperCollins *Publishers* India

First published in the US by Balance 2023
First published in India by HarperCollins *Publishers* 2024
4th Floor, Tower A, Building No. 10, DLF Cyber City,
DLF Phase II, Gurugram, Haryana – 122002
www.harpercollins.co.in

2 4 6 8 10 9 7 5 3 1

Copyright © Heartfulness Institute 2023, 2024
Illustrations by Uma Maheswari G.
Heartfulness Meditation practices used with the permission of the Heartfulness Institute.

P-ISBN: 978-93-5699-779-0
E-ISBN: 978-93-5699-864-3

The techniques and methods contained in this book are the result of the author's experience, and this publication is sold with the understanding that the author and publisher are not engaged in rendering medical, mental health, or other professional advice. If expert assistance is required, the services of a professional should be sought. The author and publisher specifically disclaim any liability that is incurred from the use or application of the contents of this book.

Any links or references to third-party resources are provided as a convenience and for informational purposes only; they do not constitute an endorsement or an approval by the author or publisher of any products, services, or opinions of a third party. While the information provided in this book is based upon sources that the author believes to be reliable, neither the author nor the publisher can control the accuracy, legality, accessibility, or content of any external site or resource listed here. Please address any questions regarding third-party content to the owners of the external resource.

Heartfulness Institute asserts the moral right
to be identified as the author of this work.

Not for sale in USA, the Philippines, Puerto Rico and Canada

All rights reserved. No part of this publication may be reproduced,
stored in a retrieval system, or transmitted, in any form or by any means,
electronic, mechanical, photocopying, recording or otherwise,
without the prior permission of the publishers.

Inside design by Bart Dawson

Printed and bound at
Replika Press Pvt. Ltd.

This book is produced from independently certified FSC® paper to ensure
responsible forest management.

O, Sadhu! The one form pervades all.
There is no difference between one drop and another;
The sea and the drop are one.
Sea in the drop and the sea as the drop,

This is the truth.
Behind the drop the sea extends,
The sea supports the drop.
To make the drop realise the ocean
Is all the Reality.

> —Ram Chandra of Fatehgarh,
> Quest of the Highest Truth—
> Hint at the Fourth Stage, Truth Eternal

CONTENTS

Author's Note ix
Introduction: Starting Your Inventure xi

READ AND ENJOY

Part 1: Your Spiritual Anatomy 3

1. Your Inner Journey: The Key to Real Transformation 5
2. Your True Potential 17

Part 2: The Center and the Soul 25

3. The Story of the Soul 27
4. Mapping the Journey to the Center 35

DO AND FEEL

Part 3: Practice and Attitude 47

5. The Heartfulness Essential Practices 49
6. The Secret Ingredient 62

Part 4: Demystifying the Chakras 69

7. Chakras: Common Traits and Locations 71
8. The Four Stages of Flowering of a Chakra 88

Part 5: Emotional Conditioning—Samskaras 99

9. The Elephant and the Chair: Conditioning that Binds Us 101
10. Points A, B, C, and D: The Feeder Factories of Samskaras 108
11. Cleaning the Samskaras: Correct Thinking and Right Understanding 116

Contents

MEDITATE AND TRANSCEND

Part 6: The Heart Region 125

12. Five Chakras of the Heart Region: The Realm of Opposites 127
13. The First Chakra: Acceptance 140
14. The Second Chakra: Peace 147
15. The Third Chakra: Love 154
16. The Fourth Chakra: Courage 162
17. The Fifth Chakra: Clarity 169
18. Freedom from Freedom: The Gift of the Heart 175

Part 7: The Mind Region 183

19. The Mind Region: A Journey to Humility 185
20. The Sixth Chakra: Selflessness 192
21. The Seventh Chakra: Stillness 200
22. The Eighth Chakra: Surrender 208
23. The Ninth Chakra: Insignificance 218
24. The Tenth Chakra: Belongingness 228
25. The Eleventh Chakra: Restlessness 234
26. The Twelfth Chakra: Settledness 238

Part 8: The Central Region 243

27. Entry into the Central Region 245
28. The Thirteenth Chakra: Nothingness 248

Conclusion 257
Glossary 259
Heartfulness Resources 265
Notes 267

AUTHOR'S NOTE

The inspiration for this book came in the fall of 2016, when I was in New Jersey conducting meditation workshops. One evening, I had a vision of the sacred anatomy—all the spiritual research on chakras, the energy centers for the evolution of our consciousness—coming together in the form of a book. That night, I wrote the first chapter, and over the next few days I completed the book's outline.

During the following six years, as I worked on this book, writing many articles on the subject, and conducting training sessions worldwide, I shared the latest research and techniques that were being revealed to me. Spiritual knowledge, like scientific knowledge, is an evolving body of work. As one's consciousness evolves, the experiences become more profound, and new knowledge reveals itself. Whenever a method or new knowledge descends into my consciousness, I test it with a group of advanced associates and gather their readings. From there, I refine the technique further and expand its usage to a broader audience. All through the process, the hierarchy of masters has guided me and inspired me to continue the work they started in the service of fellow human beings.

Spiritual Anatomy is a comprehensive collection of spiritual research on the soul's anatomy and journey. The journey commences from the heart, the pulsing center that unlocks the portals of growth and enlightenment. The heart is the inner guide, the real guru on the journey to the Absolute. We are all connected intellectually, morally, and spiritually through the invisible connection of our hearts, weaving us all into a common grand destiny.

The road to that destiny is paved by pioneers. Hidden in plain sight, even from their own discerning minds, the pioneers are catalysts

Author's Note

of change. Their silent acts of self-transformation will bring about a tipping point of consciousness that will change the future of humanity. Together their hearts beating as one will advance the way of love that will elevate the human condition from belligerent rhetoric, growing intolerance, and rising inequity. These pioneers represent the tip of the arrow in the silent revolution of consciousness.

And today, I introduce you to one of them: You.

Yes, you, who had the option to attend to that pending chore, catch up with a friend, go for a run, or take a nap, but instead chose to pick up this book. Something moved you to make this choice. Some inspiration echoed between the heart and the mind, and you acted. And your action advances the way of love.

The loving energy produced when you live a life guided by the heart goes beyond yourself. It is like a wave of pure air, capable of enlivening the human spirit. In the way of the heart, to work on oneself benefits the multitude. Individually you may be one, but collectively you are beacons illuminating the darkness, like the stars in a dark sky. The collective action of love-filled hearts from various paths will converge and strengthen the wave that will uplift humanity.

The guiding mantra for *Spiritual Anatomy* is read and enjoy, do and feel, meditate and transcend. This applies whether you are an avid reader of wisdom books and identify yourself as a regular meditator or you are just starting out on your journey of self-transformation.

Spiritual Anatomy is written to help you achieve your fullest potential and accelerate the tipping point of our collective consciousness. Nothing would give me greater joy than to see you soar into the realms of the Absolute.

Thank you for taking the first step.

Daaji

INTRODUCTION

Starting Your Inventure

Spiritual Anatomy is the story of an extraordinary adventure where the main character, your consciousness, undertakes an epic voyage to the shores of ultimate reality and steps beyond. For the central role you play in this story, you might call this book the *Story of Inventure*, your inner adventure. Embarking on the inventure means starting down the path to fulfill the incredible opportunity that human life represents. We come from an infinite source, and our soul, the life force within, embodies that endless potential. Your inventure is the journey to actualize that potential.

Spiritual Anatomy offers an in-depth understanding of the journey of consciousness. It charts a path wherein one can attain levels of consciousness that are usually thought of as unattainable without rigorous practices and extreme levels of sacrifice. Through a simple and natural practice, conditions are created within one's heart that express themselves in the form of the qualities. Contentment, peace, love, courage, clarity, generosity, and many other qualities blossom in one's being as their journey progresses. Beyond that, what this journey promises is the flowering of a human being to realize the self and become one with the Source within this lifetime.

The quintessence of nature is simplicity and purity. In your inventure, you come closer to your true nature, and arrive at higher and higher levels of simplicity and purity in your consciousness. The process is simple and natural. Aided by a heart-centered meditation at the core of your inventure, you will find that *Spiritual Anatomy* is a practical guide with descriptions, maps, tips, and techniques, grouped

Introduction

into three sections: Read and Enjoy, Do and Feel, and Meditate and Transcend. The chapters in Read and Enjoy explore the significance of spiritual anatomy and the origin of the soul. The section Do and Feel provides an overview of the core Heartfulness practices, explains the characteristics of chakras (our centers of spiritual energy), and offers guidance to overcoming the limitations on our consciousness. In Meditate and Transcend, you will find an atlas to the chakras to help you preview experiences and conditions that arise throughout your spiritual journey.

Over the years, I have received many questions from practitioners worldwide, and a select few appear throughout the following chapters. In addition, I have included a self-assessment called The Awareness Atlas. Designed by researchers at Heartfulness, it's a consciousness scale that can serve as a barometer for self-growth.

While some of the ideas in this book may feel esoteric, there is no reason to take them on blind faith or even belief. Some of you will trust in these ideas because I share them from my experience and direct perception, but what matters most is your *own* experience. Take a scientific approach, and let the evidence of your own experience guide you—after all, spirituality is the science of the soul. Take the information shared here as a hypothesis and test it out in the laboratory of your heart. Let your practice unveil the gifts of higher consciousness that await you.

With that in mind, I encourage you to keep a journal to record your meditations, take notes, and jot down any questions or doubts that you may have. Understanding comes from experience, and experience comes from practice. And to practice, well, you need more practice. That's where repetition helps. To further support you, a website, https://www.spiritualanatomy.com, has been created to house links for online classes, color illustrations, and a forum to share your questions. Most of all, I am here to support you. As the spiritual guide of the Heartfulness movement, it is my honor and my duty to accompany

Introduction

the thousands of souls who join us in meditation each day. It would be a joy to share this journey with you and learn from each other. Please write to me at https://www.spiritualanatomy.com, and I can answer your questions. Time is short, the journey is long, and now is the moment.

Good luck with your inventure.

READ AND ENJOY

PART 1

YOUR SPIRITUAL ANATOMY

1.

Your Inner Journey: The Key to Real Transformation

A long time ago, a saint and his disciples showed up at the gates of a kingdom seeking refuge. The guards offered food and water to the guests while another guard ran to inform the king. When the guard reported, the king thought for a moment and asked for a pot of water. He summoned the guard to take the pot and offer it to the saint.

The saint accepted the pot as if he'd been waiting for it. He smiled at the guard and asked for a fistful of sugar, which he mixed into the water. The saint stirred the water to make sure the sugar dissolved, then asked the guard to return the pot of water to the king.

The guard, now thoroughly confused, took the pot and raced back to the king. He offered the pot to the king and was about to speak when the king gestured for his silence. The king asked his minister to taste the water, who sipped and said, "The water tastes sweet, your highness."

A smile appeared on the king's pursed lips. "Guard," he ordered, "usher in the saint and his entourage with the greatest respect." Then he turned to his minister and said, "Please make sure they are afforded all comforts for their stay and extend the stay for as long as they need."

If, like the soldier, you are wondering, this is what transpired: When the request for refuge reached the king, he sent a pot full of water to the saint. It was a cryptic message, *We are already at capacity. How shall we accommodate all of you?*

To which the saint responded, *Just as the sugar dissolves in the*

READ AND ENJOY

water and merges with it, we, too, shall integrate into your kingdom and infuse the sweet goodness of virtue and nobility in your people.

The king valued the saint's wisdom and knew that the presence of the wise soul would ennoble his people.

Within each of us is this same daily struggle between the king and the saint. The king represents the everyday hero, the one with responsibilities, desires, aspirations, problems, wishes, opportunities, constraints, virtues, and vices—all packed into this life. We have so much on our plate that there isn't room for anything more.

The saint and his entourage represent our higher potential—the possibility of purpose, growth, and evolution that are knocking at the gate of our attention, ready to enhance our life provided we give them a chance. *And we do* because, deep inside, a voice inspires us to pursue the promise of transformation.

The process of sugar dissolving in the water is the story of integration and merger—the highest ideal of our spiritual lives. The goal of our spiritual anatomy project is to integrate a fragmented existence by merging with higher levels of consciousness and achieve our true potential.

Now, when I say "anatomy," what comes to mind for you? More than likely, you thought of your physical anatomy. Possibly vivid images from the high school biology textbook of the blue veins, reddish muscle fibers, and ivory-like bones. Physical anatomy is an integrated system of organs working together. Similarly, mental anatomy is a connected system of consciousness, ego, intellect, and thinking that work together to create our ideas and emotions. Much is written about the physical and mental anatomies and how to nurture them. But there is a third, lesser-known system, called the spiritual anatomy. When awakened, this subtle energy system of the soul integrates our physical and mental anatomies, making us one with the universal existence and infusing lasting sweetness in our lives.

Your Inner Journey: The Key to Real Transformation

Growth Through Integration

The word *integration* comes from the Latin integer meaning "whole," "intact." When you tend to your spiritual anatomy, you integrate your physical, mental, and spiritual anatomies to function in harmony as a unified whole. With integration, there is consonance between what you feel and what you wholeheartedly express. The heart and mind are aligned, and the alignment creates the circumstances for your growth.

Yogic philosophy has a lot to say on the significance of integration. A definition of yoga is "yoga is samadhi."[1] The words *yoga* and *samadhi* have multiple meanings, and a popular definition of *yoga* is "to unite." Samadhi, commonly understood as ecstasy or trance, is a much grander idea. *Samadhi* means "the state that prevailed before creation came into existence." And that was a state of absolute balance, a state of oneness. So "yoga is samadhi" conveys "a state of inner integration where everything is in balance, order, and harmony, resembling the state before creation."

Imagine yourself in that state of absolute balance, what could you achieve? For a moment, consider the opposite—a state of entropy and imbalance where, lacking peace, the mind is distracted and eventually our life is disjointed and fragmented. Contrast with a state of integration and balance and how that could transform our life.

Growth by integration is a journey in which we incrementally ascend through states of consciousness. It is like a long expedition, with camps for rest and reflection. During those resting moments, we acclimatize to the surroundings and integrate with the environment before proceeding onward. Consolidating what we gathered, as we ascend, our spiritual vision expands from the mundane to the magnificent. This will take time, but interest and effort speed the process.

I refer to this grand journey as the *spiritual anatomy project*. In

READ AND ENJOY

Sanskrit, *yatra*, a sacred journey to the center within, and you, the traveler, are the *abhyasi*, the one who practices. I also use the words *aspirant* and *practitioner* for the abhyasi. No one can force you on the yatra or compel you to meditate. It is a willful undertaking inspired by the heart. But when you do, the heart sets out to speak to you, and you will learn to master the exceptional ability to listen and then muster the courage to abide by the heart's innate wisdom.

The language of the heart is inspiration. When you meditate on the heart, its inspiration flows through your consciousness, creating ennobling thoughts. But if consciousness is blocked with prejudice and bias—spiritual poisons—the heart's inspirations cannot achieve their true potential. Think of the mineral kimberlite gushing up from deep in the Earth's core, cutting through the Earth's layers. If its path is blocked, it loses speed and gets stuck. But when rising unhindered, kimberlite can furnish a diamond.[2]

Think of all the year-end resolutions, commitments, unexecuted promises blamed on willpower, a lack of resolve, and a ruinous habit of judging oneself weak. What we don't realize is that the blocks in our consciousness frustrate our thinking and stall our resolve.

Through the gift of meditation, those blocks can be removed.

When you start your yatra, your spiritual anatomy project, you begin unblocking your consciousness. As a result, the heart's impulses flow more freely, inspiring feelings that create positive thoughts of growth and change. Your thoughts are the mind's feedback to explain, interpret, and rationalize your feelings.

For example, when you feel upset after receiving criticism, your thoughts help you rationalize it by thinking, "I'm hurt because I put in a lot of effort and expected praise." Similarly, when you're excited about a vacation, your thoughts can interpret this emotion by saying, "I'm thrilled because I need a break and have been looking forward to exploring a new place." In both cases, your thoughts provide cognitive feedback to explain and interpret your feelings.

Your Inner Journey: The Key to Real Transformation

Feeling is the cause, thought is the effect, and action is the result. "I think therefore I am" is preceded by "I feel therefore I think." Your spiritual anatomy project works from the center to the circumference: You don't simply change on the outside, you transform from within.

What happens when there is real inner transformation? Instead of seeing a glass as half full or half empty, you see the possibility of the glass designed for twice the capacity. New perspectives emerge, your field of action expands. You perform growth-oriented actions that feel good, encourage you, and create more inspired feelings.

Let's revisit the sequence:

Inspirations from within ⟶ *Change your feelings* ⟶ *Change your thinking* ⟶ *Change your actions*

As your consciousness is unblocked and evolves, you create a virtuous loop of inspired feeling stoking positive thought resulting in purposeful action—a transformation engine. When this engine starts revving, you arrive at a new awareness that makes you realize a conscious purpose and meaning in life, and you work toward that end. You no longer resist life experiences; instead, you imbibe the lessons from the roadblocks you face.

The result of such a transformation is happiness.

For perhaps the first time in your life, you experience happiness that is no longer conditional, that doesn't demand a material incentive. Your happiness is a settled and centered state of being. When you arrive into this happiness, you realize the elementary difference between happiness and pleasure, the McNugget variant of happiness. Nothing amiss with pleasure! We dine at fine restaurants, delight in the company of friends, enjoy a vacation, all of which bring temporary joy to our lives. We *like* pleasure. Sometimes quite a lot! But we *crave* happiness.

Discovering the conscious experience of lasting happiness is an early step in the journey toward integration. You soon discover the mechanisms of inner peace, compassion, and joy leading to sublime levels of happiness of extraordinary worth because that kind of inner peace is sustainable. What I am sharing here is a matter of experience, and you can witness it in your own journey in a short period of time. Such are the results you get from working on your spiritual anatomy.

You may be glad to know that the evidence of science and the wisdom of meditation point to the same truths. In her book, *The Awakened Brain*, Dr. Lisa Miller describes her cutting-edge research on the science of spirituality using MRI studies, genetic research, and epidemiology. About the benefits of working on one's spiritual core, she writes, "We begin to live beyond a 'pieces and parts' model of identity and a splintered, fragmented view of who we are to one another, and to cultivate a way of being built on a core awareness of love, interconnection, and the guidance and surprise of life."[3] The journey from the limited idea of individual self to feeling the universal connection we share with creation to becoming one with creation is the journey of consciousness.

In the future we will see and more and more that science and spirituality echo the same message: Working on the spiritual anatomy evolves our consciousness. An evolving consciousness infuses greater meaning and purpose into life and helps in achieving our true potential. So how can you move in this direction? How do you commit to the spiritual anatomy project with the devotion it requires? Willingness and interest are the keys.

What's Needed from You?

A bird needs both its wings to fly straight. To lead a life of growth and purpose, integrate the spiritual and the worldly life by making everyday acts of life spiritual. Infuse your spirit, your heart, into everyday acts. When you speak, speak from the heart. When you look at someone, look with compassionate eyes. When you see a family enjoying a meal, offer a silent prayer for their well-being. When you see people suffering, help.

The world is starved of hearts expressing themselves with generosity

Your Inner Journey: The Key to Real Transformation

and nobility. Your spiritual actions are silent, heroic gestures that touch the hearts of others. The spiritual anatomy project starts with you, from where you are in life. The responsibilities of family, work, and community are the training ground for love, acceptance, sacrifice, and forgiveness, the foundations for your growth.

All you need are willingness and interest. When you practice of your own volition and invest in self-transformation, you integrate your life with the energy of your soul. You elevate the role of your heart from a biological pump to the vehicle of consciousness.

If you are curious about spiritual anatomy, this book will still serve you well. If you are only interested in the basics of meditation to improve your focus, manage stress, and develop better habits, this book has great resources for you, too. This is your project, and you decide the trajectory you want.

I am here to help. The journey can be long, and it would be nice to have friends along the way. My life's mission is to prepare love-filled hearts blooming as celestial spiritual flowers in the diverse garden of humanity and living fearless, inspired lives. This book is a sincere effort to fulfill that mission, and I hope it inspires you to follow the path of self-realization.

THE AWARENESS ATLAS

If you want to drive from San Francisco to New York City, the simple instruction to drive east may be enough to get you started. But as you progress on the journey, you require more detailed directions, information about places to stay, scenic spots along the way, and so on. The journey from generic to specific is a natural progression.

Similarly, the spiritual journey starts with a general level of self-awareness. As our consciousness evolves, our awareness becomes more refined. We develop precision in understanding the nuances of our inner journey. We experience deeper levels of fulfillment and connection.

The Awareness Atlas is a tool for you on the inner journey. Carefully designed by a team of researchers at Heartfulness, this set of twenty-three questions is an aid for self-reflection. I invite you to take this questionnaire now so that you can reflect on your starting place and then return to it once or twice a year as a check on your growing awareness. This may seem, in some ways, like an opportunity to evaluate yourself, but please think of the questionnaire as a chance to uncover your blind spots. After all, without awareness, we cannot grow.

Taking the Questionnaire

Find a quiet place to answer these questions. It shouldn't take you more than ten to fifteen minutes. I recommend recording your answers in a journal, though a copy of the questionnaire is also available for download at https://www.spiritualanatomy.com. As you read each statement, reflect on how you have behaved over the past two weeks, rather than whether you agree or disagree with the statement and place a checkmark in the appropriate box.

As an example, one question reads, "I accept the struggles and lessons in life." You would consider the challenges you accepted and those that troubled you over the previous two weeks, then select your answer.

One note: A few of the questions ask about the "wisdom of the heart." The term "wisdom of the heart" refers to the wisdom that dawns when you rise above the noise of thoughts, desires, judgments and emotions.

Your Inner Journey: The Key to Real Transformation

NEVER — RARELY — OCCASIONALLY — FREQUENTLY — ALMOST ALWAYS — ALWAYS

RELATIONSHIP TO OTHERS

1. I am receptive to the feelings, needs, and suffering of others.
2. I notice how others react to me at the time of an interaction.
3. I notice my reactions to others at the time of an interaction.
4. I consider the feelings, needs, joys, and suffering of others.
5. I consider the perspectives of others and learn from them.

LISTENING TO THE HEART

6. I listen to the wisdom of my heart (the wisdom that arises when my preconceived notions, desires, judgment, and emotions are silenced) and trust what it tells me.
7. I feel guided in life by the wisdom of my heart.
8. When making decisions and interacting with others, it is easy for me to connect with the wisdom of my heart.

READ AND ENJOY

		NEVER	RARELY	OCCASIONALLY	FREQUENTLY	ALMOST ALWAYS	ALWAYS
9.	To make decisions in any situation, my heart (inner wisdom) guides me from a place beyond emotion and thought.	○	○	○	○	○	○
10.	I trust my intuition.	○	○	○	○	○	○

CONNECTION WITH HIGHER SELF

11.	I feel supported by a deeper reality underlying all of creation.	○	○	○	○	○	○
12.	I feel that I am part of something greater than myself.	○	○	○	○	○	○
13.	I feel a spiritual aspect to my identity, beyond my worldly identity.	○	○	○	○	○	○
14.	I feel that my consciousness is expanding.	○	○	○	○	○	○
15.	I have a feeling of wonder and awe about life.	○	○	○	○	○	○
16.	I have a sense of being one with all beings in the Universe.	○	○	○	○	○	○

ACCEPTANCE AND LETTING GO

17.	I cheerfully embrace situations that are hard, uncomfortable, or challenging.	○	○	○	○	○	○
18.	I cheerfully adapt to life circumstances in order to grow.	○	○	○	○	○	○

Your Inner Journey: The Key to Real Transformation

	NEVER	RARELY	OCCASIONALLY	FREQUENTLY	ALMOST ALWAYS	ALWAYS
19. I embrace all experiences of my life with joy as they unfold.	○	○	○	○	○	○
20. I accept the struggles and lessons in life.	○	○	○	○	○	○
21. I use my self-awareness to realize I have choices in how to respond to situations.	○	○	○	○	○	○
22. My emotions, feelings, and thoughts remain balanced (stable) no matter what is going on within and around me.	○	○	○	○	○	○
23. As my awareness and consciousness change, I adapt my behaviors in order to be compatible with these changes.	○	○	○	○	○	○

Reflecting on the Answers

Remember, your responses are not good or bad, but rather an opportunity to develop a keener awareness of where you are. If you are as objective as possible, your answers for each question can give you a sense of those areas where you might want to focus attention and grow through your spiritual development.

For example, you may notice that you are only "occasionally" aware of your reactions to others at the time of an interaction (question 3). As your journey progresses, you can revisit the questions to see what has changed. You may, for example, find that now you are "frequently" aware of your reactions at the time of interaction,

READ AND ENJOY

suggesting a gradual increase in your awareness of others—a sign of the compassion that blossoms naturally through your journey inward.

In other cases, your score may decrease over time as you become aware of the deeper meaning of the item at hand. For example, at the start, you might give a score of "frequently" to question 18—"I cheerfully adapt to life circumstances in order to grow." As your journey continues, you might develop a greater appreciation for the need for cheerful acceptance and realize that there is room for improvement. Thus the next time you complete these questions, you might score some items as "occasionally" or even "rarely," indicating that you now have a greater awareness of subtle but important aspects of your reaction to life's circumstances. The going down of scores can also be interpreted as the bending of the branches of a tree laden with fruit. The more you have grown, the more you yield.

The questionnaire and your answers become mile markers on your voyage of consciousness. Every once in a while, return and answer these questions again. How does this help? You may have noticed that when we reread a wisdom book, we discover something we missed before. A new idea, a new concept, or a deeper understanding. The book hasn't changed; you have. Like that, your entries over time will reflect the distance you have gone in your Inventure.

2.

Your True Potential

Once, there was a king who had three sons. The king wished to choose an heir who was wise and would take care of the people. So he built three palaces and asked each son to decorate one. The king announced that the people would choose which palace looked the best. But there was a catch: The decoration budget was five copper coins. With such a puny budget, how could one decorate an entire palace?

Angered by the ridiculous ask, the first son scattered bales of hay, bamboo, and straw to show his contempt. The second son thought over the problem for a little longer. He commissioned a local artist to draw charcoal sketches of the king and placed them in every room. The third son sat in the palace in silence. He prayed for guidance to understand the meaning and purpose behind the test. Above all, he wanted to see his father smile.

The answer came, and he placed candles and incense sticks all over the palace. He had some money left over, so he got a sign painted that read, "House of the People." By evening, when the people visited the palaces, everyone was drawn to the golden glow of the candle-lit palace. When they read the sign outside, they brought flowers, carpets, and furniture. Within hours the palace was decorated, and the people helped the king choose the rightful heir.

We all have limited capital, and that capital is *time*. It doesn't matter whether you are rich or poor, literate or illiterate, young or old; everyone grapples with time poverty. The five copper coins exemplify the idea of time poverty—lots to be done and not enough time. The actions of the third prince show what's possible when we discover a greater purpose and meaning in life and work toward fulfilling that potential.

Life is an opportunity to fulfill our potential. Sadly, most of us remain as potential, a seed that never germinates to become a flower. Flowering in a human being is what we call realization. In order to flower, we must become vulnerable, authentic, and open to change. Perhaps now you see why so many of us choose to remain seeds: We're protected by that outer shell—the shell of ego and comfort. So, unless we break through the shell of ego and comfort, we do not transcend the limitations and become limitless.

The spiritual anatomy project unlocks your limitless potential. We work on the body for physical growth, and the laws of biology limit the body's growth potential. The mental realm has more growth potential than the physical. But here, too, after a while, you hit a ceiling for various reasons like age and a slowing learning curve. Compared to the body and the mind, the soul embodies limitless potential. Think of it this way. Between a block of ice, a gallon of water, and water vapor, what has the greatest potential to expand, to grow? It's water vapor. The subtler the medium, the greater the growth potential.

Now, I want to clarify that when I talk about your potential, I don't mean your potential for achievement—to succeed in your job, to buy the right house, to marry the right person, to complete a dozen marathons. I am talking about your inherent potential: your spiritual capacity. It is the core of what makes you human, and what brings you closer to love and connection.

When we neglect our spiritual growth, we miss the chance to realize our full potential. You may not realize it now, imagining that the opportunity will always be there for you. But I would compare it to the feeling of watching the train pull away just as you arrive on the platform, or missing your flight even after you've run through the terminal to make it. You were nearly there. The regret of realizing that you didn't live up to your potential is a heavy burden on one's soul.

Studies have shown time and again that in their final days, people don't regret not working harder in the office or not buying fancy clothes. What they regret is not having poured more love into their lives. They regret not having spent more time with their loved ones and not having their heart thrive in kindness and compassion. They regret the things that they did not attempt.[4] More powerful, a study conducted in 2018 found that most people regret not taking actions that would have made them their ideal selves.[5]

What do we mean by the ideal self? This is the part of us that hopes, dreams, and aspirations are made of. Achieving goals gives us satisfaction, but when we discover our real purpose and march toward it, our ideal self finds its true fulfillment. The light of an awakened heart guides us in this effort. Like the prince who took some time to interiorize himself in the heart and then found his purpose, working on your spiritual anatomy helps you actualize your potential.

The Soul and Its Systems

When scientists want to explain the building blocks of the material world, they look to the periodic table. That table is an integrated system for classifying elements by atomic weight, atomic number, and elemental properties. The Spiritual Anatomy, too, has building blocks that we can quantify: The Soul and its components, the chakras, koshas, and subtle bodies. Let's define each one of them, starting with the soul.

To answer the question "What is the soul?" let's go to the beginning of a person's life, the time of birth. Have you seen a baby being born? Even if you haven't seen a birth, you might have heard a newborn announce her arrival into the world. It's a soft cry that's so full of

READ AND ENJOY

life and so sweet that its memory is etched in the hearts of most parents. But if the baby does not cry, that silence is brutal. Doctors rush to help. After their efforts, if the baby still does not cry, then the family cries out in grief.

Why did the baby not cry? Because something that needed to accompany the body at birth, something that triggers the body into action, was missing. The missing entity is the *life force*. The energy that makes the difference between the living and the dead. The life force keeps you going until the moment it decides to leave the body.

When there is no life force, there is no life experience. Your mind and body function because of the life force. There are many names by which cultures identify the life force, including *soul*, *spirit*, *atma*, *ruuh*, and *neshameh*. One that stands out to me is the name *Kaaran Sharir* in Sanskrit, meaning "the causal body," the cause for your existence. The soul is the subtlest part of your being, the part with the highest potential.

Chakras, which are the centers of the soul's spiritual energy, are the key focus of this book. Koshas are the sheaths around the soul, and there are five of them. Subtle bodies are many, and the four most important ones are thinking, intellect, ego, and consciousness. The chakras are the centers of the soul's energy, distributed through the body. You can think of chakras, subtle bodies, and koshas as the organs of the soul, working together as one integrated system.

In the spiritual anatomy project, we focus on the chakras. For one thing, they encapsulate the subtle energy that powers our transformation. But more importantly, the energy of the chakras pervades the entire spiritual anatomy. It's like having many lights connected to one dimmer switch: When you turn on the switch, all lights turn on at the same time. When you increase or decrease the dimmer, all of them respond.

Soul
Supported by

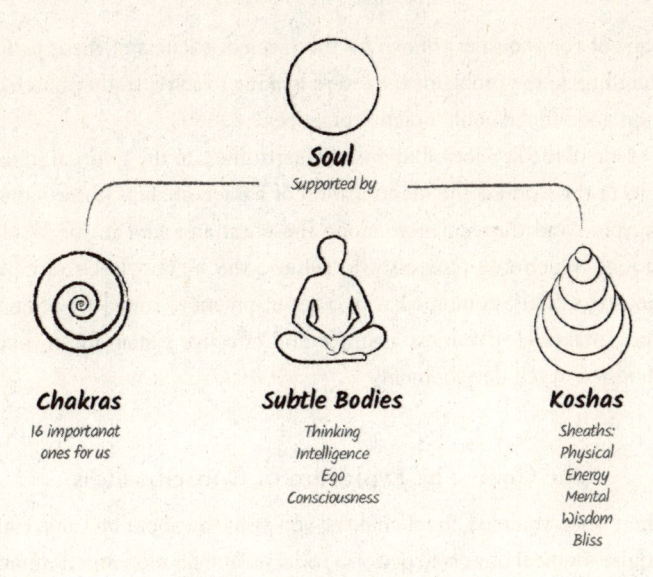

Chakras
16 importanat
ones for us

Subtle Bodies
Thinking
Intelligence
Ego
Consciousness

Koshas
Sheaths:
Physical
Energy
Mental
Wisdom
Bliss

Chakras: A Brief Overview

Just as a river, in its descent, forms waterfalls, channels, and tributaries, the soul, after incarnating in the body, expresses itself at various locations known as chakras. The chakras are the spiritual energy centers of the soul, and there are many of these whirlpools spread across the body.

One way of looking at chakras is to treat them as we do the longitudes and latitudes on a map. We don't see the lines, but we can pinpoint a physical location using the coordinates. Similarly, chakras are energetic entities in the spiritual anatomy, and we can locate their positions on the physical frame.

The most general consensus is that that there are seven chakras. Besides yogic literature, texts in Jainism, Buddhism, and Sufism contain descriptions of chakras, though each tradition points to a different number. These are not contradictions or disagreements. These are maps of consciousness drawn by the revered teachers of these paths according to the problems they were looking to solve, so they charted maps and offered contemplative practices.

One of the key contributions of Heartfulness to the spiritual traditions of the world is the identification of sixteen chakras (three along the spine and thirteen more along the chest area and in the head) through which one progresses to achieve the highest levels of consciousness. This, combined with a set of practices suited for today's times, makes Heartfulness a simple and effective system for anyone interested in self-development.

Our Goal: The Evolution of Consciousness

Often when you read about chakras, you also read about how one can acquire mystical powers to perform miracles and develop superhuman abilities. Levitation does, admittedly, sound fun, but the quest for mystical powers is not our goal. Our goal is to evolve our consciousness, to discover greater meaning and purpose in life, and to achieve our highest potential. Through our spiritual journey, we progress from a human to a humane to a divine level, and ultimately transcend even that.

It's a grand project and one that is exclusive to human beings. What makes human life special is the opportunity to grow one's potential willfully. The caterpillar grows into a butterfly, even if it does not wish to. Its inbuilt genetic design will make it what it ought to be. But for human beings, it's different. We grow physically, mentally, and spiritually, and our growth across these dimensions comes from the choices we make and the actions we take. The freedom to evolve is exclusive to human beings, and that's why across traditions, human life is celebrated as a gift.

There are many paths that can foster one's growth and evolution. One path I confidently recommend is the Heartfulness Way and its

Your True Potential

practices. You may already be following some other system, and the techniques I share here are complementary. You can adopt them along with whatever else you may be following.

The role of the essential practices (which you'll learn in chapter 5) is to create the conditions for the chakras to enliven. Think of enlivening a chakra as a flower blossoming from a bud. As chakras enliven, the subtle bodies evolve. The ego becomes humbler, intellect transforms into wisdom, and thinking evolves into feeling. The koshas, the sheaths around the soul, are also transcended. The net result: Your consciousness evolves, and the soul's potency grows. We do not act directly on consciousness—our body benefits when we work on the arms, legs, chest, and core muscles. Similarly, consciousness is a beneficiary of the work done on the systems of the soul.

As our consciousness evolves, our range of awareness widens, and our perception is refined. With the help of refined perception, we make better decisions in life that are growth oriented. The qualities of the heart take center stage and benefit us in day-to-day life. For example, if you are a manager, you become a better listener and lead your teams with greater success. If you are a homemaker, your poise will create an enriching environment at home for your family. If you are a teacher, you create a receptive classroom learning environment. In this way, qualities like acceptance, peace, love, courage, and clarity begin to blossom in your life, and you become resilient.

There is a flip side also to growing awareness. We start seeing everything as it is without veils. We come face-to-face with everything within us, we see the beauty and the ugliness, we see the opposites and the paradoxes, we see the summit and the abyss within. It can be overwhelming to confront our innermost thoughts and experiences, and it's one of the reasons why people don't like to meditate. It's the story of "Mirror, mirror on the wall...." When something ugly shows up, breaking the mirror won't help. It's not the fault of the mirror. It's not the fault of one's consciousness.

READ AND ENJOY

Once you anchor in the heart and embark on the spiritual anatomy project, you tap into the abundant resources of the heart. Courage, strength, and tenacity begin to develop. The moment we are ready to change, all of nature's forces come together to help us transform. In the process, we become the extended hands of Mother Nature. Not that she needs our help, but she likes to see her children like her: limitless. The spiritual anatomy project takes you from the finite to the infinite, from the ephemeral to the eternal, and from a limited consciousness to the limitless Absolute: the Center.

ASK DAAJI

I come from a religious background, Daaji. We pray regularly and celebrate religious holidays. Do I need to stop these practices to be successful in growing spiritually?

All religions teach about the concept of God's omnipresence, love, and the idea that we are all children of God. The question is not about teachings or observation of belief; the question is about experience. Religions teach, and spirituality helps you experience those teachings firsthand. Do we feel the presence of a higher power? Do we feel universal love? Do we truly believe in the depths of our hearts that we are a part of something much grander?

The tools for experience are meditation, contemplation, and prayer. The Buddha, Jesus, Nanak, Mohammed—all meditated to experience the truth. Your religious practices and the spiritual practices of Heartfulness are not in conflict. When we work on our spiritual anatomy, we progressively experience the truth in our hearts.

It's important to respect the religion we were born into, but it's also crucial to take the next step toward diving into the ocean of spirituality. The yatra takes us from religion to spirituality, from spirituality to reality, from reality to bliss, and from bliss to nothingness.

PART 2

THE CENTER AND THE SOUL

3.

The Story of the Soul

When the heart is at peace, the mind is at ease. Your spiritual anatomy project channels the hallmark quality of the soul: peace. In this peace, you begin the journey to return to a state of inner balance, order, and harmony, similar to the state before creation, the original state. At times, we wonder what the original state was before creation.

Imagine this. You are standing in an open field under a crystal-blue sky. Trees dot the meadows around you, and you hear a stream bubbling nearby. From this setting, crop out all the trees, the meadows, and the stream. Now what do you see? Vast stretches of land and the blue sky. Now imagine all the land is gone, the entire planet disappears. You are floating in the cosmos amid the ethereal glow of stars and the cosmic hum of the galaxies. Now, make the cosmos disappear. All the stars, galaxies, and other celestial bodies are gone. Nothing remains. There is no light or matter around you. All around is the infinite nothingness of space enveloped in indescribable darkness and pristine silence. This was the original state before creation. A state of perfect balance and total integration, exemplified in the idea of "yoga is samadhi." From the original state, creation burst forth.

Your spiritual anatomy project is an endeavor to re-create the original state within yourself. A state of absolute peace where there is no entropy of emotions. A settled state of pure being where you are one with the universal existence, free from all contradictions. It's a life of balance, inspiration, and excellence. Such human beings, centered in the highest, personify the promise that human life represents.

We become one with the original state by merging with it. For two entities to merge, they need to be the same. An oil drop can never merge with the ocean. It will only float on the surface. A tree will never merge with the sky no matter how tall it grows. To merge with the infinite Source, you need to become infinity, too. The final merger is the coming together of two infinities. Imagine how much you have evolved to arrive at that infinite state. You become infinity itself.

The Center: The Source of Absolute Vibration

How did creation come forth from the original state? Through direct perception in a state of superconsciousness, the teachers of Heartfulness observed that in the original state, there existed the Center. The entire creation was merged in the Center in the most subtle form. A single egg contains the entire human being in a subtle form, and the seed contains the tree in a subtle form; so did the Center contain within itself the seed for the entire creation. The seed was in the form of *absolute vibration*.

Here is a way to think of absolute vibration from the perspective of energy and matter. Matter is made of the finest subatomic particles like quarks, hadrons, leptons, and so on. These particles are so subtle that they resemble waves of energy more than matter. They have a directional spin that decides their charge and mass. For example, two up quarks and one down quark make a proton. Take two down quarks and one up quark, and you get a neutron. Combine the atomic Legos of two protons and two neutrons, and you get a helium nucleus. Sprinkle a few neutrinos into the mix, and you have a helium atom. We know that atoms come together to form molecules, which then form compounds. In summary, the wavelike subatomic energy fused together in countless combinations to create matter in its infinite forms.

But what created the wavelike subatomic energy? The raw material that created it must be something even subtler and more essential. Something that's absolute vibration created the subatomic energy, which in turn became material energy, and then became matter. The Center is the source of absolute vibration. The absolute vibration facilitated the creation of energy that then became matter.

Science shows us how energy converts into matter through Albert Einstein's famous equation $E = mc^2$, and matter converting into energy is a common observation: wood burning to create heat, food getting digested to give us energy, and so on.

Your spiritual anatomy project is a way to experience how energy transforms to its absolute. In your yatra through the chakras, you transcend material vibrations and move to subtler states of consciousness. Along the way, you gather evidence of the transformation from matter to energy to the Absolute occurring within you.

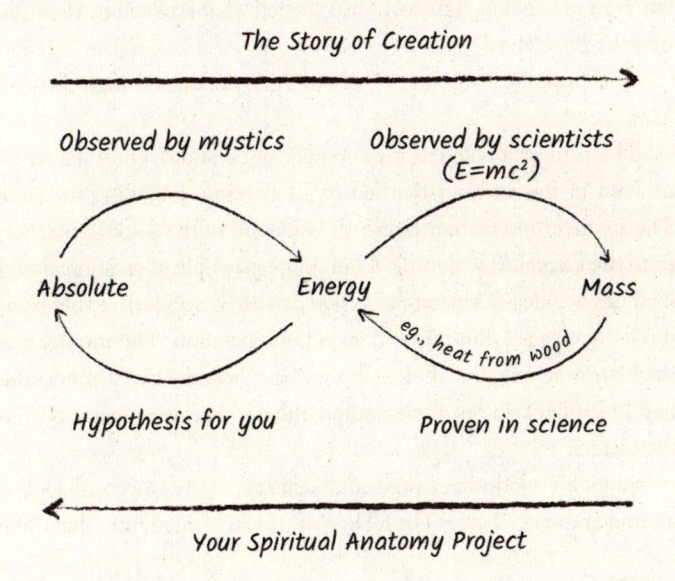

The Story of Creation

Observed by mystics   Observed by scientists
                           ($E=mc^2$)

Absolute   Energy   Mass
                        eg., heat from wood

Hypothesis for you   Proven in science

Your Spiritual Anatomy Project

The Moment of Creation and the First Mind

In the original state, the Center was present. Beneath the Center, there was latent motion. Think of latent motion as the potential for motion—the coils of a wound spring that contain all the potential of motion within itself. In that latent motion, one more thing was present. It was the *idea* of creation. The idea of creation is referred to in Heartfulness as the stir, or *Kshob*. For creation to begin, a pulse, a trigger, was needed. A switch is to be turned on to complete the circuit. Kshob, or the stir, was the switch.

At the time of creation, the stir triggered latent motion, and the revolutions created crevices in the Center. From the crevices absolute vibration burst forth and started flowing outward. Into the vast nothingness of space, the absolute vibration of the Center was unleashed.

Imagine the immensity of the first wave of creation. When nothingness was infused with absolute vibration, it resulted in a celestial bonanza of creation. The first wave created what is called in Heartfulness the *First Mind*.*

The currents of absolute vibration began flowing through the First Mind.

The soul originated at the moment of creation. The First Mind ushered in the currents that led to all creation, including the soul. The moment of creation is also the moment of the soul's separation from the Center. If you think about it, the principle of creation always includes the idea of separation. When a mother gives birth to her baby, it is a creative act, but it is also an act of separation. The mother and the baby were one, but after birth they have become two distinct entities. In similar fashion, after creation, the soul became separated from the Center.

Suddenly alone as a pure and separate entity, the soul looked around and said, "I am." The feeling of "I" was created from that time,

---

* In yogic literature, the First Mind is called *purusha* and creation is referred to as *prakriti*. The idea of the First Mind is found in many religions and referred to by many names: Supernatural, God, Para-Brahma, and so on. I use *First Mind* because it is not bound to a certain religion or sect. It is not confined to forms. And it helps us look beyond an attribute-filled, judgment-dispensing God.

and it continues. As the soul looked around, it feared. Fear is created from the illusion of estrangement and the feeling of I-ness. Fear was the first impression to be deposited on the soul.

The soul, being a part of the Center, inherited the same stirring force that triggered creation. In human beings, this force was inherited in full potency, and it manifested in the form of the *mind*. Other living things also have a mind, but the human mind is unique because of the potency it absorbed from the Center. The human mind can turn the spotlight of attention inward and redirect the course of inner growth. Minerals, microorganisms, plants, and animals all have some level of intelligence, but the human mind is distinct because it can evolve willfully.

Now, the soul equipped with the mind existed as a separate entity, and over time the idea of estrangement from the Center strengthened in the soul. In the months following birth, the newborn child depends on the mother for everything. But over time the child starts acquiring a sense of independence. Young children mimic their parents. They dress like Mom or Dad, have make-believe conversations and tea parties. Similarly, the soul mimicked the Center and got busy with its own creation with the help of the mind. The soul's activity fostered the maturing of the subtle body, which consisted of consciousness, ego, intellect, and thinking that enveloped the soul.

The working of the mind began to contribute further layers around the soul. With each added layer, the feeling of estrangement between the soul and the Center kept growing. Now, the human being exists in the physical form, consisting of the physical body, the subtle body, and the soul. The pure awareness of the soul filters through the layers of the physical and subtle bodies. There was a time when you had an unobstructed view of the mountains, but now you see the mountains from behind the clouds and smoke, wearing three or four pairs of sunglasses. As layers got added, pure awareness became blocked, and what was once just a feeling of estrangement from the Center became a reality. Though most of us no longer feel the embodied reality of our connection, we are souls, part of the Center, covered in mental and biological layers.

I use the words *Source, Absolute,* and *Ultimate* as synonyms for *Center* to avoid the monotony of language, but I prefer the word *Center* because it signifies an inward journey and is apt for the spiritual anatomy project.

In meditation, I once tried to observe the moment of creation. I found myself riding on the first wave, and I slipped deeper and deeper into meditation, so much so that within minutes, I was drowned and could no longer observe. The first wave was so immense that even witnessing it became impossible. Even though it was unleashed billions of years ago, the first wave continues to expand, creating new galaxies, planets, worlds, and souls.

If the idea of an expanding Universe sounds like the physics of cosmology, you'd be right. Even the idea of a stir in the Center that triggered an imbalance and led to creation finds close parallels in physics. James Cronin and Val Fitch in the 1980s were awarded the Nobel Prize for their discovery of asymmetry between quarks and antiquarks. It was the tiniest asymmetry in the balanced state that then led to further steps in creation.

Similarly, elder saints across cultures have left behind works that touch upon the idea of creation and dissolution of the Universe. Yogic philosophy mentions that the current Universe is one of many cycles that will eventually dissolve and give rise to the next cycle. This view is now becoming more mainstream in physics, too, with the idea of the "Cyclic Universe" theory. According to this theory, the Big Bang was not the beginning of time but the bridge to a past filled with endlessly repeating cycles of evolution, each accompanied by the creation of new matter and the formation of new galaxies, stars, and planets.[6]

Many of the teachings that have been handed down for centuries are spiritual truths revealed through direct perception. These truths find close parallels to theories posited by scientists. I do not see them in opposition. Many concepts from science are evidencing long-held spiritual wisdom, and however you come to this information, it points to the existence of a center from which all action emerged. Science and spirituality both reinforce the idea of consciousness as something beyond matter and the physical body, a nonmaterial vibration that propels us forward and directs the course of our lives.

The Soul's Origin and Your Spiritual Anatomy Project

Think of the soul's story from the perspective of consciousness. The soul was a drop separated from the Source. From the time when the soul was pure consciousness, aware of its true nature, to today, when the soul needs to be reminded of its real home, it would seem that we have lost our way.

But here is a more inspiring view of the whole affair. Let's say your father gave you a million dollars and said, "Go and invest this capital. Make something of it." After many years, you go back with a hundred million dollars and your father is delighted with your growth. Like that with your spiritual anatomy project, you can go back and merge with the Center, with a more potent soul. *But Daaji!*, you might protest, *I could also lose all the money and disappoint my father. Is it not better to keep the million dollars?* And you are right. When it comes to money, winning, losing, and becoming greedy are real possibilities.

But in the soul's march to the Center, there is no winning or losing. There is only doing. And when you do, the Universe supports your intentions and rewards your progress because you are now aligned with nature's evolutionary plan. With each meditation, you rekindle the soul's memory of the original state. In the depths of meditation, the soul speaks to you. Through its marquee silence, the soul inspires you and guides you. And each time you follow its inspirations, you are filled with unexplainable peace and happiness. Through incremental experiences of profound peace and happiness, you realize the innate craving of the soul to become one with the Center.

And the keyword is *realize*. Knowing "I am the soul" is a logical conclusion. Believing "I am the soul" is blind faith. But realizing that "I am the soul" is something fantastically profound. That's why in spiritual literature across cultures, the highest goal is *self-realization*, not self-knowledge or self-belief. As you go inward, the realization strengthens, and you reach higher levels of integration. From strength to strength, you add to the potency of the soul.

4.

Mapping the Journey to the Center

In May 1972, in Greve Strand, a town thirty kilometers south of Copenhagen, the local radio station aired an interview. A spiritual teacher was visiting from India, teaching the Danes how to meditate. Many in town found the idea intriguing, and two young journalists named Michel and Toni (Michel sporting long sideburns and both wearing bell bottoms) showed up for the interview. The man they were interviewing was Ram Chandra of Shahjahanpur, my teacher and guide. He was addressed as Babuji (meaning "respected sir") by his students.

Michel started the interview with the question, "What is the purpose of a human being, of human existence?"

"The purpose is only realization, or to realize one's own nature, which is divine," replied Babuji.

This led to a conversation that delved into questions like "Does divine nature make us God?" "What are we supposed to do as humans?" "Will civilization end?" and so on. Around fifteen minutes into the interview, Michel, who was curious to learn more about Babuji, asked, "And now may I ask you another question? It may be a silly question, too, but can you explain who you are?"

"I am what I ought to be," replied Babuji.

I wasn't there in person when the interview happened, but I have heard the recording many times. Each time I listen to it, I can hear how Babuji's answer, charged with precision and wisdom, changed the energy in the room. *Bravos* and *ahas* from those in the room can be heard in the background. The interview continued with questions on humanity, creation, and nature, until Michel looped back and asked, "Babuji, who am I?"

"You are what you are," replied Babuji.

Again, a precise answer with so much to unpack. The interview, which was in a good flow now, abruptly ended. The reason: Michel and Toni ran out of tape! I can't think of a better place than the abrupt ending to continue our discussion.

Consider these two statements, inspired by Babuji's answers: "I am what I am" and "Am I what I ought to be?"

The statement "I am what I am" helps you take stock of where you are. It points out the status quo. The question "Am I what I ought to be?" challenges the status quo. It points toward the horizon. The "ought to" is not the pressure from society or family to conform to or become something. It is the calling, the inspiration from within, to lead an authentic life. When you undertake the soul's journey to the Center, you begin to infuse your spirit into everything you do. You become more aware, responsible, and dutiful. Not that you were not all this before, but now the light of the soul infuses a different beauty into life. You bridge from what you are now, to who you ought to be: the truest expression of your potential.

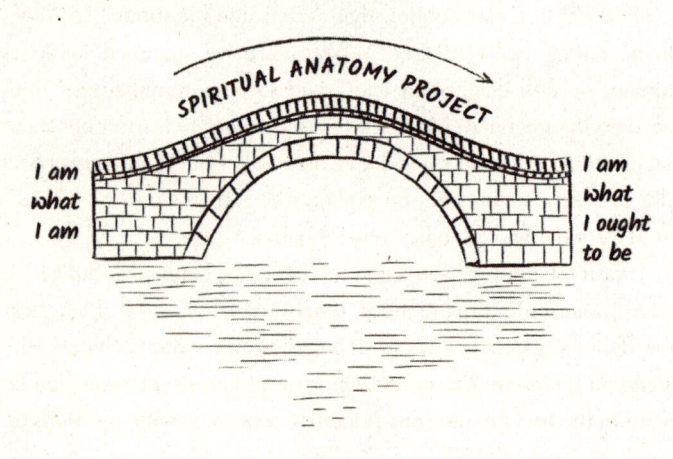

Mapping the Journey to the Center

In your duties as a teacher, a homemaker, a salesperson, a captain of industry, a doctor, a son, or a soldier, you realize the soul's plan at work. You appreciate the lessons you learn in the school of life and live with the depth that comes from authenticity. Sometimes in the past, your duties might have felt like burdens, but now you know the purpose they serve in your evolution. Your thinking changes. Your gaze shifts. As spiritual teacher and author Eckhart Tolle put it, "Life will give you whatever experience is most helpful for the evolution of your consciousness. How do you know this is the experience you need? Because this is the experience you are having at the moment."[7]

In the chapters so far, I wrote about the story of creation, the Center, the soul's purpose, and the evolution of consciousness. There is a lot to process. In times where using voice-guided maps is second nature to most of us, the idea of journeying to an unknown destination, the Center, without a map or any visual tool can seem abstract and even overwhelming.

Here is where the spiritual research of Heartfulness helps us. In this book, I share the research on sixteen chakras that form the map the soul brought with it. It's the map to trace the soul's journey back to the Source. If one can practice as prescribed, these sixteen chakras blossom and raise one's consciousness to the original state. Following the map of the sixteen chakras helps you transcend the esteemed milestones of salvation, liberation, bliss, and other achievements, and takes you back into the heart of infinity, the Center.

The possibility of rising to your highest potential and becoming one with it in this very life, while attending to all your duties and responsibilities, is available. That's what this path is.

The Map to the Center

When we are on a mountain-climbing expedition, we use a topographical map to study the mountain. From the highest point in such a map, descending altitude is depicted in contour lines. The topographical map also shows the locations of the base camps for the expedition. We rest at these camps to acclimatize our bodies to altitude conditions. So, too, is the ascent of consciousness toward the Center.

Each chakra is a camp where we experience a particular condition, such as contentment, peace, awe, surrender, or belonging. The condition is inherent to the level of consciousness at that chakra. In time, that level of consciousness becomes the new normal for us, showing up in the qualities we exhibit in our behavior.

Babuji created a topographical map of consciousness that we can use as a tool in this journey. It is a map of concentric circles that gives us a snapshot of the journey. The idea of representing the journey in concentric circles has a deep meaning. The circle represents unity, wholeness, and completeness. It is unbroken and continuous with no beginning or end, signifying infinity.

Each chakra is an infinity by itself. One can spend lifetimes just going around experiencing a chakra, like an ocean swimmer who keeps swimming the surface of an endless ocean. The idea of concentric circles represents crossing over from one infinity to another as one transcends one chakra to another, like the pearl diver who dives deeper and deeper in search of oysters.

For your easy reference, you can print a copy of this map from the website and stick it in your study, so it becomes easier to refer to it.

In the map to the Center, you can see Center, the highest point. The bands formed by the concentric circles are levels of consciousness represented by a chakra. For example, between circles 1 and 2 is the consciousness represented by the first chakra, between circles 2 and 3 is the consciousness represented by second chakra, and so on. The energy of most chakras extends only to one circle, but there are chakras whose influence extends to two or three circles. You'll notice, for example, that chakras 12 and 13 cover many circles, indicating the vast contours of consciousness these two chakras hold.

Mapping the Journey to the Center

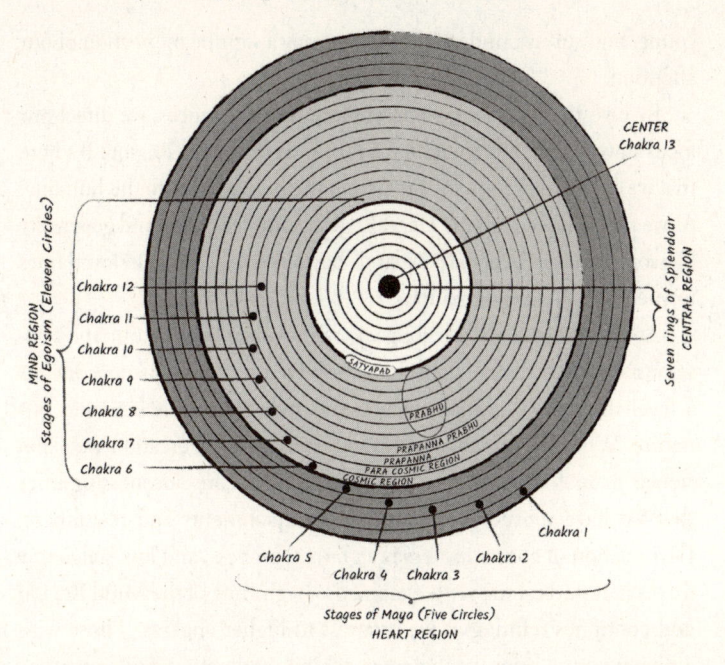

Diagram showing concentric circles with labels:
- CENTER Chakra 13
- Seven rings of Splendour — CENTRAL REGION
- Stages of Egoism (Eleven Circles) — MIND REGION: Chakra 12, Chakra 11, Chakra 10, Chakra 9, Chakra 8, Chakra 7, Chakra 6
- SATYAPAD
- PRABHU
- PRAPANNA PRABHU
- PRAPANNA
- PARA COSMIC REGION
- COSMIC REGION
- Chakra 1, Chakra 2, Chakra 3, Chakra 4, Chakra 5
- Stages of Maya (Five Circles) — HEART REGION

Another thing to notice is that on the map, bands of circles are labeled to depict a region of consciousness. For example, the Heart Region is a collection of five chakras in the chest and neck. Once you have crossed the five chakras of the heart, you cross the Heart Region. Similarly, the Mind Region covers chakras 6 through 12, and the Central Region is the thirteenth chakra.

Same Map, Different Perspectives: Human, Humane, Divine, and Beyond

At the start of our journey, we exist at the human level of consciousness. For many of us, our initial level of consciousness is instinctive. Our bodily needs like the drive to eat, mate, care for our young, and survive understandably occupy a significant portion of our attention.

By investing our energy into contemplative practices, we direct our focus inward and embark on our journey in the Heart Region. It's here that we elevate our consciousness from the human level to the humane. As we progress through the Heart Region, kindness, care, and generosity blossom. Our circle of care expands beyond our immediate loved ones to encompass more of creation.

As we continue on our journey, we advance from a humane consciousness to a divine consciousness. Divine consciousness means a level where love guides our actions, and selflessness becomes our nature. When we feel love within our hearts for all creation we experience an enchanting and joyful state. A divine consciousness signifies that we have moved beyond personal attachments and resistances. Divinization of consciousness is a gradual process, and love's alchemy drives it. It starts at the sixth chakra, the beginning of the Mind Region and continues refining as we progress to higher chakras. Those with a divine nature prioritize balance, exhibit moderation, and epitomize acceptance.

After crossing the Mind Region, one enters the Central Region, the most expansive region of all. Here, all contradictions are dissolved, all polarities settled, and one arrives at the state of universal existence. In the Central Region, consciousness is transcended. Now, one is at the root, which is the potentiality that creates consciousness.

In summary, the map to the Center is the grand design of the spectrum of consciousness that we traverse in our yatra. It highlights the progression from human to humane to divine and beyond. The map to the Center is a useful tool in your daily practice. For example, when you want to know the chakras of the Heart Region or the Mind Region, this map shows it to you. As you go deeper into the topic, this map can become the map of qualities or attitudes one develops. This is a map for you, and you adapt it to your journey. Depending on how you approach your spiritual anatomy project, the map can help you notice "This is where I am" and "Here is where I want to be."

Your Daily Life and Your Spiritual Goals: They Go Together

Given the vast expanse of the inner journey, you may wonder again whether the journey to the Center is possible within your day-to-day life. Perhaps it feels too lofty or aspirational. You may think, *It's easy for you, Daaji, to believe and experience, since you have devoted your life to practicing Heartfulness and guiding others. But what about me? My life is busy. I have many responsibilities and preoccupations. Is it possible?*

It's a valid concern.

And, to answer it, I'd like to tell you my story.

During the summer break of 1976, when I was nineteen years old, I decided to become a monk. I wanted to get away from all distractions and focus all my energy on self-realization. So, one fine morning, I left home. I had no money in my pocket. My only belongings were the clothes I was wearing—a cotton shirt, trousers, and a pair of sandals. I quietly sneaked out and went to an old temple of Lord Shiva, near the river in my village, as the chosen spot to begin my holy journey.

When I arrived at the temple, I was delighted to see a group of *aghori babas* resting at the temple. I hadn't seen aghori babas hang around at the temple before, and I took it as a sign of approval of my decision from the Almighty. All day I hung around this group and I noticed that an elderly person was their group leader, and everyone else took directions from him. By late afternoon, the leader called me to him. Despite his fiery appearance—locks of hair and blood-orange robes—when he spoke, I was surprised by the affectionate voice concealed behind his gruff exterior. When I went closer to him, without asking anything, he said, "Dear son, go back home."

His voice had enormous confidence and regret. I looked into his eyes, and they were drowned in sorrow. He said, "I have been an ascetic for fifty years and I cheated myself. I have not achieved anything spiritually; now I am a beggar roaming the streets from one temple to another. Even if I wanted to, I could not go back home now. Everyone at home has forgotten me. And suppose I did go back, for all these years of asceticism, I have nothing to show for it."

I listened to him quietly. He paused for a minute and looked out toward the river. Then gathering himself, he said, "Son, I can see your search is genuine. Go back home and serve your parents. This is not the way for you."

His wise and practical words struck a chord in my heart. I had no logical argument to refute this man's life experience. I took his advice and walked back home. After a grand span of twelve long hours, my monkhood ended! I sheepishly slipped back into our home and realized that no one had missed me. They all assumed I was having fun during the summer break! That same year, those prophetic words of the elderly Baba came true. A few months after our encounter, I started on my spiritual path with Heartfulness and have never looked back.

Which is not to say that I just traded one path of ascetic spiritual devotion for another. Remember the image of the bird with two wings: the worldly and the spiritual? I have spent almost five decades on this path, and life has continually offered me opportunities to integrate spirituality into every strand of my life.

In 1981, I arrived in America as an immigrant with twenty dollars in my pocket—the proverbial story of an immigrant landing on the shores of opportunity. Over the years, my wife and I raised a family with two boys, and we had our share of tough times making ends meet. Eventually, I built a thriving business of family-owned pharmacies in New York City. I supported many family members and friends in starting their businesses. What supported all my efforts was my meditation practice. Answers to complicated decisions like managing working capital, ordering inventory, and capacity planning would flash by me in meditation. When patients came to me, I dispensed the medicines and along with it the caring connection that many still remember even though I haven't filled a prescription now in decades. At home, too, spirituality was the way of life where I discussed deeply spiritual topics with my children, who delighted in such conversations. Like all of us, I faced many problems and uncertainties and continue to do so.

Does my practice eliminate my day-to-day problems? Not exactly. But it gives me the strength and endurance needed to gracefully accept them and learn the life lessons they bring my way.

Across the globe, millions today practice Heartfulness. Everyone has their unique journey, but what's common is the goal and the practice that takes us there. The practice makes it easier to infuse your heart into all aspects of your life. Centering in the heart, we interiorize ourselves and become loving, accepting, and empathetic. Interiorization, one of the many fruits of meditation, helps us recognize the heart as the central, sacred place one should operate from. In our daily life the heart becomes the habitat for our integrated development.

The secret is finding a practice that integrates seamlessly into your daily life. Understanding comes from experience, and experience comes from practice. The goals you wish to achieve, the answers you seek, and the transformation you want to create are all possible through practice.

ASK DAAJI

I am curious and willing when it comes to evolving consciousness, but I admit that I'm a skeptic at heart. How can I proceed in my journey?

We often think of spirituality in opposition to science, but I do not believe this to be the case. One of the definitions of science is *the application of reason to experience*. Spirituality is, at its core, an experience, and there is much to be gained by applying the same careful observation and logic to our spiritual lives. You wouldn't continue a diet plan if it doesn't help you. You wouldn't spend time on a course if it didn't help you improve your skills. Why should it be any different when you work on your spiritual anatomy? Your inner progress should be measurable. For this, we borrow from the scientific method. In the scientific method, we take a hypothesis and then conduct experiments to prove whether the hypothesis is true or not.

Take the same approach to spirituality. Whatever I teach, take it as a hypothesis. Your heart is the laboratory. Experiment there and measure your experience. Arrive at the truth through your own encounters. Till then, it's only a theory, a belief that you uphold.

DO AND FEEL

PART 3

PRACTICE AND ATTITUDE

5.

The Heartfulness Essential Practices

Heartfulness is precisely the feeling the word evokes: a life guided by the wisdom of love. Where there is love, there is inspiration, enthusiasm, and energy. There is courage and compassion. There is hope and growth. Heartfulness practices imbibe the essence of love. It is a system of Raja Yoga adapted to support the busy and challenging lives that we all lead today. To that end, there is no *You must do this* or *You have to follow this* in Heartfulness. The system is designed to align with the body's natural rhythms and energy flow, helping one progress faster. For this reason, the system is also known as the Natural Path, although the name Heartfulness is more prevalent now.

Heartfulness practices offer self-paced techniques that evolve your consciousness and integrate your spirit into daily life. Each day becomes a day of experience, a day of positive change that creates a microshift inside, which keeps you going further. The essential practices of Heartfulness include relaxation, morning meditation, evening cleaning, and nighttime prayer. (Later in the book you will find supplemental practices to deepen the meditative state and to overcome fear and anger.)

As we have talked about, willingness and interest are the only prerequisites for the practice. If you are someone with good self-discipline, that's wonderful. But if you are someone dealing with a few blows in life, someone recovering from pain, or some other challenge that dented your confidence, don't worry. The practices are self-paced and simple, and whatever time you invest, it's helpful. If you have only ten minutes to meditate, start with that. If you can spare ten minutes in the

DO AND FEEL

evening to do your cleaning, do that. If you are commuting to work and feel like meditating, go ahead. This is your practice to fulfill your deepest aspiration. You decide how and when you want to get there.

The Heartfulness practice works in the depths of your heart, inspiring your free will. It ignites an interest in yourself—to become a better person, to become kinder, more generous, more courageous, and more loving. And this transformation usually happens without you being acutely aware of it. You might feel a change taking place within, but it's only when others point out and remark, "Hey, you've changed. What are you up to these days?" Then you ponder over how you have changed.

It's important to point out that all spiritual training at Heartfulness is offered for free. Since the Heartfulness movement's inception in the late 1800s, training has been free. One cannot sell spirituality. It can only be shared with whoever is willing. It doesn't matter which country, caste, creed, or religion you belong to. If the heart is willing, spiritual essence descends into it.

Relaxation

Relaxation offers progressive calming to the body. It also helps empty the vestibules in the body. There are twenty-eight vestibules from head to toe, and they act like dumpsters that collect the excessive blocks within the system. Relaxation empties the vestibules. You can do the relaxation at any time, and it is especially useful before starting meditation.

HEARTFULNESS RELAXATION

1. Sit comfortably and close your eyes softly and gently.
2. Begin with your toes. Wiggle your toes. Now feel them relax.
3. Feel the healing energy of Mother Earth move up into your toes, feet, and ankles. Then up to your knees. Relax the lower legs.

4. Feel the healing energy move farther up your legs. Relax your thighs.
5. Now, deeply relax your hips, lower body, and waist.
6. Relax your back. From your tailbone to your shoulders, feel your entire back relaxing.
7. Relax your chest and shoulders. Feel your shoulders simply melting away.
8. Relax your upper arms. Relax each muscle in your forearms and your hands, right to your fingertips. Feel the energy gently flow out from the fingertips.
9. Relax your neck muscles. Move your awareness up to your face.
10. Relax your jaw, mouth, nose, eyes, earlobes, facial muscles, forehead… all the way to the top of your head.
11. Feel your whole body completely relaxed. Scan your system from top to toe, and if there is any part of your body that is still tense, painful, or unwell, feel it being immersed in the healing energy of Mother Earth for a little while longer.
12. When you are ready, move your attention to your heart. Rest there for a little while. Feel immersed in the love and light in your heart.
13. Remain still and quiet, and slowly become absorbed within.
14. Remain absorbed for as long as you want, until you feel ready to come out.

Meditation

Morning hours are best suited for meditation since starting your day with meditation can help you set the right tone for the rest of the day. Additionally, the body's energy flow is inward during the early morning hours, and meditation is the act of going inward. So, meditation in the early mornings means you are going with the flow of nature's currents, and it's easier to slip into a deep meditation. If you're not a morning person, don't worry. You can fit meditation into your routine once you wake up and get fresh. The peaceful state of mind that comes with meditation can help you approach the rest of your day with greater ease and clarity.

Choose a place where you can meditate without being distracted, preferably at the same place and time daily. Fixing a time is especially helpful because it helps you slip into meditation with greater ease. Turn off your phone and other devices. (Yes, all the way off, not just on silent mode.) Sit with your back upright but not rigid. Be comfortable. Gently close your eyes, and if you need to, take a couple of minutes to relax your body using the Heartfulness Relaxation. When you're ready, turn your attention inward and begin.

HEARTFULNESS MEDITATION

1. Turn your attention inward and take a moment to observe yourself.
2. Then, suppose that the Source of divine light is already present within your heart, and that it is attracting you from within. You are drenched in love, feeling every cell of your being drowned in this subtle vibration, with an attitude of joy.
3. Gently relax into that feeling. If you find your awareness drifting to other thoughts, do not fight them but also do not entertain them. Let them be, while kindly reminding yourself that you are meditating on the Source of divine light in your heart, and direct your mind back to that feeling of joyful presence.
4. Allow yourself to become absorbed within.
5. Remain absorbed within this deep silence for as long as you want, until you feel ready to come out of meditation.

The idea of all yogic practices is to make the mind resonate with the stillness of the soul. When the mind resonates with the stillness of the soul, that is the moment of realization. In that moment, we become whole. We become centered. This centeredness gives one a settled feeling.

A steady and settled mind feels happy. If that settledness is not there, then one keeps jumping from one thing to another without any resolution. There will be no closure, and one is left with a feeling of dissatisfaction and a loss of inner peace. Settledness is the key, and meditation done correctly will automatically make you feel settled.

ASK DAAJI

I have a constant chatter of thoughts going on in my mind. I want to meditate, but I am not sure I can. What do you advise?

One of the most common questions I receive from new meditators is the challenge of thoughts arising during meditation. The mind's nature is to produce thoughts, just as the eyes are meant to see and the ears to hear. During the day, the constant chatter of thoughts does not bother us that much, but during meditation, we become acutely aware of the disarray created by thoughts. We notice the mind wandering from one idea to another. Meditation helps us appreciate the need to regulate the mind and channel its capacities.

Within a few weeks of Heartfulness meditation, the chatter of thoughts goes down significantly. If thoughts bother you excessively, from time to time, you can try one of these tips:

1. Try doing some breathing exercises before you begin your meditation.
2. If there are many thoughts during meditation, try to pause breathing for a few seconds and then continue the meditation.
3. If thoughts persist, gently open your eyes. Stay seated and take a few deep breaths. Then close your eyes again.

DO AND FEEL

> One of the other things I would do is to read some spiritual literature. Perhaps it is a page from this book, some poetry you like, or a particular religious text. Often, it will put your mind in a spiritual space where it is easier to slip into presence with the heart and meditate.

Cleaning

The second pillar of your practice is evening cleaning. It is your detox and rejuvenation routine. At the end of the day's work, at around sunset time, doing the cleaning helps you eliminate all the emotional complexities and impurities gathered during the day. Cleaning is like taking a dip in a serene pool and rejuvenating yourself. It's suggested to do cleaning in the evening because at this time the energy flow is outward, so it becomes easier to expel the heaviness from the system.

The key is to have a nonjudgmental attitude toward whatever complexities and impurities are being removed. Simply affirm that all complexities and impurities are being cleaned, and be confident in the affirmation you offer.

> **HEARTFULNESS CLEANING**
> 1. Sit in a comfortable position with the intention to remove all the complexities and impurities accumulated during the day.
> 2. Close your eyes and relax.
> 3. Imagine all the complexities and impurities that are leaving your entire system.
> 4. Let them flow out from your back in the form of smoke, from the area between your tailbone (at the base of your spine) and the top of your head.

The Heartfulness Essential Practices

> 5. Remain alert during the entire process without brooding over the thoughts and feelings that arise. Try to remain a witness to your thoughts.
> 6. Gently accelerate this process with confidence and determination.
> 7. If your attention drifts and other thoughts come to mind, gently bring your focus back to the cleaning.
> 8. As the impressions are leaving from your back, you will start to feel lighter.
> 9. Continue this process for twenty to twenty-five minutes. Initially you can start with ten minutes and build your capacity.
> 10. When you feel light within, you can start the second part of the process.
> 11. Feel a current of purity coming from the Source entering your system from the front. This current is flowing into your heart and throughout your system, saturating every particle.
> 12. You have now returned to a more balanced state. Every particle of your body is emanating lightness, purity, and simplicity.
> 13. Finish with the conviction that the cleaning has been completed effectively.

Prayer

There is an experience from Shri Parthasarathi Rajagopalachari's (or Chariji) time that I want to share. After Babuji, Chariji led the Heartfulness movement. He was a prolific teacher, a relentless worker, and a giant among men. I spent many years under the tutelage of Chariji. Once, while traveling in Europe with him, we were stranded because of a storm and were put up at an airport hotel. Rooms were scarce, and I was in the same room with Chariji. Not to disturb him, I remained quietly in my bed in the morning. I noticed him sitting on the corner of his bed with his eyes closed, and he seemed to be melting away into thin air. Suddenly the atmosphere in the room changed—it was vibrating with a very special energy.

When he was done, I asked, "Master, what were you doing? It was so special. It was unique. I have never seen anything like this with my eyes open."

"Oh, I was praying," replied Chariji.

What did I learn from this experience? Chariji was there but not there. He had totally submitted, dissolved himself in thin air. We should offer prayer like that.

Prayer is a state of being, a song that hums in the humble heart. The words of any prayer are but a bridge to lead you into a state of interiorization. In this state one is carried on the waves of love into the depths of the heart, into a union with the higher self.

Before going to bed, take a moment to reflect on your day. Consider what you did well and where you can improve. Make a quiet determination to do better and turn inward for guidance from the Source as you repeat the words of the prayer below. Meditate for a few minutes over the true meaning, feeling the words resonate in your heart.

A few notes here on the use of the word "Master" in the first line of this prayer. It refers to the inner guide, the Source already present within each of our hearts. In the East, people use the words *guru* and *master*, more so than in the West. In Heartfulness literature also, you will see these words used. The word *master* always refers to the source within. The role of a teacher is to help you realize the inner connection you already have.

When I use the word *master* for my teachers, it is out of my reverence and respect for them. In my eyes, they are masters of spirituality because they mastered the self and integrated spirituality into all aspects of life. Using the word *master* in this context is no different from using it to refer to a master painter, master sculptor, or master carpenter—all of whom have mastered their craft.

And what about the word *guru*? It is a Sanskrit word. The literal meaning of *guru* is "one who dispels darkness." The guru is someone who dispels the darkness of ignorance through the light of knowledge.

The Heartfulness prayer I share here was conceived in the early 1900s. In deference to the teachers who came before, the language of the prayer has been kept intact, though we recognize that it may be challenging for some. You are welcome to change the word *master* to *Source* or *God* or change *slaves* to *servants* if those resonate more for you. I offer it here in its original form with the hope you can connect with the essence of the prayer and benefit from it.

HEARTFULNESS PRAYER

Sit comfortably, gently close your eyes, and relax. When you are ready, repeat the words of the prayer quietly to yourself:

O Master!
Thou art the real goal of human life.
We are yet but slaves of wishes
putting bar to our advancement.
Thou art the only God and Power
to bring us up to that stage.

Now silently contemplate these words a second time and go even deeper into this feeling. Allow yourself to be absorbed in the feeling beyond the words. Allow yourself to melt in this prayerfully meditative state as you go to sleep. In the morning, reconnect yourself by silently offering this prayer once before you start the Heartfulness Meditation.

How to Find a Teacher

If you would like to work with a teacher as you begin your practice, there are three options. All of these are free and available for anyone to use. We would be glad to see you.

DO AND FEEL

Option 1: Learn to Meditate with a Preceptor

Preceptors (or prefects, trainers) are trained to offer instruction in the practice of Heartfulness. Preceptors typically undergo years of training and individual practice, after which they volunteer for this work. The meditation sessions they offer are also called sittings, and they are an essential support for individual meditation as well as group meditations. The key role of the preceptor is to support you in your practice. For example, if you are struggling with intrusive, bothersome thoughts during meditation, you can call a preceptor to get a couple of one-on-one meditation sessions.

If you are new to Heartfulness, I recommend at least three introductory sittings to help you orient to the Heartfulness practices and understand them well. Thereafter, you can also work with a preceptor to receive individual sittings as your schedule permits. No fees are charged by the preceptor. It is a volunteer service. To find a preceptor near you and start the meditation practice, go to https://heartspots.heartfulness.org, and there you can find preceptors in your area.

Option 2: Join the Heartfulness Masterclass

You can join a three-day masterclass online and learn the essential Heartfulness practices. Here is a link for the masterclass: https://heartfulness.org/us/masterclass/.

Option 3: Download the Heartfulness App

Download the Heartfulness app (available on the Apple store and the Google Play store). You can set up your profile on the app and start your practice. When you sign up on the app, first start with the three introductory sessions. After that, you can request individual meditation sessions on the app.

Yogic Transmission:
The Catalyst for Your Journey

Seventy-three generations before Lord Ram Chandra of Ayodhya, there lived a great yogi. His name and other details of his life are unknown. What is known of him is that he devoted much of his time pondering over a method that could help human beings achieve freedom from problems and realize their full potential. This yogi was a highly elevated soul, swimming in the Central Region (described later in the book). After pondering long over the subject, the great yogi discovered Transmission.

Transmission can be defined as the utilization of divine energy for the transformation of a human being. I use the word *energy* because I don't have a better alternative. Energy has a wide spectrum. The material world is a dense expression of energy in the form of matter. There is a subtler expression of energy that we call life energy, or *prana*. Then there is a spectrum of energy that remains as it is, unchanged like a catalyst, and enriches whatever it touches. That energy is Transmission, also called *pranasya-prana* (the life of life) or *adi shakti* (the original force).

Transmission is the spectrum of energy resembling the absolute vibration that emerged from the Center. Using Transmission, the inner journey is greatly accelerated and helps one make progress that otherwise would have taken hundreds of lifetimes.

Because of Transmission, the merger with the Center—the highest goal—has become possible within one single lifetime. Previously, it would take an untold number of lifetimes to elevate one's consciousness back to the level of the Absolute.

For reasons unknown, the knowledge of harnessing Transmission for human transformation was lost over time. Maybe the teaching tradition did not spread far and wide. Maybe there was a downfall in

DO AND FEEL

society, and this wisdom was lost. Or perhaps Mother Nature's plans were different, and in due course the knowledge faded away. Whatever the reason, the knowledge of Transmission was lost. Transmission as divine energy would still descend because of the right environment created by saints and devotees through their love and devotion. But this was not the same as having a meditation system designed with Transmission at its core.

For thousands of years, this was the status quo. In 1873, the status quo was disrupted with the birth of Ram Chandra of Fatehgarh. From childhood, he had a deep awareness of his purpose, which was to lay the foundation of a spiritual legacy. His thirst for the divine and unrelenting craving to become one with the Absolute made him an ardent student of the self. It is said that within seven months of rigorous practice, at the age of twenty-one, Ram Chandra achieved self-realization—a feat etched in golden letters in the ethereal records of spirituality. Moreover, Ram Chandra of Fatehgarh rediscovered Transmission and started using it to serve the people who came to him.

The word spread of a guru with whom people meditated and were transformed. Locals from nearby villages began thronging at the gates of the master, who spoke little, asked for no money, did not insist on any orthodoxy, and offered meditation that transformed whoever came. Out of love and respect for him, people began addressing him as Lalaji (meaning "respected sir" in the Hindi language).

After Lalaji, his protégé—who also shared the name Ram Chandra (of Shahjahanpur) and was fondly called Babuji—continued to refine the system. The spiritual partnership of Lalaji and Babuji created the system of Heartfulness meditation, which is a gift for all of us. Today we have a simple system with a universal appeal and that is suitable for a normal householder with many duties.

The research team at Heartfulness is conducting various studies all over the world, in collaboration with scientific laboratories, academic centers, and universities, to measure and explain the effectiveness of meditation aided with Transmission. These are early days, yet we are already seeing promising results from the projects. Studies looking at brain wave patterns in EEGs have shown that Heartfulness meditators (i.e., those who meditate with the benefit of Transmission), both new and seasoned, are able to experience deeper, calmer states when compared to nonmeditators.[8] Other studies have also reported reductions in stress and burnout,[9] epigenetic modulation,[10] and improvements in well-being and sleep quality,[11] thus pointing toward the beneficial impact of Heartfulness practices aided by Transmission on human lifestyles and quality of life.

What the science helps us validate, we have already experienced in our own hearts. The conviction of one's own experience is critical for inner progress and is not to be discounted. Experience helps you cast the veils of belief aside. It unmasks doubts and helps you on the inner journey. Equipped with the practices and an understanding of the goal, the coming chapters of the book will reinforce the mantra: Read and Enjoy, Do and Feel, Meditate and Transcend.

6.

The Secret Ingredient

Once there lived a seer who meditated with great austerity. One day, a young villager was touched to see the seer drowned in meditation. Out of reverence, he bowed and offered his greetings in silence. The seer felt the young man's presence and opened his eyes. He was pleased to see the young man and asked if he would also like to meditate. The young man was a simpleton, and even though he didn't know much about the inner journey, he readily agreed. So the seer asked the man to sit under a tree next to him, and guided him through meditation.

As they meditated, a bright ball of energy descended and spoke to them: "Blessed souls, your efforts have knocked at the gates of the Lord, and you both shall be liberated soon."

Hearing this, the seer said, "Thank you! My prayers have been answered. When will that blessed moment arrive?"

"In the third life from now, you will be liberated, holy one," said the light.

Hearing this, the seer became downcast. Perhaps he was expecting liberation in this life, maybe at that very moment. Who knows?

The young man then asked, "When will I be liberated?"

"Count the leaves on the tree you are meditating under," the light said. "It will take that many lives, and your liberation is guaranteed."

Hearing this, the young man started dancing with joy. The seer couldn't understand this behavior and asked the young man, "Why are you dancing up and down? What's the matter with you?"

"Didn't you hear, sir?" the young man asked. "The Lord just

The Secret Ingredient

granted me liberation. How does it matter *when* I get liberated? One day, I will be right up there with the maker."

As soon as the young man spoke these words, the light said, "Son, your attitude is worthy of the Lord's court. This life shall be your last, and you will be liberated at the end of it."

So saying, the light disappeared.

This story has many lessons, but the biggest takeaway is about the *attitude* with which we approach life. In the case of this story, gratitude transformed the young man's destiny. In all walks of life, the right attitude ennobles our actions. Your attitude is the secret ingredient to your success.

Be it meditation, writing a letter, or making a sandwich, the attitude with which we work adds a dimension that shapes our inner being. In any task, what we do accounts for 5 percent, and the remaining 95 percent is the attitude with which we do it.

You acquire your attitudes through your upbringing and life experiences. You also inherit some of your attitudes from your parents. You can also actively cultivate attitudes. How you *think* or *feel* about something or someone is guided by your attitude. Attitudes are so ingrained in us that we aren't aware of how they shape our destiny. Your life is an expression of your attitudes.

Your active focus on cultivating beneficial attitudes helps to accelerate your progress in your spiritual journey. Think what happens when you are digging a well for water. You dig from the top and keep digging deeper (outside in), while the water under the earth is also gushing up to meet the surface (inside out). When it comes to your spiritual journey, the outside in is your cultivating attitudes, and the inside out is the meditation practice doing its work. The two work in tandem.

What are some attitudes that we should cultivate? Why these

attitudes specifically? There are three core attitudes that will serve you in your journey, which I call the mother tincture attitudes.

The Mother Tincture Attitudes

In some forms of medicine, there is the idea of a mother tincture. It is the base formulation from which other medicines of varying potency are created. The concept of the mother tincture applies to cultivating attitudes also. Some core attitudes are like the mother tincture, from which other attitudes emerge. From the early days of your practice, keep an eye out for developing the core attitudes. It will lay a strong foundation for your inner development. It will also help you in your day-to-day affairs.

The three mother tincture attitudes are:

- Sense of urgency
- Humility
- Liveliness

These three are not in any order of priority. They are all equally important. Whichever appeals to you, set your intention on it. Your intention is the subtle force that activates the will and helps you actively cultivate these attitudes in your day-to-day life. Let's take a look at each in more detail.

Sense of Urgency

In any endeavor, a sense of urgency is crucial. It is the *first step* to creating change. Without a sustained sense of urgency, efforts become lukewarm, and complacency sets in. In your journey to the Center, a sense of urgency helps you focus on your priorities. Make a habit of asking yourself this question: "What's the most important thing to do in this moment?" It will help you re-center and cultivate a sense of urgency toward your goal.

The Secret Ingredient

As urgency increases, your eagerness to get to the goal also increases. Questions such as "What am I here for?" "What do I need to do?" and "What is my goal?" become more frequent. Each time these questions surface in your mind, they leave a ripple of restlessness in your consciousness. These ripples linger like the ones on a quiet lake disturbed by a pebble thrown into it. The more your consciousness evolves, the greater the ripples of restlessness. You could say that the spiritual anatomy project is an endeavor of growing restlessness for the goal.

But don't worry—the restlessness I am writing about is nothing like when you are late for a flight or your takeout is delayed. Neither is it the unhealthy restlessness that leads to anxiety and other problems of despair. This is spiritual restlessness. It propels you toward the soul's true purpose: to grow and evolve. If you have been in love, recall the restlessness with which you waited for your lover. Amplify this many times, and you can get a whiff of the restlessness I talk about.

The spiritual restlessness created in your meditation finds an ally in the sense of urgency you cultivate. Together, they help you stay focused on the goal. Alertness, initiative, and agility are natural outcomes of a sense of urgency.

Now, be mindful that urgency is not desperation. Urgency is a positive driving force you create, but desperation is a knee-jerk reaction grounded in fear or scarcity. A sense of urgency helps you focus on making progress toward the goal daily, whereas desperation creates a flurry of activity that fatigues you. A sense of urgency helps you counter inner entropy and creates protection against a lukewarm approach to life.

Humility

Humility is the most sublimated state of ego. Humility is not flattery or servility. Instead, humility is a sign of great self-awareness, where you are aware of your smallness in front of a much bigger ideal. Such awareness gives you a feeling of insignificance that helps you grow. A humble person is respectful by nature and cultivates reverence in one's heart. Just as a tree laden with fruit bends naturally under the weight of its gifts, a human being bearing spiritual fruit becomes increasingly accessible to one and all.

Humility attracts grace. When a low-pressure area is created in the atmosphere, the wind rushes in to fill the void. In the same way, when you create space within by sublimating the ego, you create a low-pressure area in the heart, which is then filled with grace. When there is humility within, grace descends automatically. And grace is a catalyst for inner progress.

Liveliness

Long-drawn faces, gloomy moods, and irritable behaviors stretch the journey. But a song in the heart, a smile on the lips, and a spring in the step make the journey livelier. Cultivate an attitude of liveliness.

Become livelier, more cheerful. Carrying the baggage of sadness, sorrow, and unhappiness will not work. You may be justified in feeling sad. How long would you like to carry that sadness with you? Is sorrow that precious? Is it worth storing it in your beautiful heart and burdening it? And in almost all cases, the reason for sadness will always be another person, who is also God's creation. So, to bring about transformation, be livelier. Throw away the deadwood that fixates you. Stay pliable in spirit. Emotional and mental flexibility comes from the openness of the heart. A sad, heavy heart cannot stay open. Only a lively heart is open and flowing.

※

A few years ago, on a summer afternoon, I was driving back home after a meeting with a team of volunteers. This was when the meditation center in Kanha Shanti Vanam was still being built. Today Kanha is a green paradise with gardens, lawns, and even a tropical rainforest. But back then, Kanha was flat, arid ground with glistening quartz and chunky boulders of granite scattered across the landscape. Summers in this part of India (about forty miles from Hyderabad) are dusty and dry, and the summer afternoon on that day was no exception.

As I was driving back to my home in Kanha, a mile away from my office, I saw a group of ten women, volunteers, clearing the gravel on the side of the road. You couldn't miss them. From afar, their colorful traditional attire stood out like spring flowers in the midst of barren land. As I drove closer, I could see how joyfully they worked, as if the hundred-degree weather didn't matter. These women came from the same small town from the heartland of Western India.

Their simplicity, devotion, and enthusiasm had created such liveliness. I pulled over and requested them to visit me at home later that afternoon. When they arrived, we sat for meditation. Their hearts had such devotion that it felt as if they were turning the face of the divine their way with the same ease with which one pulls a branch to smell a flower. A few minutes into the meditation, I felt a strong jerk in the Center. Once in a while, it happens that the pitch of someone's devotion rises so high that it creates a reverb in the Center. It's rare, like the sighting of a thousand-year-orbit comet, but it happens. But what came next melted me away in love.

Like clockwork, there was jerk after jerk in the Center during our meditation. One after the other, the loving calls from the hearts of these women were echoing in the Center. I hadn't witnessed this before, and I haven't seen this happen since.

It was such a moving experience, and after the meditation ended, I requested that they stay on for a little longer. We all had some coffee and spoke for some time. One of my associates took a picture of us. I still have this picture in my study as a reminder of what the innocent purity of hearts can evoke in the highest.

And what was the secret to this momentous experience? Their

DO AND FEEL

attitude. Their approach to life and to one another created something that compelled the descent of the highest grace. Their beautiful souls represented the purity and simplicity of their attitudes. If you implement anything from this book in your life, let it be the cultivation of attitudes that ennoble your life.

PART 4

DEMYSTIFYING THE CHAKRAS

7.

Chakras: Common Traits and Locations

My five-year-old granddaughter has these books with vibrant illustrations of carnivals, cityscapes, and other settings. Hidden in these busy images is Waldo, the lanky Brit with his trademark red-and-white-striped T-shirt and blue jeans. On his own, Waldo is unmissable. But when Waldo is thrown in with all the clutter, spotting Waldo is quite a task.

Observing inner changes is much like finding Waldo, but with a big twist. *You know what Waldo looks like.* But in the inner landscape, you must first learn what to look for. So, in this chapter we will be doing two critical tasks. First, we need to know what we're looking for, so we'll learn the most common traits of the chakras, such as their elemental constitutions, colors, movement and vibrations, location, and emotional qualities.

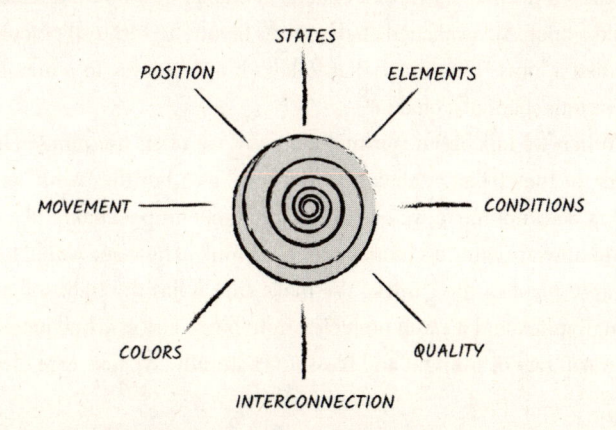

DO AND FEEL

Our second task will be locating all sixteen chakras on the body. This will help you correlate the traits of the chakras with their locations. As you engage with the chakras more deeply, these traits will help you tune in more precisely to their energy and the inner states they create. This understanding makes you proficient in appreciating the inner growth. It's like finding Waldo. Spotting him the first time is tricky, but once you do it, the next time is easier. With each successful attempt, your confidence grows and you enjoy the journey more.

States: Knot, Chakra, and Lotus

When the soul descends into the body, it does so like water descending from a mountain and flowing across the plains. At various points during its descent, the water forms whirls and currents. The soul, too, expresses and collects its energy at various places of the body, which we call chakras. The word *chakra* means "a wheel," symbolizing the spinning-vortex-like nature of these energy centers.

Across cultures, there are many terms to describe a chakra. Of particular significance are the terms *knot*, *chakra*, and *lotus*. Each indicates a distinct status of a chakra. A chakra in a bud-like state is called a knot. An awakened chakra that's blooming with full potential is called a lotus. The image that follows is an easy way to remember the various states of a chakra.

When we talk about spiritual anatomy, we often use phrases like "work on the chakra," "chakra is touched," etc., but the "work" on a chakra does not mean we do something to open up a chakra like we would unwrap a gift. It's more nuanced. Think of how one would tend to a rose plant in the garden. We make sure it has the right soil and enough water, and it's well protected from bugs. The rose bud receives the warm rays of sunlight and blossoms naturally. We take care of the

Chakras: Common Traits and Locations

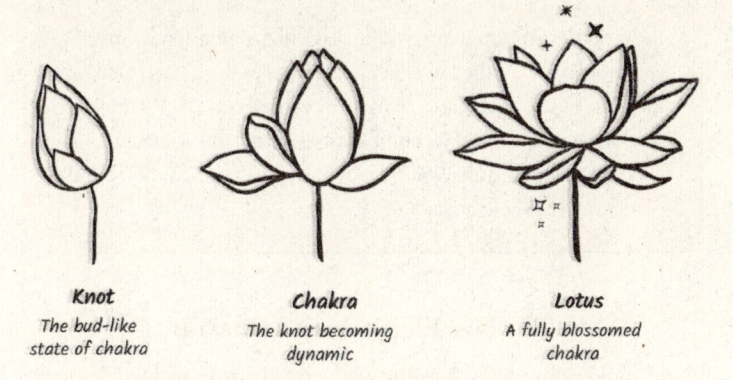

Knot
The bud-like state of chakra

Chakra
The knot becoming dynamic

Lotus
A fully blossomed chakra

plant and the bud blossoms on its own. In the same way, when you meditate on your own, in sessions with Heartfulness trainers (preceptors), and in group meditations, work happens on a chakra.

The field around the chakra is cleaned and the intervening spaces between the chakras are cleared. After the field is purified, impulses of transmission are given to a chakra. This allows the chakra to flower, and its energy descends into the heart, creating inner conditions. Cleaning and applying Transmission is a layered process that takes place throughout the spiritual journey. Bear in mind that, often, you will feel the work happening *after* meditation, as well as during. As their awareness grows, many practitioners notice that even during routine activities like taking a walk or cooking the inner work continues.

POINTS: SPECIALIST CHAKRAS

There is a particular category of chakras that I refer to as points. The points are unique and they hold a specific role in the spiritual anatomy. For example, in our body, the nose plays a specific role in

> the much larger respiratory system. Like that, points have a specific and crucial role in the larger anatomy. Besides the sixteen chakras, there are four points that we will focus on in this book. Working on these four points helps us build a strong and stable spiritual foundation. Later in the chapter, we will locate the positions of the four points and the sixteen chakras.

The Five Elements and Chakras

Yogic philosophy states that the Universe is made of five elements: earth, space, fire, water, and air. Of course, our modern understanding of matter tells us that certainly there are many more elements than these five. What the elders intended was to observe the five distinct attributes of matter. They made a qualitative observation and not one based on the atomic nature of the elements. Each of the elements represents a unique attribute.

Earth is used to describe solidity.
Air represents movement exhibited by a gas.
Water represents the liquid state.
Fire signifies the attribute of matter to transform from one state to another. (For example, when we heat water, it becomes steam.)
Space is the base, the fundamental material. It was never created; it was always there. It represents the idea of nothingness.

With this understanding, when you look at the human body, you find that we are indeed made up of the five elements. The solidity of the body is the earth element. The various fluids in the body signify the water element. Our breathing is the intake and outflow of the air element. The digestive process of breaking down food into energy represents the transformative attribute of the fire element. All through the body, the space element is present. The space between cells, the hollowness of blood vessels, intestines, and so on—all signify space.

The five elements are not limited to the physical anatomy alone. They also play an important role in spiritual anatomy. Within each chakra, the qualities of the five elements are present, and each chakra has one prominent element. Think of it this way: Pick up a clump of soil and hold it in your hand. The earth element (solidity) is dominant, isn't it? But trapped in that clump of earth is the air element. Some moisture (water element) is also trapped in the soil. When the sun heats the soil, it bakes and becomes harder, so the transformative quality of fire is also there. And finally, between the particles of soil, the space element is present. Still, as we hold it in our hand, we would recognize its earthiness first. So too, it is for the prominent element of a chakra.

Conditions at a Chakra

Of all the traits we cover in this chapter, understanding the conditions created when a chakra is worked on is perhaps the most important. When a chakra blossoms, the energy bracketed inside is released gradually. We feel this energy in the form of emotional conditions created in the heart. When we nurture these inner conditions and make them a part of our nature, they express themselves as qualities in our behavior. In this way, we gradually reprogram our nature by developing the qualities that help us grow and evolve.

Conditions are the steps we ascend on the path to infinity. Transmission and the guru's work create conditions that we experience. For example, at the first chakra we develop acceptance, and at the second chakra we develop peacefulness, and so on. When we feel these conditions within, we work with them to imbibe them. When we make use of the condition by immersing ourselves in it, we grow. If not, the conditions are lost.

AN INTERCONNECTED SYSTEM OF CHAKRAS

Babuji coined a term, *invertendo*, to capture the inversions of truth that we see in nature. Invertendo shines the spotlight on the paradoxes that we observe in nature's design. For example, the lower one goes (humility), the higher their consciousness rises. The more emptiness one creates within, the greater the grace that descends in their heart. The more centered one becomes, the more one's consciousness travels.

Babuji observed that in the spiritual anatomy, the interconnections between chakras are an example of invertendo. To understand it, consider dividing each chakra into upper and lower parts. As a chakra begins to flower, both its upper and lower parts are awakened. The vibrations from one chakra's upper part resonate with the next chakra's lower part in the sequence, creating a relay race–type flow for the energy.

Because of the interconnection, similar vibratory patterns are observed across sets of chakras. The odd-numbered chakras share certain patterns, and even-numbered chakras share a different pattern. Understanding interconnection is a significant discovery because it helped design a meditation practice where one can work in parallel across the anatomy instead of serially taking up one chakra after another.

Think of it this way: You are building a house. An efficient way to build the house is to line up the masons, electricians, plumbers, and carpenters on a schedule and ensure that once the foundation is laid, the masons start the structure. While the masons work on the structure, electricians can run the conduits for the cables. The parallel work is efficient and synchronized.

Contrast this to hiring a civil worker and digging the foundation. After this work is over, you go hire the masons. Once the masons are done, you start figuring out electrical systems. Such sequential work is inefficient, and often there is rework.

Chakras: Common Traits and Locations

> The Heartfulness system takes advantage of invertendo to work across the anatomy. That's why, at times, practitioners feel vibrations at several chakras in the same meditation. The specific work may be happening at one chakra, and its echo effects are felt at the other chakras. Preceptors sometimes conduct exercises to help practitioners become more sensitive to the interconnected nature of chakras. In these sessions, they work on a single chakra for the entire group and then ask the group to share their experiences. It's common to see the participants report stronger vibrations at one chakra and milder vibrations at other chakras, indicating that the work on one chakra has had ripple effects on others.

Colors at Chakras

In meditation, practitioners often observe various colors, especially in the early years of practice. For instance, when work happens at the first chakra, a yellow light may appear during meditation. Similarly, depending on the chakra, you might see white, pink, orange, red, green, or bluish colors. These colors can appear as a gentle glow, a gradient, or as a flash in your meditation. When moving from one chakra to another, there is often an intermingling of colors. Not everyone notices colors. Some individuals may observe colors, while others may be more attuned to vibrations, movement, or feelings that arise during meditation. Ultimately, what's most important is to stay attentive to the sensations or experiences that arise during the meditation without judgment or expectation.

Movement and Vibration

Chakras spin along the vertical axis like the hands of a clock. Some chakras spin in a clockwise direction, while others move in a

DO AND FEEL

counterclockwise direction. Then there is one chakra that is, shall we say, moody. All chakras have a direction, but it is in the first five chakras—which form the Heart Region—that the movement is most palpable.

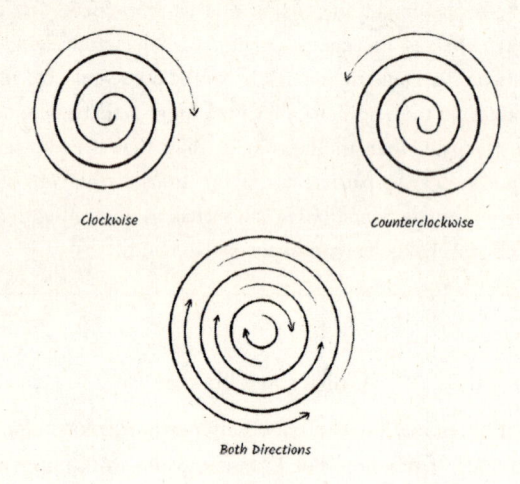

Clockwise

Counterclockwise

Both Directions

Movement of Chakras

The chakras form an energy field, and the energy field of each person is unique. Even identical twins would not have energy fields that are alike. An echo of the energy field can be felt physically. You may feel it as a gentle buzzing, rotating movement at the chakra's location. Sometimes you also feel other sensations, like the chakra throbbing, pulsing, pinching, and even giving you a tickle. These are all types of vibrations one feels when a chakra is worked upon.

There are times when even during routine activities like reading, working in the kitchen, or watching TV, you may feel some vibration in the chest area, the soles of your feet, the palms, or at the back of your head. Observe these signs. They point to some work that started during a prior meditation and is continuing, or some new work that has started in your system.

Chakras: Common Traits and Locations

When you notice something like this, close your eyes gently and center yourself by connecting to the heart with love. Direct your attention to the area where the work is happening. You need to be gentle, almost like shifting a baby who fell asleep in your lap back onto the bed. Tuning in when you get an inkling of work will help you appreciate the spiritual work happening in the system.

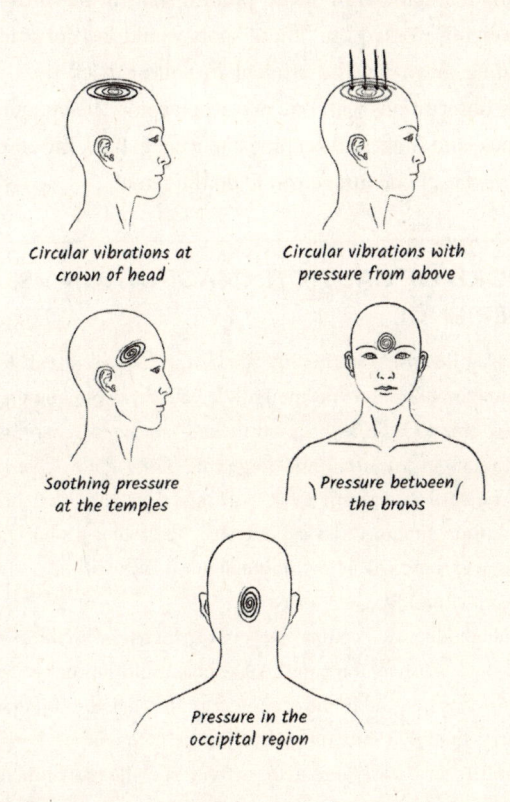

Circular vibrations at crown of head

Circular vibrations with pressure from above

Soothing pressure at the temples

Pressure between the brows

Pressure in the occipital region

At times, in the crown area of the head, you may feel circular vibrations or a gentle pressure pushing downward. At other times, you may feel sensations similar to a feather moving through your hair.

DO AND FEEL

Occasionally you may also feel pressure at the temples and the occipital regions. These could be signs of spiritual work. Instead of instinctively scratching your head, take a moment to center yourself and try to feel what might be occurring.

The movement of the chakras, especially the heart chakras, may also show up on the skin as mild skin pigmentation. During the early years of my meditation, I noticed pinkish spots at the heart chakras that were being worked on. These spots would last for a few hours before fading away. I was a student in college back then. When I shared my observations with one of my preceptors, he encouraged my attentiveness and suggested keeping a journal to track my observations and experiences. I encourage you to do the same.

A WORD OF CAUTION: IMAGINATION VS. EXPERIENCE

There is a downside to this information, of course. It can trigger your imagination, and you mentally create these phenomena. An effective way to keep a check on mental fancies is by writing our observations in a journal and forgetting about them. Over time, when we read our journals, we will notice patterns that help us separate imagination from experience. Also, when we have a real experience, there will be no doubt about it. You will be certain of what you witnessed.

Additionally, avoid comparing your experiences with those of others. Though we share the same goal, each person's journey is unique. The attitudes we exhibit, the eagerness for the goal, the conditioning we carry, the environment we live in, the company we keep, and many other factors are unique to us. With such diversity inherent to our lives, comparison can only confuse us. It breeds doubt and competition that can distract us from the main goal. So, remain focused on cultivating the right attitudes and continue with the practice.

Chakras: Common Traits and Locations

Locating Points and Chakras

We are a living atlas, carrying the map to the Center with us. The topographic map of circles of consciousness can be charted on the body with the latitudes and longitudes of the chakras. In this section, you will learn the locations of all sixteen chakras and the four points that play a vital role in the spiritual anatomy project. Try to memorize the locations of the points and chakras, and stay attentive to any effects you may feel at these locations. Nurturing one's curiosity with interest and observation will make the yatra an engaging journey.

Points A, B, C, and D

To locate the chakras, we first locate four points called A, B, C, and D on the body. As I mentioned before, points are specialist chakras, and each has a specific foundational role in guiding the energy flow through the chakras.

Start at the base of the sternum, where the rib cage cavity begins. Measure one finger width (using your own finger) down from the sternum. Then move four finger-widths to the left. This is the location of point B.

Two fingers above point B is point A.

Point C is on the bottom rib, directly below point B.

Point D is two fingers to the left of point C, directly underneath the left nipple.

Take your time to locate all four points on your body. When I did this exercise, I took small round stickers and stuck them on my chest at these points. Then I looked at myself in the mirror to get a clear idea of where these points were located. It's crowded real estate, with so many points packed into a small area, and it's helpful to be certain of the physical location.

Over time, you will become adept at identifying vibrations at

DO AND FEEL

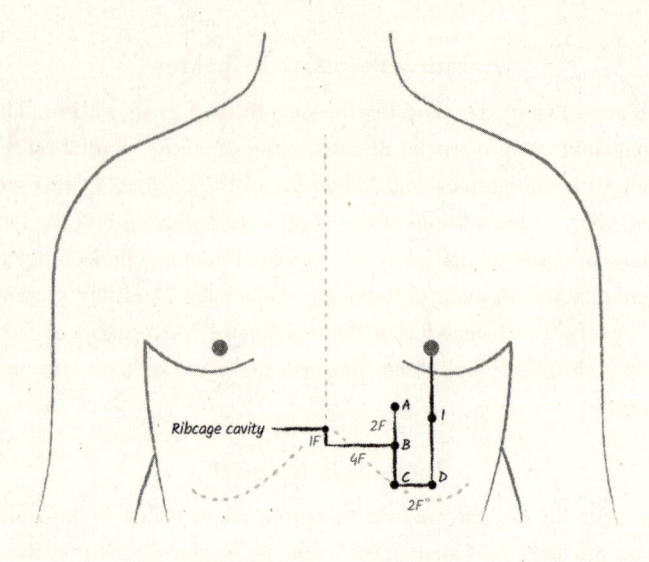

these points. It takes patience, and it's essential to allow your heart to guide you. Take an interest in it, but don't push yourself too hard. It will happen naturally. Initially, learning a new skill takes effort, but eventually, it becomes automatic, similar to how children learn to ride a bicycle. They start with a tricycle, progress to a bicycle with training wheels, and ultimately they can ride effortlessly while chatting with friends, singing songs, and even without holding the handlebars.

Now that we have located points A, B, C, and D, let's locate the chakras.

The Sixteen Chakras

Let's begin by locating the first chakra (heart chakra), which, as we can see in the figure, lies exactly between the left nipple and point D. You can also find the first chakra by measuring approximately three finger-widths (3f) up from point D.

Now, looking at the following image, you can see that the second

82

Chakras: Common Traits and Locations

chakra is on the right side of the body, the mirror image of the first chakra.

Next, imagine flipping the first and second chakras upward so they're a mirror image above the nipples. These are the third and fourth chakras.

The fifth chakra is precisely where the two collarbones meet at the base of the neck. The fifth chakra is also called the throat chakra. Chakras 1 to 5 are the heart chakras, or chakras of the Heart Region.

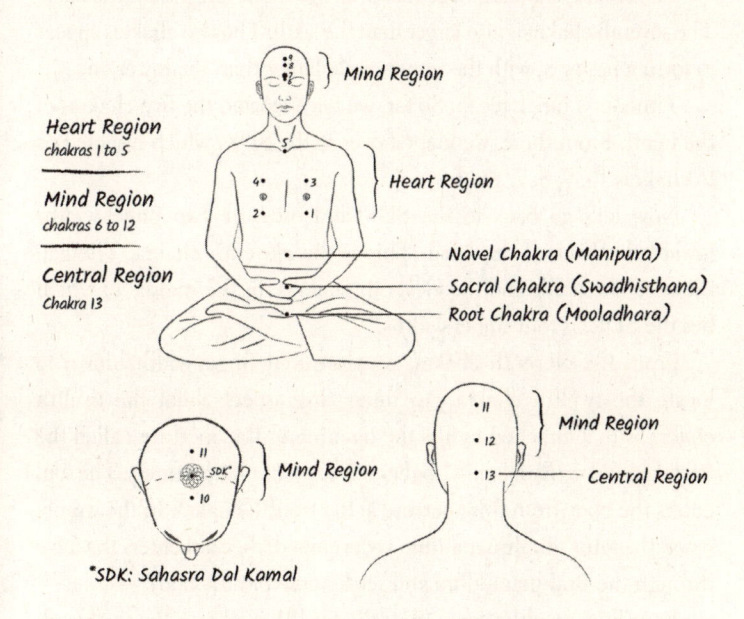

Heart Region
chakras 1 to 5

Mind Region
chakras 6 to 12

Central Region
Chakra 13

- Mind Region
- Heart Region
- Navel Chakra (Manipura)
- Sacral Chakra (Swadhisthana)
- Root Chakra (Mooladhara)
- Mind Region
- Central Region

*SDK: Sahasra Dal Kamal

Now we move to the chakras of the Mind Region.

The top portion of your ear is called the helix. Place your right index finger on the right helix and your left index finger on the left helix. Draw lines upward from the helixes until they meet at the mid-scalp. This is the location of the crown chakra, also called the thousand-petaled lotus, Sahasra Dal Kamal, Sahasrara, or SDK, as

DO AND FEEL

I will refer to it in this book.* From SDK, two finger-widths toward the forehead is the tenth chakra.

From the tenth chakra, measure four finger-widths toward the forehead, and that is the ninth chakra. From the ninth chakra, measure two finger-widths forward, and that is the eighth chakra.

Three finger-widths down from the eighth chakra, slightly above the eyebrows, lies the sixth chakra. Exactly above the sixth chakra, overlapping slightly, is the seventh chakra.

The sixth chakra is a little forward, and the seventh is on the back. The seventh chakra is also larger than the sixth. The two chakras appear to form a figure 8, with the upper circle larger than the lower one.

Time for a quick recap. So far, we have located the five chakras of the heart. From there, we looped over to the SDK, which oriented us to chakras 10, 9, 8, 7, and 6.

Now let's go back to the SDK and measure two finger-widths toward the back of the head. This is the eleventh chakra. The gap between the tenth and the eleventh chakras, in the middle of which lies the SDK, is four finger-widths.

From the eleventh chakra, measure four finger-widths down to locate the twelfth chakra. An interesting aspect about the twelfth chakra is that attached to it is the opening or the aperture called the *Brahmarandhra* (*brahman*—"higher self"; *randhra*—"aperture"). The soul enters the body from this aperture at the twelfth chakra. In the womb, when the fetus's Brahmarandhra is developed, the soul enters the fetus through the Brahmarandhra and settles down in the body.

Four finger-widths down from the twelfth chakra is the thirteenth chakra, the Central Region, the seat of the Center within the human frame.

---

* Since we don't work on the SDK on the way to the Center, we don't include it in the count for the sixteen chakras. There is a reason why we don't work on the SDK, which we will touch upon in chapter 24, when we talk about the tenth chakra.

The Root, Sacral, and Navel Chakras

If you have been counting along with me, you will notice that we have located four points and thirteen chakras. "But Daaji!" you will say. "You have said that there are sixteen chakras. Where are the other three?"

Besides the thirteen chakras we have located so far, there are three additional chakras along the spine. These three are the root, sacral, and navel chakras. These three lower chakras are common across the animal kingdom, and their primary role is in sustaining physical existence.

Root chakra: The root chakra plays the role of making one feel grounded. It provides the primary support for existence and perpetuates the most fundamental need of survival. In Sanskrit, it's called Mooladhar (*mool*—"primary" or "main"; *adhar*—"support").

Sacral chakra: This is the dwelling place of the lower self and is responsible for procreation and sensuality. In Sanskrit, it's called Swadhisthana (*Swa*—"self"; *adhisthana*—"dwelling place").

Navel chakra: Located at the navel, this chakra generates the ego aspect of domination and ruling. The sense of pride and power comes from here. In Sanskrit, it's called Manipura, whose name means "the dwelling place of jewels" (*mani*—"jewels"; *pura*—"city").

The main purpose of these three chakras is to ensure our survival. They are responsible for actions that deal with food, sex, power, dominance, and so on. These needs are primal and instinctive, and that's why these chakras are filled with power.

In Heartfulness practices, the focus is on purifying the system and awakening the heart chakra first, which then leads to the activation of higher chakras. As the system becomes purified, energy from the higher chakras flows down and nourishes these lower chakras. This cascade effect is similar to how walking for heart health can lead to overall health improvements and stronger calf muscles. Meditating on the heart benefits both higher and lower chakras.

The cascade approach also saves time by addressing multiple

chakras simultaneously. Without it, one would need to observe strict discipline and austere practices to manage the effects of power released in the lower chakras. These practices can be time-consuming and difficult to follow.

The heart chakra and others above it are dormant in animals. Because of this, animals cannot evolve their consciousness willfully. Awakening the heart chakra and evolving consciousness is possible for humans but it requires our willing and joyful participation. Human beings can think and evolve, which is why many cultures celebrate human life as a blessing of the Almighty.

The three chakras—root, sacral, and navel—along with the thirteen located in the chest and the head, add up to sixteen (13 + 3) and a bonus of four specialty chakras, the points. You now have the traits of chakras, the locations, and the interconnection mapped out. Knowing what you know so far will add a different flavor to your practice. The Meditate and Transcend aspect of the book comes alive even more now.

One important thing to remember: Do not worry about doing something "wrong" while you practice. We develop mastery only through practice. Also, understand that there may be days when you miss practice, but don't give up because of that. Whenever you realize you are off track, press the reset button and resume with fervor.

> **ASK DAAJI**
>
> Daaji, I struggle with reading what is going on inside my mind and body. How can I improve in this area?
>
> To make sense of the world outside, you have the toolbox of the five senses. You can smell the roses, see the sunset, feel the touch of your beloved, and taste the finest life has to offer. Since birth, our attention has been directed outward toward the external world.

Chakras: Common Traits and Locations

Our attention is easily distracted, like a kitten chasing a red laser dot; it's all over the place.

When you embark on the spiritual anatomy project, you mark a turnaround. Through meditation, you focus your attention inward, like shining a spotlight on the stage of the soul. It takes some time to explore the landscape and get used to the inner view. You need to cultivate sensitivity for inner exploration.

To develop sensitivity, your attitude in meditation should be like that of a cat waiting for a mouse. So much alertness is needed. But most people get so absorbed that they go deep into meditation and can't observe much. It takes time to develop the sensitivity to understand the work happening within. Start with small steps. For example, identify where you felt heaviness or lightness in the chest. Left side or right? Upper half or lower? How was the flow of Transmission? How was your condition before meditation, and how was it after? What thoughts did you have? Start writing all these details in your journal, and your sensitivity will grow.

But sensitivity can be a double-edged sword. Let's say you are very sensitive. Then you are an open door for all the good, bad, and ugly around you. Could you tolerate everything that came your way? So, a lower sensitivity threshold is Mother Nature's way of protecting you. As you become more accepting, generous, and forgiving, you become more sensitive. If you are already sensitive, use your gift by working on yourself. Develop higher levels of acceptance and generosity. That will make the sensitivity tolerable, and you can use it when necessary as a tool.

8.

The Four Stages of Flowering of a Chakra

If I ask someone, "How was your meditation?" the most common answers I usually get are, "Oh! It was deep," "I had many thoughts," "I think I fell asleep," "I felt lighter," "I felt relaxed," or something along those lines. Describing a meditative experience is difficult because, in some ways, we are trying to distill the ocean into a teacup. The sensitivity to observe and the vocabulary to describe are both required, and they take some time to develop. Often, it's easiest to describe how we feel at the end of meditation.

A condition is what you feel at the end of meditation. Peaceful, joyful, blissful, light, agitated, restless, content, irritable, happy, emboldened, settled, and compassionate—these conditions are the gifts of your practice. Each time you sit to meditate, the bracketed energy inside a chakra is released gradually. This higher-potency energy gently flows into the center of our consciousness, our heart. We feel this energy in the form of conditions in the heart.

You need to be vigilant in nurturing the condition. When you protect and nurture the condition, it grows into a meditative state that carries you. But if you lose the condition by, say, checking your phone immediately after meditation or getting into some useless chitchat, then you revert to the previous state. It's like drawing water from a well with a bucket full of holes. By the time you pull up the bucket, it's almost empty. It happens to most of us. We enjoy an excellent condition, and within a few hours what was created is lost. But when you nurture a condition, then you build on that condition and allow a newer condition to descend.

The Four Stages of Flowering of a Chakra

A condition is something that you work in and work with, meaning you can work in the peaceful condition created after meditation and stay connected with it throughout the day. You can also work with the peaceful condition and make it grow into harmony and joy.

At first, a condition will only descend after deep meditation. With practice though, your consciousness can evolve to a level where, on demand, you can recall conditions of peace, joy, or any other condition in yourself, much like ordering a dish from a menu.

The journey through the chakras to the Source relies on the conditions created in the journey, which serve as the steps to infinity. In the first chapter, I wrote that the heart's inspirations lead to feelings, which in turn lead to thoughts and actions. But what triggers inspiration in the first place? Conditions. The condition within triggers inspirations that grow into feelings, thoughts, and actions. Feelings, thoughts, and actions power the transformation engine that helps you design your destiny. At the heart of it, your meditative practice creates conditions that untether your consciousness and help you grow.

Conditions ⟶ *Inspirations* ⟶ *Change your feelings* ⟶ *Change your thinking* ⟶ *Change your actions* ⟶ *Self-Transformation*

You may ask, "Daaji, what creates conditions?" The blocks in consciousness affect the creation of conditions. But a bigger factor in creating conditions is the secret ingredient: your attitude. The attitude you bring to meditation determines the altitude from which the conditions descend into your heart. Contrast an angry, irritated, and disinterested attitude with a loving, tender, and melting attitude. Which heart will attract conditions that propel inner growth?

When you nurture conditions with the right attitudes and take a keen interest in observing them, you can appreciate how the flowering of chakras helps your consciousness evolve. You can notice the finer subtleties of inner change. For example, you can experience how the blossoming of the second chakra and later on the eighth chakra creates unique flavors of peace. Over time terms like *heavy peace, very light peace, shallow peace*, and *drowning peace* become part of your vocabulary. All these conditions and many more are created as chakras flower.

The flowering of a chakra happens in four distinct stages, and in these stages, it goes from being a knot to a lotus. Each stage serves a specific purpose, and once that purpose is fulfilled, the next stage commences, much like the launch stages of a rocket that propel it to reach escape velocity and settle into orbit. There are four stages in which chakra flowers. These are:

- Coexistence (Salokyata)
- Nearness (Sameepyata)
- Identicality (Saroopyata)
- Merger (Sayujyata)

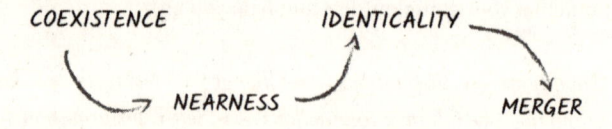

COEXISTENCE → NEARNESS → IDENTICALITY → MERGER

Stage One: Coexistence (Salokyata*)

In coexistence, your consciousness is raised to the level of the chakra you arrived at. The sudden shift in consciousness can be a peculiar experience for some. It's like moving to a new country. The language, culture, and cuisine are all different. You need to adjust and adapt to the new place that has different weather and winds. In coexistence, your consciousness, which was well settled, is now on new turf. It is a

---

* In Sanskrit, *Sa-lok-yata* means "coexisting in the same world"; *lok* means "the world." Every chakra is a world in itself.

The Four Stages of Flowering of a Chakra

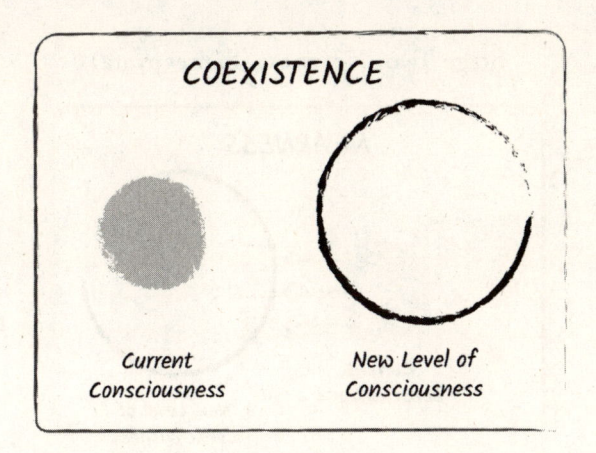

COEXISTENCE

Current Consciousness

New Level of Consciousness

condition in which you feel awakened, alert. The mind perceives the presence of a pervasive divine force, ennobling you to elevate your consciousness. Coexistence can make some people feel a little restless or feel mild heaviness in the head. The internal dissonance or discomfort in coexistence is a sign of progress. But some people stop meditation because of their subconscious resistance to change. Without thinking much of it, one day, you stop meditation because you don't feel like it. One day becomes two days. Then you meditate on your own again for a day or two, but the interest is less. After a few fits and starts, you lose the rhythm and meditation drops off.

Please remember, whenever you don't feel like meditating or you feel uneasy, it's a sign that your consciousness is trying to adjust to a new inner environment. It's like lifting more weights in the gym than you are used to. You feel discomfort in the beginning, but after a few days of repeating the new cycle of weights, you overcome the resistance and enjoy the new threshold.*

---

* If you find you are struggling, I invite you to visit with a preceptor through the Heartfulness app or to schedule a one-on-one meditation.

Stage Two: Nearness (Sameepyata)

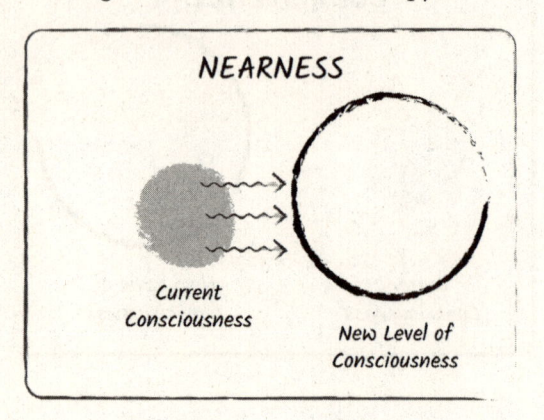

NEARNESS

Current Consciousness

New Level of Consciousness

In *coexistence*, you entered the fringes of a new world. Any uneasiness felt during coexistence calms down with the help of your practice and the sittings. In a matter of days, the peculiarity and newness you experienced lessen.

In Sanskrit, *sameep* means "nearness" or "closeness." It is the stage where you begin to adjust to the new level of consciousness and enjoy the new condition. Your heart feels like *savoring* the condition more, and you feel like staying absorbed for longer after meditation. You find yourself slipping back into meditation. During the day also, you feel like closing your eyes and savoring the condition.

A helpful tip at this stage is to practice mini meditations. Take a few minutes during the day and meditate. Before lunch or when you get up to get a cup of coffee, take five minutes and meditate. These mini meditations enhance the condition.

The feeling of a pervasive divine force transforms into a feeling that everything around you is absorbed in divinity. Some experience it as awe. They can't quite explain why looking at a flower or a bird, or just sitting in silence fills their heart with joy. Nearness continues to

Stage Three: Identicality (Saroopyata)

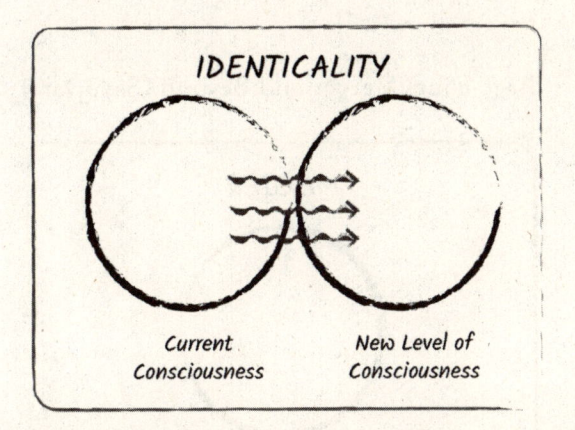

IDENTICALITY

Current Consciousness   *New Level of Consciousness*

Once you are familiar with the various conditions at a chakra, you develop identicality. The word *saroop* means "identical in form." In identicality, your consciousness is akin to the new level. How do you come to know that identicality has begun? The feeling of lightness is one key sign. Lightness in the heart makes the weight of all mental activity lighter. Your thoughts seem lighter; your interactions have a lightness where you don't get sucked into unnecessary discussions.

The analogy of immigrating to a new country is fitting for the stages of the flowering of a chakra. The first time you arrive at immigration is the stage of coexistence. Over time, as you become familiar with your surroundings and settle down in the new country, you're in the stage of nearness. Once you are well settled, all feelings of being an outsider are gone. You identify yourself as one with the new country. This is the stage of identicality. Your consciousness is in resonance with the new vibratory level. You are aware that something significant has changed within.

DO AND FEEL

You feel grateful and settled but nature wants you to keep growing. So the urge to move further starts taking shape in your heart. As a result, a feeling of negation begins in the heart. Negation is a silent realization that lays the groundwork for the *merger*, which is the fourth stage of the opening of the chakra.

Stage Four: Merger and Beyond (Sayujyata)

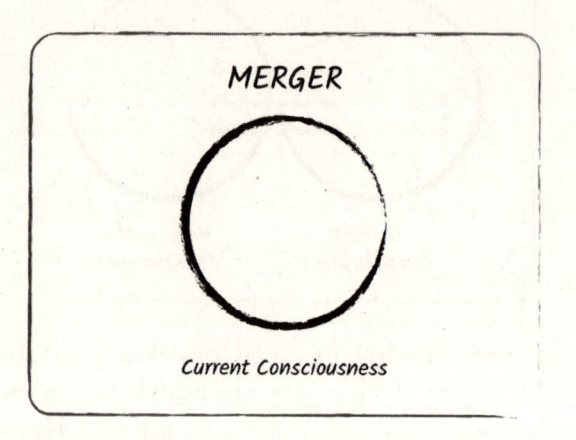

MERGER

Current Consciousness

Yuj is the Sanskrit word for "union." It's the same root word for *yoga*, too. *Sayujyata* is the final stage of the blossoming of a chakra. Your consciousness is now in complete resonance with the higher vibratory level. There are no ripples, only total uniformity. The previous stages of coexistence, nearness, and identicality are a thing of the past. Now the stage is all set for the finale: merger.*

A drop falls into the ocean. Is the drop in the ocean or the ocean

---

* In Sanskrit, merger is called *Layavastha* (*laya* means "dissolution," an aspect of merger; and *avastha* means "state"). As you move from one chakra to another, you keep merging with various states of consciousness, and the final merger is with the Center.

The Four Stages of Flowering of a Chakra

in the drop? Merger with a chakra leads you to a trancelike state in meditation. There is a feeling of oneness in which the prevailing consciousness has dissolved into the new level of consciousness. This is now the new normal for you. Securing the condition at a chakra is possible only through merger of consciousness. If you are separate, then there is a possibility of losing the condition, but when you have merged, nothing can take it away. So merging gives security.

Merger begets tenderness in the heart. When you feel these signs, make the inner condition dynamic by expressing it in your behavior. When you speak, act, think, or look, infuse your inner condition into these actions. This will create balance between inside and outside and stabilize merger.

Merger creates love, and love dissolves the ego. When the ego dissolves, consciousness expands. With merger, your consciousness becomes one with the new level. When the merger is complete, in some of the subsequent meditations, condition is as if everything is gone. There is no impression upon the heart, not even that of existence. The meditation is not deep or absorbing, but it's not superficial, either. You feel only a sense of profoundness. Sometimes such a condition can confuse meditators. They worry that something has blocked their consciousness because they don't feel anything. But in a few days, this condition makes way for the next cycle of flowering of the chakra.

The Flowering of a Chakra Is Like the River Flowing into the Ocean

The flowering of a chakra is not a onetime occurrence. Just as a river continuously flows into the ocean without ever declaring its merger complete, securing a merger with a chakra doesn't mark the culmination of one's journey at that level. The merger with a chakra allows the qualities of the chakra to express in one's consciousness. There is no limit to how generous, loving, or compassionate one can become.

DO AND FEEL

Once we cross a consciousness threshold, we move to the next chakra while the work to attain mastery at the previous chakra continues.

Think of it this way. You open one store, and it starts doing good business. Now you have accrued enough capital to start the second one. From the operations of the two stores, you get capital to start the third store, and so on. But this doesn't mean you can forget about the first store or the second one. You still need to operate the stores that opened earlier and make sure that they continue to grow. If the stores don't perform, then you can't open newer stores.

Similarly, you move from one chakra to another as soon as you gather enough momentum. For example, the spiritual energy and conditions you experience at the first and second chakras propel you to the third; and while you are at the third chakra, work continues to secure merger with those lower chakras. In this way, your vertical journey toward higher consciousness continues even as you deepen the conditions of each lower chakra. This process of rising and merging enables us to grasp and master the different conditions encountered at each stage of the journey.

The key question to ask at this stage is: What clogs the field around a chakra that prevents it from blossoming? Earlier in the chapter, I wrote that the blocks in consciousness that inhibit the descent of conditions in the heart. Coming up next, we understand more about the blocks and how to clear them so the chakras can blossom.

SUGGESTED PRACTICE: AEIOU OF THE INNER CONDITION

The beautiful conditions created in meditation are like seeds that can grow and expand into deeper meditative states. The practice of AEIOU helps you retain the condition and nurture it so it grows into a newer meditative state.

The Four Stages of Flowering of a Chakra

A means Acquire the condition. *E* means Enliven the condition. *I* means Imbibe. *O* means become One with it. *U* means Unite with it.

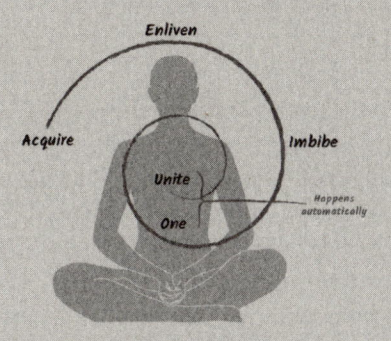

4-5 minutes after meditation

Acquire. We acquire a condition through meditation. Enliven, Imbibe, One, and Unite take place after the meditation is over and you are ready to get up. These four steps allow the condition to settle and expand. They take a total of four to five minutes.

Enliven. What you acquire in meditation is the seed of a condition. It is a possibility that you can actualize through conscious attention and willingness. For example, if, after meditating, you feel peace, keep your eyes closed and allow every cell of your body to enjoy that peace. Then, from that physical feeling of peace at the cellular level, let it be drawn inward to your subtle levels. As you inhale, feel that peace flowing down and into every part of you; on the exhale, imagine sharing that peace with the Universe.

Imbibe. Once the condition is enlivened, savor it like you would savor a nice meal or appreciate a beautiful painting. By savoring what was created in meditation, you allow the condition to assimilate within you.

DO AND FEEL

One and Unite. After a few minutes of quiet imbibing, automatically you become one and unite with the inner state. End with the gentle affirmation: "My thoughts, words, and actions are imbued with the inner spiritual state within."

Tips

After meditation, stay seated in the same pose for AEIOU. Allow the physical awareness to take over gradually; don't rush into it.

It is also advisable to avoid drinking water immediately after meditation. Just wait for a few minutes. Water has the unique property of changing the inner condition. For example, if someone is upset, we offer them a glass of water, which helps them feel better. But drinking water as soon as you open your eyes after meditation will dilute the meditative state within.

Avoid any loud conversations or phone calls as soon as meditation ends. The condition we acquire after meditation is subtle, and your attention with tenderness will help it settle within.

PART 5

EMOTIONAL CONDITIONING— SAMSKARAS

9.

The Elephant and the Chair: Conditioning that Binds Us

In a popular study published in the *Journal of Psychopathology and Clinical Science*, the football fans of Dartmouth and Princeton were given a questionnaire after they watched the same game. The researchers wanted to understand what the fans thought happened in the game. The results were astounding. The "game" was many different games. The fans had different versions of the events that transpired for the same game. And each version was just as real to a particular person as other versions were to other people.[12] Each fan had their own version of reality. This study was done way back in 1954. Since then, a large body of research shows that people see the world through their own filters. Their attitudes, beliefs, and biases define their perceptions of themselves and the world.

All of us suffer from this kind of conditioning. It constrains our spiritual growth, and we have many blind spots. Only when we evolve our consiousness can we become aware of the filters blocking our awareness—the habitual thoughts and feelings that arise—and start to remove them.

We Are Victims of Hijacked Awareness

When your consciousness is free-flowing, you feel transcendent, connected. Think about how you feel when you are joyful, cheerful, or grateful; the heart opens up, allowing the consciousness to flow unhindered. But the moment your heart encounters something you don't like, its reflex action is to contract the consciousness like the

DO AND FEEL

touch-me-not plant. The moment you touch it, the leaves contract. Your consciousness is also like this, expanding and contracting, always in flux.

The flux in the field of consciousness is caused by your likes and dislikes, which hijack your awareness. If you tune into the chatter of thoughts in your mind, you will notice that most of the chatter is connected to your likes and dislikes. Something you like catches your attention, creating a loop of thoughts. Then something else you dislike grabs your attention and creates its own cycle.

Though the idea of likes and dislikes may seem innocuous, the actions and reactions they trigger cause blocks in our consciousness. The blocks choke the flow of consciousness by clogging the chakras and trapping the vibrant spiritual being in shackles. Each time you try to create a wave of change, the blocks quell the nascent wave. Each time the inspiration gushes upward, it gets blocked from becoming a diamond. But how did these blocks form?

> **YOUR LIKES AND DISLIKES**
>
> The next time you are in a busy place, take a moment to notice your thoughts. You can do this in a restaurant, on a crowded street, or on the airplane. Watch your thoughts as you observe people boarding the flight. Do you hear the chatter of judgments for their looks, what they wear, what they carry on, how they talk, how they stow away their luggage, and so on? It's a stream of consciousness seasoned with likes and dislikes. Most of us unconsciously judge ourselves and others. Our journey is to move from judgment to acceptance to compassion to love.

Likes, Dislikes, and Knots

Your likes and dislikes trigger your emotions, and your emotions create the blocks that affect the chakras. Let me unpack that with an example.

The Elephant and the Chair: Conditioning that Binds Us

Let's say in your childhood a dog bit you and tore into your calf. The trauma of the dog bite aside, you also had to deal with painful shots to prevent infection. The whole episode left you with bad memories, and ever since, even as an adult, you keep your distance from dogs and feel nervous around them.

Now, imagine you have a little daughter, and you're out together taking a walk in the park. She sees a dog in the park and starts playing with it. While you stiffen in fear, she leans down to knead the dog's ears and pulls its tail. The dog is enjoying the obscene pampering it gets from your little one. While you grow increasingly nervous, your daughter is busy making some of her happiest memories.

Why did your reactions differ? Simple: Because your child's memories are different from yours. The child, you could say, has a *beginner's mind*. With no prior experience, she sees this dog as it is in the moment: loving, playful, and happy. On the other hand, your mind calls up the past traumatic experience. What's inside you creates your view of what's outside. The memories inside create the emotions through which you process the world. Your past conditions you and, without mitigation, runs your present.

Usually, you go through life processing the experiences that come your way. Reading a book, driving a car, walking to the store, cooking dinner, and taking a shower are examples of experiences we take in and process before moving on to the next one. While doing so, if you are joyful, grateful, or cheerful, the heart opens and consciousness flows unhindered. You feel a deep sense of connectedness with your surroundings. If not, these experiences are ambivalent, they pass by, and that's also fine.

But when something triggers your likes or dislikes, it prevents you from taking in, processing, and moving on. You get stuck in that moment. You resist the experiences you don't like, and you become attached to the experiences you do like. Whether it's attachment or resistance, like or dislike, the flow of consciousness is blocked. Subsequent experiences have to overcome these blocks to capture our attention.

DO AND FEEL

Take a moment to scan back through your life and think of the incidents when you resisted, or you became attached. "I was betrayed," "I detest that person," "I want that business at all costs"—the more the I-ness (ego), the stronger the emotions. Such strong emotions hog your attention. You may be driving, eating dinner, showering, or speaking with a friend, but your mind is brooding over the blocked incident. Be it attachment ("Oh! I loved her so much!") or be it resistance ("How could they do that to me?"), the result is the same. You are stuck with a block that hijacks your attention.

In his best-selling book, *The Untethered Soul*, Michael Singer writes about the blue Ford Mustang. You see a blue Mustang that looks like your girlfriend's car, and you think you see two people hugging. Those few seconds are enough to keep you blocked and you miss all other cars, trees, and drivers. Years later, the same emotions bubble up when you see a blue Mustang with a couple. The unresolved emotional blocks create deep impressions with exceptionally vivid detail and long-lasting memory of the emotional turbulence. The yogis call these impressions samskaras.

Samskaras: The Blocks in Your Consciousness

When water flows over the same ground, it carves out a channel for itself. Over time, this channel widens and makes way for a gushing river. Now when it rains, that is the only path the water takes. Your samskaras also carve a pattern of behavior in you. How you think, how you react, and what you like or dislike are all the results of samskaras. The life you are leading is your samskaras unfolding in front of you.

Modern psychology has deep insights in this regard. Research into areas like neuroplasticity, trauma, light bulb memories, and habit formation shows how we store emotional memories within, and they condition our behavior. The much-repeated line "Neurons that fire

The Elephant and the Chair: Conditioning that Binds Us

together wire together" conveys the same idea of rainwater deepening the same channel year after year for the water to flow.

Most people never realize how much their samskaras condition them. They are the invisible filters through which they look at the world. A good example is how something as strong and mighty as an elephant is broken down and conditioned.

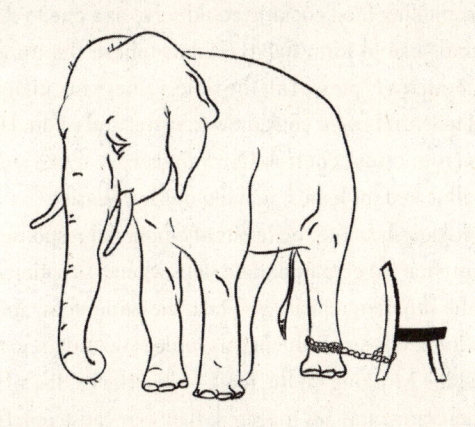

First, when the elephant is a baby, he is tied to a tree with a rope. The elephant isn't yet strong enough to snap the rope. As the elephant grows, he feels helpless each time he is tied and stands in one place. Eventually, he becomes so conditioned that he no longer believes he can break free. This elephant can then be tied to a light plastic chair and stay put, even though he could tear down entire forests if he wished.

Samskaras Form Habits of Emotional Response

The unresolved emotional blocks fester inside us and create samskaras that instigate behavior patterns. Each time a situation arises, the same behavior pattern is enforced, and as a result, we form emotional habits.

And what's so special about a habit? Once a habit is formed, it occurs *automatically*, without much thought or effort. All it needs is a

DO AND FEEL

cue, some type of trigger, and then the programmed behavior follows. For instance, when you turn on the coffee maker in the morning, the rest of the steps follow automatically. Turning on the coffee maker serves as the cue for the habit to unfold. Feeling bored could serve as a cue to mindlessly scroll through social media or check email. Other examples of habit cues: Seeing your workout clothes may prompt you to exercise, or smelling food cooking could serve as a cue to start eating.

Our minds like to form habits. Habits relieve the mind from the pressure to be *actively* present all the time. Otherwise, imagine if every day we had to learn how to cook, how to drive, and so on. Habits allow life to happen in cruise control. Our minds have a vast storehouse of memories allocated for habits, making our lives easier.

The samskaras become the habits of emotional response. They create a program that triggers automatic steps when a situation arises. And each time the situation repeats, you take the same steps, and the samskaras are reinforced. Smell the pizza—order take-out; see a dog—step aside; see a blue Mustang on the road—curse the ex. It's all automatic.

And when samskaras are triggered, they can cause emotional chain reactions. In a chain reaction, one neutron is enough to trigger an uncontrolled explosion. Samskaras can be like that. They can create disproportionate emotional responses and make you feel weak and helpless. The stronger your emotional reaction, the heavier the samskara. Traumatic incidents like loss of a loved one, violent encounters, heartbreak, or abuse, all form deep samskaras that weigh on one's soul. Regardless of their origin, samskaras are the plaque that clogs consciousness.

Remember the three states of a chakra: knot, chakra, and lotus? How do you think the chakra, a wheel of energy, became a knot in the first place? It's because of the samskaras. They clogged the field around the chakra and suffocated it. The result is blocks in consciousness.

It's important to remember that attachment and resistance both create samskaras. Whether the cage is made of iron or gold, it will imprison you. By tending to our spiritual anatomy—bringing

The Elephant and the Chair: Conditioning that Binds Us

awareness to the emotions, memories, and experiences that block our merger with the highest qualities—we can clean away these samskaras and return our knotted energy centers to chakras. In this way, we give ourselves the opportunity to experience them blooming.

Remember that emotional blocks come up in our behavior because they need resolution. Anger arises in everyday life because those emotional blocks seek resolution through love. Irritability comes up to be resolved through kindness. Grief burdens the heart, seeking the light of compassion. Fear bubbles up to be purged through courage.

Unaware that these emotions seek resolution, our instinctive reaction feeds rage to anger, amplifies irritability into hate, drowns grief into depression, and feeds anxiety to fear. Such instinctive reactions change when you do the cleaning.

The practice of cleaning creates space inside your heart; daily meditation fills this space with conditions that create wisdom. Bit by bit, you develop correct thinking and the right understanding of situations. It is through correct thinking and right understanding that you begin to reprogram yourself and unblock your consciousness.

Forming samskaras doesn't mean you are a terrible person or a lesser human. Samskaras are what they are, a part of the emotional cause-effect equation. The important thing is that you do not become bound by these blocks. You are bigger and stronger than the samskaras that bind you. Inside you, a beautiful spiritual being lies shackled. Your spiritual anatomy project will unleash this being. The rope that tied the elephant only needs to be cut.

10.

Points A, B, C, and D:
The Feeder Factories of Samskaras

John Snow was a physician and epidemiologist in mid-nineteenth-century London, where cholera outbreaks were a common occurrence and thousands of people died from the disease every year. At the time, the policy was to drain swamps and spray disinfectants in the air because it was thought that cholera was airborne. But Snow was skeptical of this theory, and he began pointing out the locations of cholera cases in London on a map. Through his investigation, he identified a cluster of cases around a water pump in a neighborhood. Snow convinced the local authorities to remove the handle of the pump, effectively cutting off the source of contaminated water. The outbreak subsided, and John Snow's theory that cholera was waterborne was later proven by other scientists also.

Snow's work is a powerful reminder of the importance of identifying and addressing the root cause of any problem. As you learned in the last chapter, the samskaras block the chakras. We clear the samskaras and that enables us to progress. But what creates samskaras in the first place? The points A, B, C, and D are the root cause for triggering the formation of samskaras. When these points are disturbed, they affect the other chakras, triggering samskara formation that destabilizes us. The points play a foundational role in triggering the formation of samskaras. The knowledge shared here will help you in understanding the finer details of how they form, and their impact on our journey.

Points A, B, C, and D: The Feeder Factories of Samskaras

Point C Is the Epicenter

Try this the next time you are in a public place, such as a restaurant, a crowded street, or an airplane. Watch your thoughts as you observe the people around you. You'll notice a stream of likes and dislikes flowing through your mind about their appearance, their clothing, their carry-ons, how they talk, and even how they store their luggage. This stream of consciousness is often seasoned with judgments based on personal preferences. Pay attention, and you may even feel a mild pressure in your chest when you have particularly strong reactions. The pressure will be felt at the location of point C (for a refresher on the locations of points, refer back to page 82).

Point C is a strategic point in the spiritual anatomy. Whenever we react to something with feelings of like or dislike, those vibrations start from point C. If your reactions are mild, the vibrations are not strong enough to form samskaras. But if the reactions are strong, then samskaras affect the points and the chakras, too.

This does not mean we shun all personal preferences. It's in our nature to have personal preferences. What we read, eat, wear, and think are driven by our personal preferences. I prefer Gujarati food, while you may prefer Italian cuisine. But if we can avoid insisting on things, or becoming obstinate and demanding, then we protect point C from getting disturbed and prevent the formation of most samskaras.

The practice of constant remembrance* is how we temper our likes and dislikes and, by extension, our samskaras. Constant remembrance is the practice of staying connected to the positive inner conditions you create through meditation and allowing them to grow.

While talking, eating, reading, driving, and anything else you do,

---

* Constant remembrance is also practiced in various traditions of the world. In Christianity, it's called ceaseless prayer, and in Hinduism, it's called Bhajan.

stay connected to your heart. That connection creates a channel for your attention to flow inward. As they say, "Energy goes where attention flows," and through constant remembrance you can divert the flow of your attention—avoiding the deep grooves of samskaras and, in time, finding new paths for your consciousness. Constant remembrance helps one transcend the paradox of likes and dislikes, thereby creating the space for inner growth.

The Paradox of Likes and Dislikes

Before we go further, let's begin with a clarification for those wondering: "Daaji, are you suggesting that we give up all desires? Are desires inherently bad?" No. We all have desires and aspirations; in fact, the spiritual anatomy project itself is a desire for self-improvement. Desire is an expression of the soul's yearning for transcendence. But because of samskaras, the energy of desire is often misdirected toward lower aims in life. It's as if a piece of iron is placed next to a compass and skews the true north. In the case of the soul's true north, the compass is cluttered with iron filings of samskaras, causing each chakra to become a pole of its own, leading us toward different directions instead of the main objective.

It's easy to say, "Overcome desire," but the reality is that it's not that simple. Repressing desire is not a permanent solution, as it may work sometimes but not always. In many cases, repression creates much heavier blocks than the desire itself. Another option is to satisfy the desire, but each satisfied desire often propagates many more in return, reinforcing the attachment. Giving up desires can create strain, while giving in to desires strengthens the attachment. So what's the solution?

Desire is the energy created by lack. While you cannot create or destroy energy, you can transform it. The energy of desire can be transformed by attaching it to something higher, such as higher values and goals. By allowing the mind to rest on higher principles and goals

Points A, B, C, and D: The Feeder Factories of Samskaras

and creating the protective barriers of discrimination and renunciation, we make better choices.

In your day-to-day life, be mindful of the sequence of desires. The sequence starts with a simple wish. From wish, it moves to desires; from desires, it moves to expectations, which leads one to demand that their expectations must be fulfilled. Demands then lead one to insist, "It is my right."

When you start demanding, you fall—you literally fall—in your own eyes. Your heart knows what you are doing is wrong, but your ego prevents you from correcting the action. If this tendency continues, then it leads to self-isolation and guilt. That's why, if you notice, the prayer in Heartfulness has the line "wishes putting bar to our advancement." The wisdom behind this line is to address the root cause: our wishes.

This flow from desire to demand to deserve (and the accompanying guilt) corresponds to the remaining three points: points A, B, and D. Understanding the flow will make you self-aware and help you take the actions needed to eliminate the root causes for triggering samskaras.

Points A and B:
Possessions and Sensory Experiences

Let's do an experiment together: I want you to take a piece of paper (this can be in your meditation journal or elsewhere) and divide the page into two columns. In the first column, write your likes, and in the second, write down your dislikes. Your list could have likes that include a luxury car, nice espresso, vacations, hot yoga, time with family, and so on. And in the column of dislikes could be falling sick, losing a loved one, heartbreak, pineapple on pizza, and so on.

Once you have at least ten items in each column, analyze the list. You will notice two things. First, your likes and dislikes reflect your

DO AND FEEL

desires. We all want what we lack. The desire for a car, the warm relationship, a great career, closure from pain, and more money are all our desires to fulfill a perceived lack in life. The second thing you will notice is that most items fall into two categories: possessions or experiences. For example, an espresso, hot yoga, and a cold shower are experiences. A luxury car, a cashmere sweater, and a vintage record album are possessions.

Desires about possessions, power, status, and worldly things disturb point A. The more you insist on having that watch, that promotion, that vacation, whatever it may be, the more samskaras you create. What disturbs point A most of all is jealousy. Your friend or a family member buys an electric sedan—one of those sleek ones from Mercedes—or a vacation home in Bora Bora, or achieves great success in their career. Do you think, *Why them and not me?* Do you question their deservingness? Such feelings linger for a while, and if they get out of hand, then point A is disturbed, and conditioning is reinforced.

Point B, on the other hand, is more closely aligned with sensual likes and dislikes. Cravings of all sorts fall into this category. When you overindulge in your sensual urges, the vibrations ripple to point B. Sexual obsession is the most prominent. Attraction is natural, and it ensures that the species propagates. But when desire gets out of hand, the mind becomes restless. Lustful thoughts bombard the mind, and the other becomes a mere object to satisfy one's passion. Brooding over such thoughts creates samskaras.

Whether the desires are related to possessions (point A) or experiences (point B), we are aware of our indulgence. The inner voice keeps tugging at us to moderate. But human emotions are complex, and it's difficult to break free from habits and tendencies. Most of the time, guilt develops when we ignore the inner voice and indulge. It's not that sex is bad or buying a TV or a car is excessive. But when your attitude is indulgent and selfish, it creates samskaras of guilt.

Points A, B, C, and D: The Feeder Factories of Samskaras

> **TRANSCENDING LIKES AND DISLIKES**
>
> There is nuance, of course, to dismantling our likes and dislikes. While a strong attachment to worldly power, possessions, or sensations is a problem, resisting worldly life causes its own disturbances. Both likes and dislikes, attachments and resistances, cause samskaras. From the example of the two wings of the bird, when any of the points are disturbed, the bird flies around in circles. Your consciousness is blocked, and growth slows down. But when we look up to a higher goal and fix our attention on it, we rise above the likes and dislikes and allow our consciousness to grow.

Point D: Guilt

All the samskaras of guilt are stored at point D. Guilt creates extreme heaviness in the system. There are many reasons why guilt develops. One common reason is when we ignore the voice of our conscience. When the heart says no, and we go ahead anyway, then we develop guilt. Our ego may brush off the thoughts, but the guilt lingers, settling down at point D.

Guilt also forms because of inactions. The errors of omission form deeper samskaras of guilt than the errors of commission. For example, we let pride get in the way of a well intended apology. Later on we feel guilty. Or consider another example in case of adults who suffer from the guilt of not caring enough for their aging parents. After the parents have moved on, the guilt becomes overbearing, and then they feed the poor and carry out other acts of charity in the parents' name. While charity gives some temporary relief, the emotional burden—the samskara—remains.

To avoid guilt, do your best with all sincerity. It may entail more work in the short term, but it will keep your conscience clear, and you will feel good about your life. Regret is a powerful tool to dissolve guilt.

DO AND FEEL

Try this: At nighttime, offer a prayer in the most supplicant mood, regretting any mistakes made unknowingly. Resolve to correct the mistakes made knowingly. When you introspect and regret with full sincerity, the energy trapped in guilt transforms into an uplifting force for change. Shed a few tears while you pray, and the emotional lightness will be of a different degree. You can test for yourself the truism of the Jewish proverb "What soap is for the body, tears are for the soul."

> ### SHAME AND GUILT
>
> Besides the errors of omission and commission, there are other actions that cause guilt. These are actions of trauma and abuse in which you endure severe hurt because of your actions and the actions of others. Think of the soldiers who suffer from PTSD and other diseases of despair; they feel guilty because they couldn't save their friends or they killed other people.
>
> In the case of victims of abuse, they are so tormented that they blame themselves for inviting the hurt. They blame their looks, their behavior, for causing the suffering they themselves endured. The sense of shame they burden themselves with is toxic. In all such cases, heart healing takes time, but it's possible to heal. It's possible to develop patterns of thinking and understanding that help you achieve closure. Compassion and radical acceptance play a key role in the healing journey.

By understanding the role of points A, B, C, and D in our emotional makeup, we work toward a lifestyle that helps prevent the formation of samskaras. It's not about giving up desires or avoiding worldly possessions and experiences, but rather transforming the energy of desire by attaching it to something higher. As we work on points A, B, C, and D, we can move toward our evolutionary goals and experience the joys of living in the present moment.

Points A, B, C, and D: The Feeder Factories of Samskaras

ASK DAAJI

Daaji, I struggle with developing constant remembrance. Do you have any suggestions for me?

I had this same question during my early years of practice. Once I asked Babuji, "How do I progress quickly?" He replied, "Constant remembrance." Babuji replied in short sentences and long pauses. Usually, I wouldn't bother him with follow-up questions, but that day, I wanted to hear more from him. So I asked, "Any tips to practice constant remembrance, Babuji?"

"Each time you change your action," he said, "connect with the heart."

Let's say you are reading, and you stand up to get a drink of water. With love and tenderness, connect with the heart. You step out to get the mail, connect with the heart. You start cooking, connect with the heart. You are at work, and the phone rings...you get the idea. Make a habit of connecting with the heart, and the immunity shield of constant remembrance will protect you. Constant remembrance helps you interiorize in the heart, link one meditation to another, and nurture the conditions you are experiencing.

11.

Cleaning the Samskaras:
Correct Thinking and Right Understanding

Imagine a lit candle. In front of that candle, you place a piece of colored glass. The candlelight now shines through the glass. But, because the glass is colored, some of the light is filtered out. Add another glass in front of the first one—a different color this time. Even less light shines through. Continue adding glass pieces until there are sixteen. How much light will shine through now? Most of it is filtered out. Over time, dust and webs scuttle and obscure the light further. When we start our journey, we are at the outermost glass. We can barely see the light shining.

Now, clean all the impurities that are around the outermost glass, and see what happens. There will be more light coming through. Remove the glass, and even more light comes. As we keep on cleaning and removing the glass pieces, even more light is visible. Finally, we remove the last one and reach the light's source, the candle.

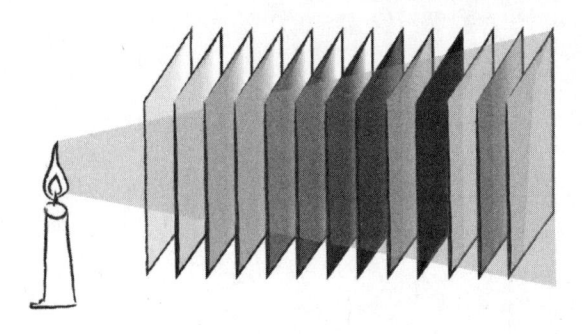

Cleaning the Samskaras

The candle is the soul, and the pieces of glass are the chakras. We let the soul's light shine through by cleaning the system and allowing the chakras to blossom. When a chakra blossoms, the energy within gently flows into our center of consciousness, our heart. We feel this energy in the form of conditions created in the heart. In this way, as we transcend the chakras more energy flows through, and subtler conditions are created.

The crucial element is the removal of the samskaras that clog the chakras and energy channels. By now, you have a good understanding of samskaras and how they form. You know that it is the programming from the past that is shaping your present. To create the future you want, you have to upgrade the program. The spiritual anatomy project empowers you to confidently take ownership of what you were, what you are, and what you ought to be. And with this ownership, you seek solutions to the questions "How can I change the programming?" and "How do I regain my pure perception?"

Ways to Clean the Samskaras

There are no good or bad samskaras. They are what they are: blocks that prevent the expansion of consciousness. Going back to the glass pieces and the candle, the candle's glow increases as you clean the glass pieces. The illuminating glow of correct thinking and right understanding pierces through the darkness of samskaras. For example, you think that someone took your money, and you were upset with them. But later on, you find that you were wrong. The right understanding gives you clarity, and the feeling of regret for blaming an honest person cleans any samskara about the whole episode.

There are many ways to clean away samskaras. The Universe's default mechanism is through cause and effect, also called *karma* and *bhoga*, where the Universe, arranging itself to support your journey, creates opportunities for you to work through your blocks.

DO AND FEEL

Let's say you and your friend have a misunderstanding that leads to a fight, and you have a falling out. Samskara of unresolved anger and hurt remain blocked inside you. The blocked energy needs an outlet. So, nature creates circumstances for you to find closure. For example, a similar situation occurs when you are again in a standoff. But this time, it's not with your friend, but with your son or a colleague from work. How do you respond? Do you choose anger or forgiveness? If you choose anger, the existing samskara becomes heavier and the block becomes stronger. But if you pause and respond with forgiveness, you transform anger into love. The unresolved anger and hurt are unblocked, and you instantly feel lighter. Correct thinking and right understanding helped you make a choice that dissolved samskaras.

Many years ago, a French abhyasi who had a tumultuous relationship with her mother visited Chariji. She shared her pain with Chariji and asked for help to heal. At that time, the lady's mother was in hospice. Chariji asked her to be with her mother and take care of her in the final days. After much hemming and hawing, out of obedience to her teacher, she went to take care of her mother. After a month, when she returned, her face was radiant, and her eyes had exquisite tenderness. She shared the story of how she and her mother bonded and how their togetherness blossomed into love. She recounted that the day her mother died, the room smelled of roses, and her mother's face was radiant. Even the hospice staff remarked about the lightness they felt in the room. When we allow our better angels to prevail, we grow.

But relying only on the Universe to create circumstances to resolve past burdens is time-consuming. We carry an immense backlog of samskaras, and we keep adding to our burdens. We've accrued so much that one lifetime isn't enough to resolve everything. And whatever is left, the subtle body carries that burden from one life to another.

I said earlier that there are many ways to clean oneself and let go of the past. Besides cause and effect, the other options are active interventions. These include therapy, past life regression, eye movement desensitization and reprocessing (EMDR), and self-hypnosis, among others.

Whatever practices of healing and self-reflection you may be using, Heartfulness cleaning (as described on page 54) complements it. It will act as a force multiplier in your efforts, and you will be amazed at how you heal and emerge stronger. The unique aspect of cleaning is that it frees you from the pain of recollecting whatever needs to be cleaned. You don't focus on the pain. You don't relive the trauma by bringing it to your awareness. Instead, you offer a nonjudgmental affirmation that all complexities and impurities are being removed. It's like a refreshing dip in the waters of purity and love, and one emerges rejuvenated.

Besides doing cleaning on your own, when you take sittings (either on the app or with a preceptor), most of the work is cleaning. Thoughts from the distant past pop up: the math exam in high school, memories of the childhood home, flashing images of holidays and other events, and so on. These are hints that any blocks created from those times are being cleaned away. As you go deeper into your practice, samskaras from the distant past are also cleaned away.

Cleaning and meditation help you understand causes and effects. They raise the height from which you were looking at the situation, and now you have a much better picture of the surroundings. Earlier, you were in the valley, and now you are higher. Cleaning and meditation nurture understanding. Samskaras are erased because of understanding. It is through understanding that we let go of the past.

Offense and Defense: Cleaning and Lifestyle

As part of the Heartfulness community initiatives, we have a national campaign in India called Forests by Heartfulness. The goal is to plant at least 30 million native and endemic trees across India by 2025. It's a vast grassroots movement with teams of climate experts, arborists,

DO AND FEEL

scientists, botanists, conservators, and community organizers. One day, the chief engineer of a large city asked for our team's help in cleaning up a lake and restoring it. He had heard of our work and knew that some members of Forests by Heartfulness are experts in lake rejuvenation. I asked the chief engineer how the lake got polluted in the first place, and he told me of the condos all around the lake that dumped their sewage into it. I told the engineer that cleaning the lake would be an expensive and temporary affair. The sewer inflow had to be fixed first.

Our hearts also have become like this lake: We dump all kinds of rubbish into its hallowed grounds. Unless we stop the sewage, it doesn't matter how often we clean the lake, it becomes a Sisyphean affair of cleaning oneself repeatedly. So, we need to cultivate a lifestyle that protects us. We need to cultivate the right attitudes and effective habits. A regularity in practice helps us defend and nurture inner purity.

Also, please be kind to yourself. Change takes time. Even if the samskaras are cleaned from the system, the habit is etched in the synaptic connections. Some of those habits may have become tendencies in your behavior. It takes time to rewire oneself. So be patient. Especially when dealing with deep hurt and trauma, be extra compassionate to yourself.

The early days of practice are crucial. You can lay a strong foundation for your journey in the initial days. This is an opportunity to create a flow in your practice. The flow, or automatism, gives you the much-needed escape velocity to break free from the bondage of samskaras. Meditate regularly, clean in the evenings, and offer prayer at bedtime. Once a week, get a meditation session from a preceptor. Do this for ninety days and see the results. And if you have been meditating for a long time and feel that you didn't give it your best in the initial days, it's okay. Press the reset button and think of yourself as a

Cleaning the Samskaras

beginner and restart. In the journey toward infinity, treat every day as day one.

A helpful tip for you on maintaining inner hygiene. Let's say you are in a restaurant, having lunch with colleagues. Some marinara sauce falls on your white shirt. What do you do? Do you wait till you get home that evening and then clean the shirt? You scramble to remove the sauce from the shirt right away. You try to clean it with a napkin and some water. When you get back to work, you grab a stain remover and try to clean the stain further.

Why would you treat the inner messes, those that could stain your consciousness, any differently? You can do an emergency cleaning—performing the Heartfulness cleaning found on page 54 but for just a few minutes. After an argument with a colleague, email fights, snapping at your child, getting upset with a video you see online, or anything else that topples your inner balance, do emergency cleaning. In a few minutes, you re-center yourself and prevent the formation of samskaras. The momentary pause in emergency cleaning creates the space for correct thinking and right understanding.

There are also situations where nothing has happened *yet*, but you know something is wrong. You enter the room, take one glance at your partner, and know it's not good. Or you're in the office and don't feel good about the vibe at work. In such moments, distance yourself for a few minutes. Find a quiet spot and clean yourself. It will help you center yourself and avoid getting sucked in.

Cleaning is all about being liberated from the fossilized energies that remain in our deepest core. Developing a mature outlook toward life with a sympathetic understanding that can make our hearts more accepting and open will happen when we find a release from the trapped energies that enslave us. A mature outlook toward life, right understanding, and acceptance are the bountiful gifts of your practice.

DO AND FEEL

ASK DAAJI
How do I know my samskaras are being cleaned away?

A growing feeling of lightness inside is a hint that something that was weighing you down has been removed. You will also notice you tend to pause more before reacting. You make room for correct understanding before reacting to a situation. Keeping a journal helps validate your growth. When you read your journal from two or three years ago, you will find that some of your reactions have been tempered or gone away. You will also notice changes like lightness, softness, kindness, and a tendency to be more forgiving.

You will also notice a greater depth in your meditations. It will also be easier for you to slip into meditation faster. One other unmistakable sign of samskaras being cleaned away is that you interiorize more and seek the counsel of your heart. You feel the growing recognition that the heart is the place where you should be permanently operating from. You are keen on leading your life from the heart and continue to explore greater depths within. All these signs indicate that the complexities and impurities inside are being removed.

MEDITATE AND TRANSCEND

PART 6

THE HEART REGION

12.

Five Chakras of the Heart Region: The Realm of Opposites

When I use the word *heart*, don't think of it as the pump in the body. The physical heart represents the heart chakra, which is the custodian of many mysteries. It is the vehicle that transports you to higher levels of consciousness. And why? Because the specialty of the heart chakra is that it is connected with all sixteen chakras. Just as watering the roots of a plant nourishes even its farthest branches, meditating on the heart chakra ensures work is done on all chakras.

There are five chakras in the chest region. Together, they are like a constellation and form a region of consciousness called the Heart Region. The Heart Region represents the five elements our elders say are the Universe's building blocks: earth, space, fire, water, and air. From animated series for children to Hollywood blockbusters, mastering the five elements through rings, stones, and other tchotchkes has been a popular storyline. In reality, mastering the Heart Region gives you mastery over the five elements. Does that mean you fly in the air and spew fire on evil powers? No. Sorry. You do something more remarkable and less gimmicky: You overcome the tendencies that have kept you tethered to lower levels of consciousness. You break free from limitations and arrive at real freedom. I'll explain.

The Heart Region is the collective consciousness of the human condition. It represents the everyday you, me, and everyone who grapples with life's daily struggles and joys. Our desires, insecurities, fears, worries, joys, pleasures, feelings, emotions, indifferences, strengths, weaknesses, and prejudices all come together in the human condition's melting pot. The mastery over the Heart Region symbolizes mastery over the human condition. In our transformation, going from mass to energy to the Absolute, crossing the Heart Region means expanding our awareness beyond materiality to a subtler level.

Mastering the Heart Region gives you the momentum you need to continue your journey to the Center. It ensures you build enough strength to reach the final goal, which lies far ahead. It's like the mountaineer who spends a long time scaling smaller summits to prepare for scaling the big one. And what is the time spent on? Most of our samskaras are deposited at the heart chakras. You spend time cleaning the region and allowing the chakras to blossom, giving you strength and confidence for the journey ahead. When you cross the Heart Region, you outgrow the instinctive nature and become a generous and benevolent humane being—liberated into a level of consciousness that we could call real freedom.

Babuji used to say, *Freedom from freedom is real freedom.* I know it's bendy, so stay with me here. To understand real freedom, we should understand the idea of freedom. Health is freedom from disease; when we are healthy, we are happy. Love is freedom from hate, wealth is freedom from poverty, and freedom gives happiness. But the freedom that comes *because* of something is conditional freedom. When you cross the Heart Region, you arrive at real freedom, free from all conditionality. You are free because it is your *nature*.

The yogis have a name for real freedom. It is called liberation, *kaivalya, nirvana, mukti,* and so on. Liberation is freedom from the bondage of opposites. Such a state creates immense poise in one's being. By throwing a pebble, you can create ripples in a pond—but try creating ripples in the ocean. No matter how hard you try, the ocean stays in its rhythm. A liberated person is like that, deep and unshakable. They have transformed a human existence into a humane one. Such people impose on no one, and they demand nothing. Wherever they may be, they radiate happiness and create happiness in others. Their freedom evokes such lightness that others forget their own burden for some time. All this and much more await you at the end of the Heart Region. Isn't this what we all seek at some level?

The Heart Region: Understanding the Opposites

Opposites characterize our world: night and day, positive and negative, hot and cold, joy and sorrow, life and death, and so on. The opposites are a part of the world's design, and the five chakras of the Heart Region embody this.

At each chakra, samskaras of opposing emotions are collected. For example, samskaras related to contentment and discontentment are collected at the first chakra. Similarly, samskaras related to calmness and disturbance are collected at the second chakra. The image below shows the types of samskaras that gather at the five chakras. An easy way to remember the opposites is to think of them as the five Cs and five Ds of the Heart Region.

How we feel at any time depends on the swings of the five Cs and five Ds. We may feel content at one level and disturbed at another level. We may feel outwardly calm but also feel displeasure deep within. Thus, our emotional state is in a flux, causing instability. The main culprit for instability is the samskaras. For instance, if a samskaric wish is fulfilled, the field of the first chakra vibrates with contentment. But, if that wish remains unfulfilled, the same chakra will vibrate with discontentment because now those samskaras are active. Any chakra can tolerate disturbance in the energy field to a certain extent. But if the emotion is intense, the excess emotional energy ripples over to other chakras. It is like the water basins that collect stormwater at different locations to mitigate the intensity of a flood.

MEDITATE AND TRANSCEND

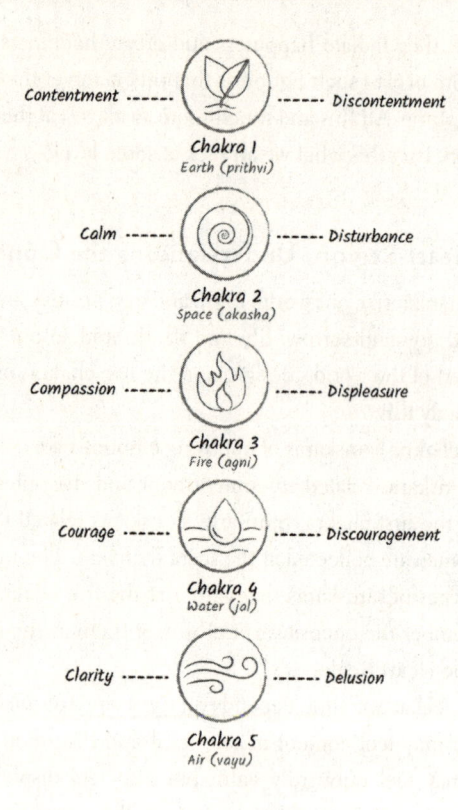

Contentment ------ ⬤ ------ Discontentment
Chakra 1
Earth (prithvi)

Calm ------ ⬤ ------ Disturbance
Chakra 2
Space (akasha)

Compassion ------ ⬤ ------ Displeasure
Chakra 3
Fire (agni)

Courage ------ ⬤ ------ Discouragement
Chakra 4
Water (jal)

Clarity ------ ⬤ ------ Delusion
Chakra 5
Air (vayu)

Consider this scenario:

Your job leaves you dissatisfied and unmotivated. This *discontentment* can trigger samskaras at the first chakra, leading to a distorted energy field. If left unchecked, these emotions can trigger further samskaras at the second chakra, causing *disturbance* and instability. To keep this from affecting your performance, it's important to change your working style, take help from colleagues, or consider a different role.

If the disturbance persists, it can trigger samskaras at the third chakra, leading to prolonged *displeasure* and eventually *discouragement*

Five Chakras of the Heart Region: The Realm of Opposites

at the fourth chakra. This can leave you feeling blocked and fearful, triggering samskaras at the fifth chakra and causing *delusional* thinking and mistakes at work.

Such a cycle of negativity can affect your performance, spoil your relationships with coworkers, and reinforce unhealthy behaviors. It's essential to recognize the five Ds (discontentment, disturbance, displeasure, discouragement, and delusion) and break away from the cycle before it spirals out of control.

Discontentment → *Disturbance* → *Displeasure* → *Discouragement* → *Delusion*
Chakra 1 → *Chakra 2* → *Chakra 3* → *Chakra 4* → *Chakra 5*

Reflect on the sequence of events with situations in your own life. Think of the times when you felt angry or upset, the times when you felt discouraged or fearful. Analyze these events and see how they came to be. Why did you lose your composure? What emotional states did you go through? Arguments, gossip, bad traffic, or anything can trigger the relay race from discontentment to delusion in seconds. When you break down the process, it seems long and drawn out, but in day-to-day life, these steps are a chain reaction. They happen as if you have no control over your emotional response.

We lose control because the samskaras at these chakras are triggering your response. The emotional energy trapped in these samskaras is unleashed, and before you realize it, the cascade of emotional reactions is underway.

Now, just because the five Cs and the five Ds sit in opposition does not mean that the Cs are good and the Ds are bad. Both the Cs and the Ds are a result of the samskaras that gather at the chakras. The dominance of any of the five Cs and five Ds indicates that the system is off-balance, and you need to center yourself. For example, let's go back to the sequence of emotions and consider the opposite sequence with the five Cs.

MEDITATE AND TRANSCEND

Let's say you were gunning for a promotion, and you got it. What happens? Your ego is thrilled. Suppose you begin to gloat about your success and feel superior to your peers. What happens to the first chakra if the gloating feeling persists? Your ego creates an imbalance, and the first chakra attracts samskaras of attachment. You start feeling entitled, a negative shade of contentment.

An inflated ego also disturbs the balance at the second chakra, where the feeling of calm gives way to smugness, a characteristic of arrogant behavior, where even small things disturb you. If such behavior continues, you care less about other people's feelings. In such a heart, compassion suffers. As a result, now your third chakra is disturbed.

So even small disturbances now make you insecure. Fear creeps in, and you become defensive, disturbing the fourth chakra. Do you think there will be clarity of conscience when there is fear and insecurity? There is only confusion and unfounded worries. The fifth chakra is now off-balance, and the chain of samskaras continues. When likes and dislikes sway you, disintegration is bound to occur.

As I said earlier, whether it's chains of steel or gold, they both tether you. If you're thinking that the pattern of triggers and cascades of emotion sounds like a primer in modern psychology, you wouldn't be far off. The belief that our past experiences subconsciously determine our experience of the present is widely held as the basis of most therapeutic work.

The concept of locating emotions on the body is finding greater acceptance in the scientific community as well. Emotional body mapping is an emerging area of research; scientists have created body maps for thirteen emotions including happiness, anger, fear, disgust, love, sadness, and so on. The striking aspect of these studies is that all the emotions are viscerally felt in the chest region, which corresponds to the knowledge you now have on the spiritual anatomy. Studies also show that the stronger the feeling in the body, the stronger the emotion.[13]

Five Chakras of the Heart Region: The Realm of Opposites

But the origins of this knowledge can be traced to five thousand years ago. In the great Indian epic, the Bhagwad Gita, Lord Krishna spoke of this sequence of events:

> When a human being dwells on the pleasures of sense, attraction for them arises in him. From that attraction arises desire, the lust of possession, and this leads to passion and then to anger.
>
> From passion comes confusion of mind, then loss of remembrance, the forgetting of duty. From this loss comes the ruin of reason, and the ruin of reason leads a human being to destruction.[14]

Remarkable, isn't it, to see how science and spirituality converge and offer insights that guide us on the path of inner development?

Overcoming the Opposites and Generosity of the Heart

You may have seen kids play on a seesaw. They keep going up and down. Only when the kids are playing does the seesaw move up and down. Once the seesaw is left in balance and undisturbed, it stays that way.

A chakra, too, tips from one end to another when samskaras create imbalance. Your regular practice helps clean the samskaras over time. In addition, constant remembrance shields you from the effect of likes and dislikes. As a result, for the most part, chakras operate in harmony.

But some situations sneak by or some deep anguish that takes time to heal can continue to bother you. In a moment of weakness, you may lash out at someone, brood over something, and set off ripples inside. How to vaccinate oneself from the samskaras and their aftereffects? How to continue the healing journey?

I pondered these questions for many years, and one day the answer came to me in meditation: Cultivate generosity. It is the key to mastering the Heart Region. Generosity is often understood as sharing your possessions and wealth with those who may need it. This is a narrow definition of generosity. The generosity of heart is about how well we accept our differences. Is your heart generous enough to accept the mistakes of others? The shortcomings of others? Forget others—what about accepting your own mistakes? Are you generous enough? Many a time, we cannot forgive ourselves. We may be unkind to others, but most of the time we are harsh on ourselves. The likes and dislikes are not reserved for others alone. They are also directed toward ourselves.

Generosity is acceptance of reality. By accepting the reality of life, people, and situations, generosity paves the way for understanding. You now understand why people do the things they do, why circumstances come into life and the role they play. You understand yourself better and see yourself fully, free from self-judgment. Your understanding of why things are the way they are helps you manage expectations, both from yourself and from others. Through generosity you overcome the sway of emotions and master the heart chakras.

Mastery over these chakras means mastery over the swings of the opposites. The swings become so subdued that the opposites don't sway you anymore. That doesn't mean the opposites go away. They remain, but their role changes. Now the opposites work together to act as an air traffic control system. They help you navigate the traffic of feelings and emotions by issuing alerts that encourage or warn you.

For example, when you feel fear emanating from the fourth chakra, treat the feedback with the importance it deserves. It's a signal from the heart to avoid an act you may be considering. Similarly, in relationships, when you feel vibrations at the second chakra, and you feel peaceful, you know there is a heartfelt resonance in that relationship. At such times, there will be lightness or a feeling of softness at the second chakra.

While feeling peace within, if you also feel vibrations at the third chakra and the feeling that you are melting away, you can infer that

Five Chakras of the Heart Region: The Realm of Opposites

this relationship will be a soulful one. A final confirmation is the heart feeling free, burdenless, expansive, light, and joyous. This feeling comes whenever something good for your evolution is going to happen. Based on such signals, you can conclude that a relationship will flower and bear fruit.

Furthermore, if when you're in a person's presence, your calmness is disturbed and heaviness is felt at the second chakra, know that you need to be careful in such a relationship. With time, if you notice heaviness at the third chakra and also feel heaviness at the first chakra, then know that such a relationship will not work out.

Then there are times when you are making a decision, and it feels as if the entire system is being crushed between two giant mountains moving closer and closer to each other. At such times, please drop whatever you are pursuing. Such a pulverizing feeling inside is an indicator that whatever you are pursuing is not in the best interest of your soul's evolution.

Be wary of making snap judgments, though. Be alert to the signals from within and distinguish between nonjudgmental feedback of the heart versus noise that comes because one is emotionally entangled in a situation that clouds judgment. A good way to alleviate confusion in decision-making is to listen to the heart's guidance.

Some of you may be thinking, *How do I make sure I am listening to the heart?* The answer is simple: When life flows naturally, our heart just observes. But when things feel forced or unnatural, the heart chimes in. For example, when we lie, we feel a sense of unease and fear, and our inner voice reminds us that we've strayed from the truth. The more we practice listening to our heart, the clearer its voice becomes. Start small by asking the heart for guidance on everyday decisions, like what to read, how to plan the day, and whether to meditate or go for a run. Operate increasingly from the heart. The more we interiorize ourselves and give the heart a central role in our lives, the more we can learn to trust its wisdom and follow its guidance.

MEDITATE AND TRANSCEND

The Five Elements and the Heart

Picasso once painted a series of eleven sketches of a bull. He started with a detailed sketch of a bull and gradually stripped away the details until he distilled the essence of the bull, its spirit, and its energy into just a few lines, creating a powerful work of art. Similarly, as we master the chakra, we distill the essence of each element into its corresponding quality, which expresses itself in our consciousness.

Earth represents acceptance. This is also why we refer to Earth as "mother." She accepts us all.

Space represents the eternal nature of the soul. Space was always there, and its essence is peace.

Fire represents love, the spirit of transformation.

Water represents courage and flexibility.

Air is invisible, but it enables visibility. It represents clarity.

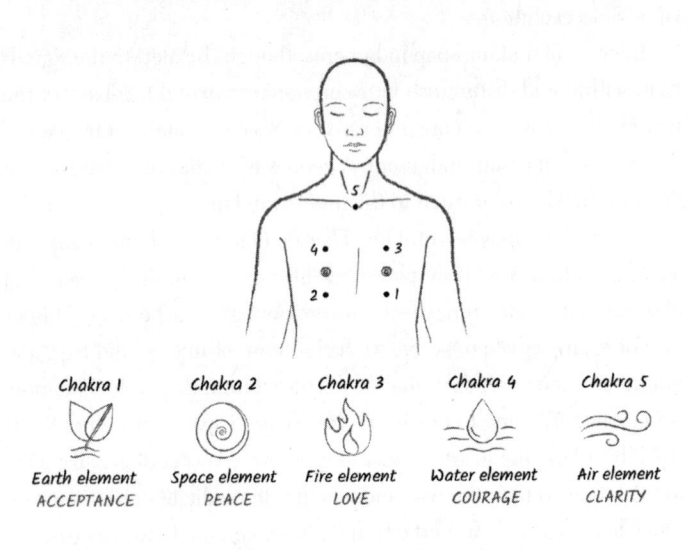

Chakra 1	Chakra 2	Chakra 3	Chakra 4	Chakra 5
Earth element	Space element	Fire element	Water element	Air element
ACCEPTANCE	PEACE	LOVE	COURAGE	CLARITY

Heart Region - 5 Elements

Five Chakras of the Heart Region: The Realm of Opposites

The quality of each chakra helps us rise above the samskaras that gather at that chakra. By developing the quality of the chakra, we transcend its opposites. For example, to rise above the swings of contentment and discontentment, we cultivate acceptance, the quality of the earth element, the first chakra. Likewise, to rise above calm and disturbance, we cultivate peace. We can see how nature's design helps us overcome the swings of opposites.

The interplay of opposites is equally evident in the five elements. For example, when the first chakra flowers, we cultivate greater acceptance within. When the water element which represents courage and flexibility is disturbed, such people lack softness. They lack softness and they are rigid.

Similarly, when the fire principle is shrouded behind samskaras, then love is lacking. There is no drive or craving, and such people struggle with self-motivation.

But before you extrapolate from this understanding, I need to point out one risk. Let's say you feel you've lost your drive. You may be tempted to work on the third chakra to spark the fire. Or, to give yourself clarity, you may decide it's a good idea to clean the fifth chakra.

Slow down. Please.

Spiritual anatomy is an integrated system, and the chakras are interconnected. The best approach for integrated development is to work at the root. Always meditate on the first chakra, the heart chakra. When you meditate on the heart chakra, its intuitive intelligence directs the spiritual energies to work across all the chakras and bring them into a state of integration. If five lights are connected to the same switch, they all glow or dim simultaneously when you flip the switch. Similarly, when you meditate on the heart, work happens across the chakras, and your heart regulates the work. Focus on the essential practices and trust the inner sensei, your heart, to guide the process.

MEDITATE AND TRANSCEND

About the journey in the heart, there is one more thing to point out. During your stay here, you catch glimpses of what lies ahead in the form of special experiences. In the early days of my practice, during one of my visits to Babuji, I developed a peculiar state of consciousness that lasted for a few days. In this state, I was totally carefree. Have you seen a dog relaxing in the shade of a tree in the blazing hot summer? Nothing bothers it. It slouches and enjoys the shade while the earth around it is scorched away. Even if someone kicks the dog, it limps away and slumps back again. My condition was something similar. I wanted nothing, and I needed nothing. Even hunger didn't bother me. If someone gave me food, I would eat. Otherwise, I would meditate, stay absorbed, and relax. This lasted for a few days, and then one day, Babuji looked at me and said, "You should be in this condition 24/7." I wondered why he said that and how he had such a clear insight into the depths of my heart.

Many years later, I understood why Babuji commented on my condition. I was given a glimpse of the spiritual condition of insignificance (*abhoodhiyat*). This condition is a very, very advanced state that arrives much later in the journey at the ninth chakra. But while I was still a beginner, I got a taste of it. We get a taste of many other conditions that await us. Such experiences inspire us to look forward to the journey.

Inspiration and experience await you in the coming chapters. The journey at each chakra is described in detail. The conditions that are created in the heart, the feelings one has during the journey, and the changes one notices within oneself are explained. What would help you enjoy these chapters the most is your own practice. Your practice opens the heart to a level of cooperation where you match rhythm for rhythm, step for step, and condition for condition, leading you to resonance with the higher self.

Five Chakras of the Heart Region: The Realm of Opposites

ASK DAAJI

How do I know I am progressing?

The easiest way to know your progress is through two individuals in your life. One is your mother. If your mother says, "You're okay, my child. You're getting less angry. You're less irritated. You're more regular. You're calm. You're empathetic," and so on, then that indicates progression doubt. When your mother endorses your progress, it's good. Second, if you are married and your partner says, "My god, what a transformation. You're more loving. You're not shouting the way you used to shout before. You're not as demanding!" that's another indicator of progress. In essence, spiritual progress can be measured by how we behave with family and friends.

If you have pets, like a dog, cat, horse, or some other animal, then when you meditate they become quiet. Their quietness will also signify your level of quietness, your level of silence, and your level of evolution. Dogs especially are sensitive to your inner condition.

You can also gauge your progress by the small things in life. When you're washing the dishes, how peaceful do you feel? Or are you just throwing the plates and utensils into the sink, making a lot of noise, and irritating everybody? Do you perform your tasks in a peaceful and orderly manner? Do you feel joy in the heart now and then for no particular reason? While going to bed, do you look forward to the morning so you can meditate? Do you feel that your relationship with the divine is becoming stronger and stronger? These are some signs that indicate inner progress.

13.

The First Chakra: Acceptance

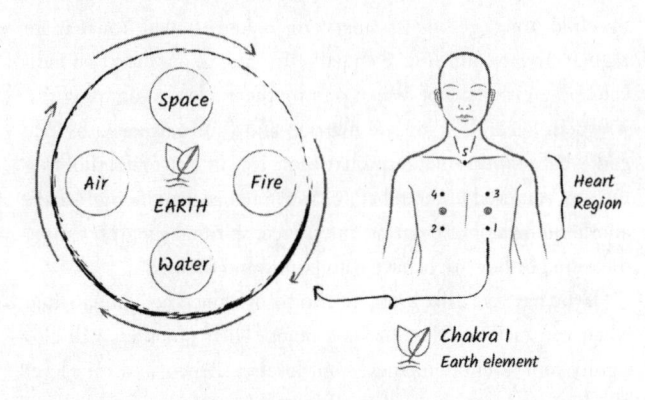

Chakra 1
Earth element

Names	Heart Chakra, Earth Chakra, First Chakra
Prominent Element	Earth
Color	Yellow (sometimes also shades of red)
Location	Lower left (chest)
Defining Quality	Acceptance
Main Feelings	Contentment, forbearance, balance Discontentment, selfishness, jealousy
Points Nearby	A, B, C, D
Similar Vibrations	6, 11, and Root Chakra (Mooladhar)
Direction	Clockwise

The journey to the Center begins from the first chakra, where the prominent element is the earth. The essence of the earth element is acceptance. Mother Earth accepts all without judgment. The seeker and the saint, the rich and the poor, the wise and the ignorant, all walk the same Earth. She feeds us, clothes us, raises us, and ultimately

The First Chakra: Acceptance

accepts our mortal remains. When you master the first chakra, you develop acceptance, and at its pinnacle, your nature becomes infinitely loving and accepting.

The True Nature of Acceptance

In 2017, a group of young people from some of the most impoverished nations, as part of an exchange program, came to Kanha Shanti Vanam, our ashram in India. They told me stories of the silent tension in their homes each day as they figured out who would eat dinner and who would skip the meal. Commenting on the food we served in the ashram—a meal of rice, lentils, and bread three times a day—they said it was more food than what they ate in a whole week. But they weren't complaining or comparing. Over the duration of their stay, they made friends, meditated well, and lived in the moment. When it was time to go home, they were jubilant. An evening before they left, they all showed up at my home and sang songs—an impromptu performance that moved hearts.

These young hearts symbolized what my master said about life: "Life is movement, change, and evolution." The movement of energy, acceptance of change, and the evolution of consciousness.

Movement, change, and evolution create a flow. Is it possible to flow if you are tethered? The samskaras tether your growth. As samskaras are cleaned, you rise above attachments and resistances by developing acceptance. Acceptance and love are the fulcrums for navigating life with grace and compassion.

Acceptance means allowing movement, change, and evolution. Instead of imposing your will on the Universe, acceptance helps you channel the Universe's will to allow you to grow and evolve. Acceptance is a wise counselor and saves you valuable time on the journey. It gives you strength and wisdom, and a state of acceptance is the secret of a well-understood spiritual life.

But acceptance is difficult. Really difficult. Accepting the traumatic loss of a loved one, a nasty breakup, failure in a business, strife in the family, and physical and moral violence, life on earth is no bed of roses. Everyone faces trials and problems without exception. Acceptance of others is the basis of good relationships. It encourages us to move past our differences and to accept and embrace people as they are.

While miseries are universal, the suffering can be reduced through acceptance. Denial only prolongs the suffering. Denial means suffering without learning life lessons. Realizing that acceptance is the way is a great breakthrough in one's life. When the first chakra blossoms, acceptance permeates your being. You don't have to make mental efforts and practice acceptance. It happens naturally, like a rose whose fragrance wafts with the air.

Acceptance liberates you. The journey from "I am what I am" to "I am what I ought to be" begins with accepting oneself. The inner lamp glows, lighting up the path ahead, making the ascent easier, and elevating the beauty of the soul.

Conditions Experienced at the First Chakra

As I have mentioned, my hope is that this book will be an atlas of consciousness for you. In that spirit, I will share common feelings and experiences aspirants have during their journeys through each chakra. Depending on their sensitivity, some feel these conditions more intensely than others. The goal is not comparison or checking boxes for "success," but rather to know so that you might experience, and to experience so that you might become. When we meditate on the Heart Chakra, we enliven that bracketed energy and are open to the gifts of a variety of conditions. The most prominent include:

Feeling the Presence of the Divine

At the first chakra, the presence of the divine is felt within and without. This means, when you close your eyes and look within, you feel the

The First Chakra: Acceptance

presence of something higher. Similarly, when you look at the sky or the sunrise, you feel the pervasiveness of the divine all around. Your heart begins to catch glimpses of something immense during the journey of the chakra. These glimpses are expressed in feelings of awe. You become charged with these feelings and admire nature and its creation.

Poise

The feeling of the pervasiveness of the divine or a higher power kindles a feeling of acceptance. You remain poised during times of calamities and troubles and times of joy and excitement. A sense of balance is paramount in this state. This means no undue attachment to anything. You expend only as much emotional energy as needed by the task. You also refrain from judging people and situations. An equal eye on all is appreciated here.

Kindred Feelings

During this phase, you feel like meditating more. You may also feel like taking more sittings. These are welcome signs. Others who are on the spiritual path feel like kith and kin. You feel camaraderie with them and feel like spending more time with those who share similar goals. The motherly qualities that develop in you make you a caring person.

> **ASK DAAJI**
>
> The qualities express when the chakras open in meditation, and I'm working to imbibe them through the AEIOU practice... so why don't I exhibit these qualities in my day-to-day life with the same intensity?
>
> The sun shines for everybody, but only those who open their doors and windows will enjoy its warmth and light. When it rains, the farmer who has tilled the land and kept it ready will benefit.

MEDITATE AND TRANSCEND

> Your cooperation helps you benefit from the gifts of nature. The first level of cooperation is your daily practice. When you practice, you sensitize the heart to the changes you need to make so you can grow. These changes come in the form of inspirations of the heart. Inspirations like "be kind," "don't be selfish," "let it go, don't react," and so on. A sensitized heart gives its guidance, and when you follow it, the inner energy of qualities flows along with your actions. If the heart says "be content" and you follow its guidance, then acceptance blossoms in your consciousness.
>
> But because of samskaras, the complexities and impurities create inner resistance. There is constant adjustment you make to let the heart prevail in such situations. The more you adjust and cooperate, the faster you will see the development of qualities. That's why some people transform fast while others spend years at it and the inner change still struggles to express itself in the outer behavior.
>
> Let me also remind you that when you get involved in the self-development journey, you are busy working on yourself. You may not notice how far you have come, but those around you remark about your poise. They complement the positive energy you carry.
>
> The key here is to cooperate and keep moving, knowing fully well that when you take one step toward the goal, the Universe leaps to welcome your next step.

Discernment and Renunciation

As your samskaras are cleaned away, the heart becomes sensitized and you begin to experience everything with greater intensity. So, while you experience contentment, acceptance, forbearance, and balance, you will also experience their opposites: Discontentment, selfishness, jealousy, and denial. The key is to accept, process, and move on.

The First Chakra: Acceptance

How do you do that? Through *discernment* and *renunciation*. They begin with the first chakra and continue to be refined as you progress on the journey.

Discernment is distinguishing what is beneficial from what is detrimental. When the heart is free of samskaras, its voice becomes clearer, and you receive guidance from within about what actions to take and what to avoid. As you advance, your discernment expands to include thoughts, helping you cultivate the positive and reject the negative. Ultimately, discernment works at the level of feelings, guiding you from a place of inner wisdom. (Remember: Feelings ⟶ Thinking ⟶ Actions.)

Renunciation is not about abandoning your job, family, or possessions, but rather putting aside the undue attachments that burden you emotionally. Renunciation is a state of loving detachment in which you focus on what's important and distractions lose their power over you. By meditating with love, you can cultivate the state of flow and clarity needed for renunciation and discernment to emerge. It's essential to take the early days of practice seriously, as any deficiency in practice during this time can have repercussions at higher levels.

Restlessness Increases

I know, it sounds contradictory, but as you journey through the first chakra, you may feel some restlessness. This is natural. As I described earlier, restlessness is an expression of the soul's eagerness to keep going further. A discerning mind can feel the difference between restlessness for the goal and the restlessness that arises from disturbance. Even if restlessness arises from mundane matters, you can now deflect it to propel your journey. Your poise helps you navigate the period of restlessness and helps you to progress further.

MEDITATE AND TRANSCEND

Reflect on the experiences, qualities, and feelings at the first chakra. So much to experience and if the beginning of the inventure is so action-packed, imagine what awaits you as you reach higher levels of consciousness.

> ### SELF-REFLECTION
>
> *To have a deeper appreciation of the qualities you develop at this chakra, consider writing two or three sentences that reflect your inner state and feelings. Take the time to answer the questions honestly, without judgment or fear of confronting difficult emotions. Periodically review your answers (ideally every six months) to gain insight and track your progress on your personal and spiritual journey.*
>
> *Think back to a time when you were open to listening to the feelings of another person. What was the condition of your heart during this time? What did you learn from this experience? What did that feel like?*
>
> *Think of a time when you resisted a difficult situation in your life. What did that feel like? What did you learn from it?*

14.

The Second Chakra: Peace

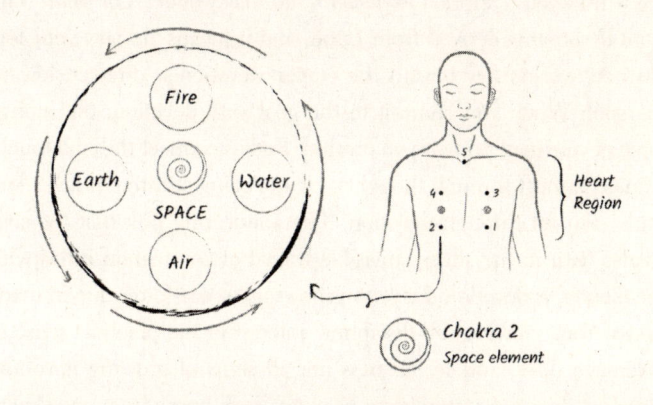

Name	Soul Chakra, Second Chakra
Prominent Element	Space
Color	Red (pinkish hue)
Location	Lower right (chest)
Defining Quality	Peace
Main Feelings	Calm, kindness, peace Disturbance, aversion, restlessness
Similar Vibrations	7 and 12
Direction	Counterclockwise

In the body, the settling place for the soul is the second chakra. For this reason, the second chakra is also called the *soul chakra* or the *spiritual heart*. At the second chakra, you experience the qualities of the soul, such as peace and compassion. You feel the presence of the soul, and its expansiveness dissolves the limitations of selfishness. The

MEDITATE AND TRANSCEND

concept of mine and his or hers or theirs becomes meaningless. You feel a sense of equality in your heart, and there is peace.

What propels the move from the first to the second chakra is *devotion*.*

Each heart chakra represents a higher level of devotion developing within you. *Devotion for whom?* you may wonder. *For what?* The word *devotion* is derived from Latin, and it means "to vow your loyalty." As we journey toward the center, devotion is directed toward the goal: When you commit to the goal with devotion, the motive force of your soul propels you onward. Bodies connect through touch. Minds connect through thoughts. Hearts connect through love. And souls connect through devotion. The connecting link that the soul carries with it, the silken, invisible thread of connection it has with the Center, is devotion. Devotion shows up in day-to-day life in many forms. Your growing self-discipline, interest in the practice, sense of reverence, love, and restlessness are all signs of growing devotion. Growing devotion is important because as you move from one chakra to another, the ascent becomes increasingly difficult. Besides samskaras, there are other factors at play that test our resolve on the inner journey.

First among these are the curvatures of consciousness. These are like whirlpools that lure you in and keep you blocked. For example, you may enjoy the peaceful condition of a chakra or the strong flow of power at another chakra, and you want more of the same. Attachment to a state of consciousness creates bondage. You get stuck there. I often get requests from meditators who want to be "knocked out in meditation" or "drowned in peace." Imposing conditions on what experience you want in meditation is an early sign of curvature. So meditate

---

* The actual term is *bhakti*. It conveys a state where intense love, deep dedication, unswerving loyalty, and the highest humility come together to help you achieve your goal.

The Second Chakra: Peace

with an open mind, and please look out for any preconditions that you may be imposing on your meditation.

Devotion helps you escape the curvatures by creating restlessness for the goal. Besides curvature, the upward ascent is made difficult because of ego. "I am such a good meditator," "My meditation is the best," and "I am better at overcoming samskaras than others" are some pitfalls of ego. Be vigilant in detecting such thoughts and cultivate an attitude of humility. Your devotion to a larger vision and a goal that inspires you will help.

Some may be wondering why we face these obstacles in the first place. The spiritual anatomy project is for self-transformation. The Universe should support you in such efforts. Why face obstacles, then? Once the samskaras are removed, it should be smooth sailing.

What you think of as obstacles are actually protective barriers designed by Mother Nature. Suppose there were no obstacles. Imagine all the chakras connected in a straight line flowing down from the Center to the heart, blocked only by samskaras. I don't think anyone could withstand the flow of that energy! It would be like releasing billions of gallons of water behind a dam, in one go, by blowing up the dam. Everything would be swept away.

To avoid shattering the system, the energy is modulated so it becomes tolerable. Little by little, you increase your capacity. Regular practice, constant remembrance, and actively maintaining your meditative state (AEIOU) all enhance and expand your capacity. The guru, in the background, prepares the field at each chakra, so there is less resistance at the consciousness level when you arrive.

The Paradox of Peace

The second chakra is the spiritual heart. The intensity of your craving and increased devotion makes your path clearer and brings you to this refined world of finer vibration. The prominent element at the second

MEDITATE AND TRANSCEND

chakra is space—the primordial element of nothingness. When we create the condition of nothingness within, the result is peace.

However, many of us mistake satisfaction for peace. For example, if you miss your morning exercise routine, you may feel restless all day. But when you exercise the next day, you feel satisfied. Most people, when they are satisfied, think they are peaceful. The peace at the second chakra is beyond satisfaction and dissatisfaction. This type of peace creates a spiritual restlessness where there is a sense of calmness on the surface, but a deeper yearning remains.

Entering the second chakra often causes some restlessness, as your subconscious resists the shift. It's similar to a child's behavior when she has to change schools because of a parent's job relocation. The child doesn't want to leave her house, neighborhood, or friends, and she may say, "I'm not changing my school." Even moving up a grade in the same school can be challenging for some children.

It's a similar experience for you at the second chakra where your subconscious temporarily resists. The most common sign of inner resistance is that you don't feel like meditating. You lose interest in the practice because your soul knows that you are about to move schools and your subconscious prefers the comfort of where you are.

Nature demands evolution and tries to push you up, yet you resist. Don't underestimate this resistance. We resist even the most mundane changes in life. Changing a pillow or sleeping on a different side of the bed is enough to mess up your sleep. Someone swaps your chair at the office, and it isn't easy to focus on your work. A shift in consciousness is a change at a subtle level so the resistance will be subtle but significant. If you are alert, you can pick up on this inner resistance and realize, "Okay, I'm about to move to the next station." Many people don't, and they drop off at this stage after a few months of practice. So, remember, when you don't feel like meditating, it is a *sign*. Call your preceptor and say, "I don't feel like meditating. Can you please help?"

The Second Chakra: Peace

If a preceptor isn't nearby or it's inconvenient for you, then use the Heartfulness app and take a few sittings.

Also, now that you know you'll face some resistance, you can do something about it in advance. Some meditations stand out where you feel "This was so good," or "I was completely lost," or "It was such a beautiful session," and so on. In your journal, write these experiences in bold letters and add this caption, "Remember this." Then in your calendar, add three to four reminders in the coming six months. Name these reminders "Read my journal." When the reminders pop up, take a few minutes to read some pages from your journal, especially the ones where you highlighted your experiences. These reminders will motivate you and help you stay on track.

Conditions Experienced at Second Chakra

The key experience at this chakra is varying flavors of peace tinged with restlessness. While you enjoy the peace, the idea of the peace giver starts taking root. You now want to meet the peace giver, and your devotion takes on a new dimension where the restlessness to meet the peace giver grows.

Feeling of Nothingness and Slowing Down

Once you settle down at the second chakra, you may experience a newer expression of consciousness. The quality of space element, nothingness, can manifest in feelings of wanting and needing nothing. Free from mundane demands, you may become forgetful or carefree, or experience a loss of ambition that may make your family members, or even you, wonder what's going on. But don't worry, this is a normal and temporary adjustment period as your consciousness adapts to the inner peace that's developing. In fact, it's a positive sign of the inner change taking place. Unfortunately, many people misread this phase and stop meditating, worried that they are losing their edge. On the contrary, your resilience is growing. The calmness and peace of the second chakra help you take things in stride. You make decisions with a cool mind. Taunts, rebukes, and criticisms from others flow by like water droplets on a windshield. As your inner peace grows, call on your devotion and continue your meditation practice.

Ethereal Feelings and Experiences

As you enter this chakra, you may feel a sensation of detachment from your physical body. It's like being on a planet with weaker gravity, where you can jump higher and move faster with less effort. This newfound sense of freedom may make you feel as though you're in a realm that's more ethereal and profound. You feel everything is connected to a higher power. You may even feel like you're enveloped in divinity, much like a rose drenched in its fragrance.

After a few months of meditation, I felt something similar. I was going back to college after spending the summer vacation at home in the village. I was waiting at the bus stop. It was a blazing hot afternoon, and luckily the bus was on time. As soon as I boarded the bus, everything around me began to dissolve. It felt like the matter was losing its density, and particles were becoming looser. Love permeated the space around me, and divine energy flowed through everything—the air, the seat, the clothes, the people, and even the trees on the roadside. I tried to shake off this feeling. I thought the sun was playing tricks with my head, but all I felt was everything being soaked in the loving energy.

For a good hour I was in this state, and then slowly I returned to my sense of normal. A dervish who was also on the bus observed me. He noticed that I was in a meditative state. When our eyes met, he said, "When the attention of the guru grips the heart, you are carried on the wings of love." I had started meditation in the Heartfulness Way just a few months earlier. I knew only my preceptors, and I hadn't even met Babuji, and this was the effect the teaching was having on me. I felt blessed to have experienced the second chakra in such a profound way.

The Taste of Liberation

Earlier I mentioned that crossing the Heart Region leads to liberation, and the condition of liberation starts manifesting from the second chakra onward. It's similar to driving toward the ocean—even if you are still a few miles away, you start feeling the cool breeze and the smell of salt in the air. Because of the shift in conditions, some people get trapped with the false sense of having arrived at a higher state, and curvature sets in. Remember, this is just the second station on the journey.

Compassion Begins

At the second chakra, you feel the presence of the soul, and that dissolves the limitations of selfishness. The concept of mine and his-or-hers becomes meaningless. You feel a sense of equality in your heart. The feelings of others touch your heart, and you feel moved to pray for one and all. This is the beginning of compassion. On the foundations of acceptance and peace, compassion begins to take root in the heart.

> **SELF-REFLECTION**
>
> *Have you had moments in life when you felt at ease within yourself and with the world around you? How do you feel inside as you bring this to mind?*
>
> *What does the word* devotion *mean to you? What are you devoted to, and how does that align with your inner growth?*

15.

The Third Chakra: Love

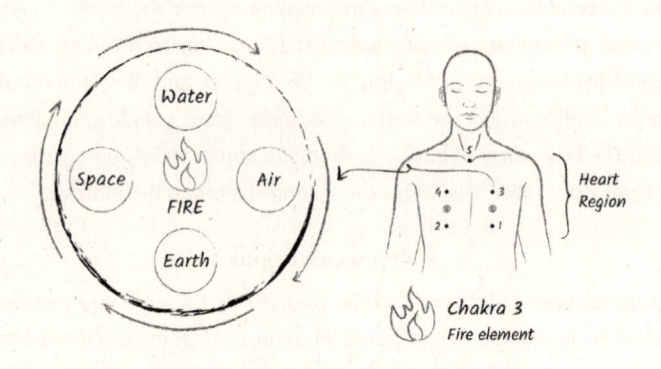

Chakra 3
Fire element

Name	Fire Chakra, Third Chakra
Prominent Element	Fire
Color	White
Location	Upper left (chest)
Defining Quality	Love
Main Feelings	Compassion, poise, love Anger, volatility, irritability
Similar Vibrations	8
Direction	Clockwise

There once was a kingdom where each year the people picked a new king. For one full year, the king would rule, and at the end of the year, he would relocate to an island where he would live out the rest of his life and the new king would take over. One year, when the new king took over, he asked some questions about the island. Then he ordered a team to start building a palace there. He also ordered a new city to be built around the island palace—all to be completed by the end of the year. When the time came for the king to make way for his replacement, he left happily to live in the new palace he had built.

There is great wisdom in not settling for temporary happiness. It is pointless to become a millionaire for a day and become a pauper the next day.

This wisdom to not settle for temporary happiness takes root when you arrive at the third chakra. The restlessness that started developing at the second chakra comes into full swing at the third. Your heart is no longer happy with these early visions of peace and acceptance. Now, you are restless for the real thing, and the embers of restlessness spark the fire of love—the very essence of life.

Understanding Love

Love is the engine of the world. It is the most beautiful thing we can give or receive. It transcends the boundaries of this earth and stays with us beyond our physical existence. In the spiritual anatomy project, the fire of love is the transformative energy that elevates our being to a higher level. When we reach the fire chakra, we gain a true perspective of love that is beyond what we previously understood.

In our daily lives, we often refer to human love, which can be painful and leave scars. However, there is another kind of love that develops in us as we progress, which is divine love. It is a flame of pure feeling that can be poured out with confidence and will never disappoint us. Delighting in this love will transform us and those around us.

Divine love is like a rare and sublime flower that we cultivate within our hearts, and its scent can carry us away from everything else. It is the key that opens the doors, a luminous vibration that twinkles even in the least of our cells. As we advance toward our spiritual goal, we become imbued with this energy and feel its effects.

Love rejuvenates our subtle bodies, and at its zenith it modifies the vibratory structure of our being. It is a dimension too subtle to be measured or quantified, and it belongs to a realm beyond the material. I hope that scientific research in this area will help us to bridge the gap between the material and the subtle, and to better understand the pivotal role of this rare and subtle energy.

From love spring many qualities, foremost among them being compassion and empathy, the fragrances of a humane heart.

Love, Compassion, and Empathy

Compassion begins at the second chakra, and when love enters the scene compassion hits a crescendo. To understand compassion, start with its opposite: selfishness or indifference. Selfishness comes from a feeling of "me, mine, and nothing else"—a self-centered state where personal fulfillment comes at the cost of others. On the other hand, compassionate people have no time to think for themselves because the idea of others is predominant. Selfishness hoards, while compassion gives and gives. Despite their opposing effects, both of these behaviors stem from the same source—passion, the energy that comes from enthusiasm and keen interest. If passion is misdirected by our desires, it can drag us down and lead to destructive behaviors. But when passion is directed from the heart, it helps us to evolve our consciousness toward our greatest potential for love, connection, and positive transformation.

Compassion at its zenith operates spontaneously, without any conscious effort to be caring, loving, or kind. There is no selection process, no decision to show compassion to some but not to others. In the animal kingdom, compassion is pervasive. A dog protecting a herd of sheep or goats will start barking when it sees a wolf. Often the dog gets mauled by the wolf. In a civilized society, compassion exists, but its radius is restricted to *my own*—my family, my sect, my community, and so on. A meditative heart dissolves these boundaries, and over time, you embrace one and all.

The Third Chakra: Love

One of the most striking examples of ultimate compassion is Lord Jesus. Even in his final moments, he prayed for his tormentors, saying, "Father, forgive them, for they do not know what they are doing."[15] That is the epitome of compassion, where one can empathize and forgive others without resentment or judgment.

The way we express compassion matters. Compassion extended with a heavy heart is not the same as being compassionate with a cheerful and joyful attitude. A positive attitude uplifts both the giver and the receiver. It is also important to be mindful of not burdening others with our compassion. When giving to those in need, it is important to ensure that they do not feel obligated or indebted. One way to do this is to serve anonymously. This can prevent the formation of samskaras in the receiver.

Empathy is a precursor to compassion. When you empathize with others, you feel their joys and sorrows in your heart. Compassion is empathy in action. Feeling someone else's hunger is empathy, and compassion is taking the step to feed that person. While empathy acknowledges the duality between self and other, compassion dissolves this separation. Dualities begin to fade away as the second chakra flowers. Then, at the third chakra, as love grows, there is no sense of who is giving or receiving, or who is sacrificing for whom. You do and move on.

Conditions Experienced at the Third Chakra

The many qualities of fire include its volatility, its ability to melt and purify, and its ability to ascend. To get gold from ore, we need to melt it. Melting signifies *transformation* from one state to another. As you meditate, you enliven the latent fire element within you, and experience various conditions, including volatility of emotions, softness of the heart, and ascension of love.

MEDITATE AND TRANSCEND

Volatility of Emotions

Most of us carry a heavy burden of samskaras at this chakra. The aftereffects of anger and irritability settle here. Anger is a tricky one, and even advanced practitioners struggle with it. When we are angry, we often cause hurt, tension, and conflict, and often the people we hurt the most are our loved ones. To overcome anger and use it to our benefit, we need to understand anger's true nature and purpose.

Anger is the energy we need for improvement. When the anger is channeled to disrupt the status quo and improve oneself, it becomes righteous anger. At the third chakra, we understand the true role of anger and learn to channel it toward self-improvement with patience, practice, and a compassionate heart.

A helpful tip for managing anger is to *postpone* it. Postponing anger is like the ripening of an alphonso mango. The raw green mangoes can cause blisters in the mouth if you eat too many right away—but allow them to sit for a few days, and one morning the entire home is filled with a sweet fragrance announcing that the mangoes are ripe. The next time you feel angry, make a conscious decision to postpone your anger and allow it time to transform. Give yourself some emotional space, and you'll find that in a short amount of time, your anger will transform into sweet compassion.

> ### SUGGESTED PRACTICE: DISSOLVE ANGER
>
> Sit comfortably and close your eyes. Imagine that you are in a gentle ocean of peace. The waves are soothing and blissful. Make the affirmation that you are immersed in the ocean of peace, and the waves are removing all your coverings of impurities and complexities. Feel the coverings dissolve and lightness grow within.
>
> Do this for no longer than thirty minutes.

The Third Chakra: Love

By making a habit of postponing your anger, you'll notice that it becomes increasingly difficult to get angry. Even in difficult situations, you may find that the strongest emotion you experience is pity, rather than anger.

From Solidity to Suppleness: The Transformative Power of the Fire Element

Sometimes we feel vibrant and engaged when interacting with people, while other times we are uninterested or cold. What causes this shift? It's a lack of fire within us. The fire element gives us vibrancy, dissolves mental blocks, and keeps our inner being supple.

At the third chakra, we experience this vibrancy. We cut through obstacles and connect with others openly and compassionately. We no longer view others solely through a lens of their shortcomings, but rather see the beauty in their imperfections and embrace them fully.

As you progress on your spiritual journey, your focus becomes increasingly fixed on the goal. This intense concentration leaves little room for worrying about the shortcomings of others. Instead, you direct your energy toward working on your own flaws. Through devotion, your heart transforms into a pure and loving space. There is a song in my native language, Gujarati, that goes like this: "Oh Lord, please descend once into this earthly abode of my heart. Once you visit me here, you will be so lost in its beauty that you will forget the home you came from." These lines summarize the silent sentiment in your heart when journeying through the fire chakra.

Ascend Toward the Goal

Fire has another unique quality. It always burns upward, even when the lighter or matchstick is held upside down. At the fire chakra, your love also ascends like a flame. But toward what does it ascend? Toward

MEDITATE AND TRANSCEND

that which is higher. Your journey has transformed the wastelands of hatred into green shoots of love. Your heart effuses love that rises toward the Source and is expressed through silent acts of compassion. Your heart melts, and your love ascends.

Many traditions practice fire worship as a symbolic ritual for ascension toward the ultimate love. Through your practice, your heart becomes a holy receptacle that lights up a blazing flame of love. Dwelling at the third chakra, you don't pretend to love; it becomes your nature.

To end this chapter, I want to share my experience at the third chakra. For years in my journey, I struggled with mastery of the third chakra. I had already had many experiences at chakras above the third, but whenever I thought I would leap beyond, some emotional turbulence or the other yanked me back. Each time this happened, it took lot of effort to lift myself up and keep going. Once Babuji appeared in my dream and told me that once I broke free of the third chakra, my progress would zoom like a rocket. So I kept working at it.

During those times, in 1986, I was traveling with Chariji in India and we were in the city of joy: Kolkata. That evening in Kolkata, there was a ghazal session (poetic verses in Urdu set to music) and the artist sang the songs that Chariji liked. It was a pleasure to watch Chariji listen to music. He would close his eyes and tap his fingers. When there was a breeze, you could see his silver hair sway in the wind as if each strand were dancing to the music. I listened to music, but that evening, I was preoccupied with observing my inner condition.

As the singer hit a high note, Chariji waved his hand in tune with the song. At that instant, I felt the movement from the third chakra to the fourth. It was like a laser beam! An unmistakable feeling of movement etching a straight line in my heart. I looked up and saw Chariji. Our eyes met. My head bowed as my hands discreetly came together in gratitude. He was at a distance. There were at least a hundred

The Third Chakra: Love

people in the room at that time. His eyes acknowledged mine, and he responded with the slightest nod. That was it.

An affirmation of the immense work done in an opportune moment of receptivity. Would it have happened had I not been alert? It could have, but not knowing is the equivalent of not having. Divine knowledge is not taught. It is caught.

> ### SELF-REFLECTION
>
> *Recall a recent time when your heart was moved by the suffering or distress of another person. What does this experience tell you about your capacity for love and compassion?*
>
> *At the end of each day, ask yourself this question: "Did I pour enough love into my day today?"*

16.

The Fourth Chakra: Courage

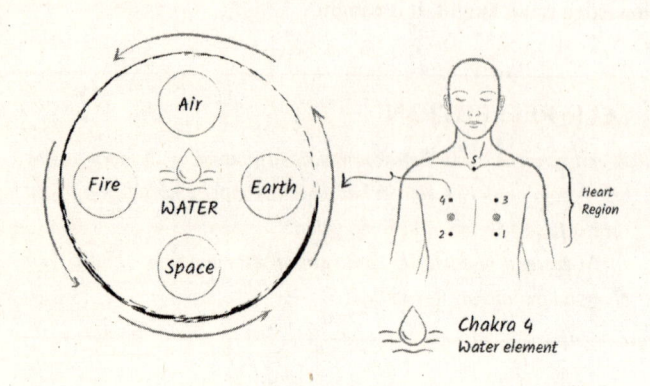

Chakra 4 — Water element

Name	Water Chakra, Fourth Chakra
Prominent Element	Water
Color	Black
Location	Upper right (chest)
Defining Quality	Courage
Main Feelings	Courage, humility, surrender Fear, worry, dismay
Similar Vibrations	9, Sacral Chakra
Direction	Counterclockwise

One stormy night, a young man crossed a river to see his beloved. He grabbed on to a log floating downstream and arrived at her home, soaked to the bone. Ecstatic to see him, she asked how he had climbed up to her balcony. He said he had used the rope she had left for him, but she denied leaving any rope. They then discovered that the "rope"

The Fourth Chakra: Courage

was a snake hanging from the balcony. The next day, after the storm had passed, the young man returned home and found that the log he'd used to cross the river, was, in fact, a corpse. Love had blinded him to the dangers and gave him the dauntless courage to reach his beloved.

As we advance from the fiery energy of the third chakra to the calming energy of the fourth chakra, the pitch of love begins to soften. This doesn't mean that love has disappeared, but rather that it has matured and become more serene. In the third chakra, emotional turmoil can conceal the pure, divine love within us. But as the turbulence settles at the fourth chakra, love comes to the forefront. The fiery energy is calmed by the soothing touch of water.

Upon reaching the fourth chakra, your consciousness shifts, and you feel reassured. Previously, you may have felt like you were pushing forward on your own, but now you sense guidance and support coming to you. Even though it's a feeling you can't quite explain, nevertheless it brings calm and marks the start of true courage. As you come to understand that you are not alone on your journey, you feel more settled.

The Courage of the Heart

It takes courage to act on the inspirations of the heart. The courage to overcome temptations, overcome lethargy, and do what is right. Listening to the heart and following its guidance takes courage, and it's not restricted to grand deeds alone. Reaching for your highest potential by following the heart's guidance requires courage every day. At the fourth chakra, you start developing this courage. Remember that the Heart Region is the realm of opposites, so while you are developing courage, you are also overcoming fear.

At the time of creation, when the soul came into being, the first samskara it formed was fear. The soul was gripped in a feeling of estrangement, and that created fear. When the soul contemplated

MEDITATE AND TRANSCEND

Why am I afraid? fear vanished. In our everyday life, fear is often the result of estrangement between the heart and the mind. The conflict between the inspirations of the heart and the desires of ego creates fear inside.

Fear can obscure clarity and love, and replace them with insecurity. This can be seen in relationships where one or both partners are insecure, constantly seeking reassurance through gifts, attention, or demands on each other's time. Relationships based on fear require constant attention and energy to maintain. In contrast, relationships rooted in love are characterized by willingness to give without expecting anything in return. Love enables two people to communicate volumes with just a look and allows them to support each other effortlessly.

Similarly, the love you merged with in the third chakra gives you the reassurance, and support you need to cultivate courage. Courage does not come from ego. Courage comes from the clarity that love gives. Ego makes you obstinate, while love gives you the courage to be flexible and to make positive changes.

People generally think of courage as the ego's reaction when we demand equality of status, justice, or position, where we need to engage in an uncomfortable discussion, become agitated, or face conflict. But in its true form, courage is an offshoot of the mother tincture virtue humility. The courage of humble people breaks through barriers. Have you seen the tiny, tender, hairy roots of a tree break through the toughest rock? These insignificant, almost invisible, and powerless roots forge the way for the mother root to drive deeper into the soil and make the tree stronger. In the same way, the most impenetrable ego barriers are broken down by the courage of a heart filled with humility.[16]

Courage is innate to us, but it can be accelerated in the company of great souls. In the epic Mahabharata, Lord Krishna displays his celestial form to prepare the warrior Arjuna for battle, instilling him with courage. Similarly, the story of young David's faith and courage

The Fourth Chakra: Courage

in slaying Goliath and defeating the Philistines demonstrates how courage can be given. Courage is a capacity given by nature as and when circumstances call for it. The transference of spiritual power from the Source into our heart is also an example of courage being given. With courage you can wage war on the tendencies that drag you down and rise higher.

> ### SUGGESTED PRACTICE: FEAR DETOX
>
> For the general fear of situations, places, events, and so on, you can use this guided limb-cleaning technique.
>
> Focusing on the left side...
> 1. Imagine that the divine current is flowing into you through the crown of your head.
> 2. Draw the current down to your heart. Now let this current move toward your left shoulder, then let it descend down your arm to your biceps, your elbow, your wrist, your hand, and then let it flow out through the fingertips of your left hand.
> 3. While this flow is going on, think that heaviness, complexities, impurities, and fears are going out of your system along with the flow. Continue this process for two to three minutes, then gently taper the flow.
> 4. Now again, let the divine current be drawn down from above your head to your heart. Let it continue down through your left lower torso, your left thigh, down to your left foot, and out through the toes.
> 5. While this flow is going on, visualize that heaviness, complexities, impurities, and fears are leaving your system along with the flow.
> 6. Continue this process for two to three minutes, and then gently taper the process.
>
> Now repeat steps 1 to 6 to detox your right side.

MEDITATE AND TRANSCEND

> **Affirm and Repeat**
>
> At the end of the detox, with confidence, affirm that you are completely cleaned of all fears and complexities, and that purity and simplicity are restored.
>
> If you feel that there is still fear or heaviness in your system, repeat the process one more time.

While courage is important, bear in mind that fear is not always an enemy. Fear, especially of the consequences of our actions, can be necessary to maintain a discerning ability. The fearlessness of terrorists who shed the blood of innocents is a clear case of courage gone astray. When the fourth chakra is activated, courage and fear both play a constructive role in our lives. Courage gives us confidence, and fear allows us to pause and introspect.

Conditions Experienced at the Fourth Chakra

As explained earlier, the reassurance from the heart and growing courage are hallmarks of this chakra. Discerning inner changes can be tricky because qualities don't develop in isolation. As you grow in courage, you may also become more loving, peaceful, and content. The other chakras are also blossoming, and so their qualities are also growing. At the same time, the opposite qualities also express themselves in your behavior, creating signals and noise.

It's like finding Waldo, but now you have more context and understanding. Regular journaling helps in keeping track of inner changes. The sections below will help you understand more about the qualities and experiences at the fourth chakra. But how do these qualities express in day-to-day life?

The Fourth Chakra: Courage

Flexibility and Flow

Flexibility is one of the hallmarks of this chakra, where water is the prominent element. When you look at water, what do you notice? Water assumes the shape of whatever object it is poured into. It adjusts. If there is nothing to contain the water, it flows effortlessly. The fourth chakra demonstrates this same fluidity.

A constantly changing consciousness needs constant adjustment. Without flexibility, adjustment is not possible. Our day-to-day life demands constant adjustment to circumstances. Whether it's financial stress, demands at work, family situations, or sickness—each day, one thing or another creates a churn that calls for your attention. At the same time, your spiritual endeavors are inviting new conditions to descend. One pulls you inward and the other pulls you outward. It's a lot of change to manage! And you need spiritual flexibility to keep up with it all.

The fourth chakra gives you the flexibility to adjust and adapt with grace. In fact, *you* don't adjust consciously anymore. The adjustment happens automatically. You can say that at the fourth chakra, total dependence on the heart with confidence and courage takes hold.

Humility and Resoluteness

At the fourth chakra, you grow in humility and resoluteness. You will find yourself less stressed and agitated. You are more centered, and you act with greater decisiveness. These changes in you are observed more by those around you and some will possibly share their observations with you. Not that you are looking for external reassurance, but it comes anyway, fortifying your devotion.

Deeper Connection with the Guru

As you progress through the fourth chakra, your relationship with the guru deepens. Having traveled a reasonable distance on your inner journey, you become curious about the system of practice and the teachers who designed it. You discover deeper meaning in the writings you may have read before, and thoughts of kindness and care flow from your heart toward the guru. You feel more open to writing to the guru, exchanging thoughts, and sharing your feelings more freely, especially in your journal.

Letting Go with Love

Surrendering, or letting go, plays a crucial role in our spiritual anatomy project, but it is often misunderstood. To put it simply, acts done with love are akin to surrender. When you think with love, see with love, speak with love, eat with love—these are all acts of surrender. And what do we surrender? The baggage of samskaras that holds us back from expressing our true selves, the hubris that makes us inflexible, and the shallowness that makes us narrow-minded. Surrendering these negative patterns frees us from bondage. The fourth chakra marks the beginning of surrender, and as you progress on your spiritual journey, you can attain newer levels of surrender, enabling you to experience deeper levels of love and growth.

When your consciousness merges with the fourth chakra, that initial fire for the goal changes into eager yearning. Your successful journey at this chakra is marked by refreshing and soothing tranquility. In this time of tranquil awareness, nature sets you onward for the journey.

> **SELF-REFLECTION**
>
> *Note an example of when you were receptive to the feelings of another person even though you disagreed with their perspective. Did that take courage?*
>
> *How does this feel compared to times when you disagreed with a person and were not receptive to their perspective?*

17.

The Fifth Chakra: Clarity

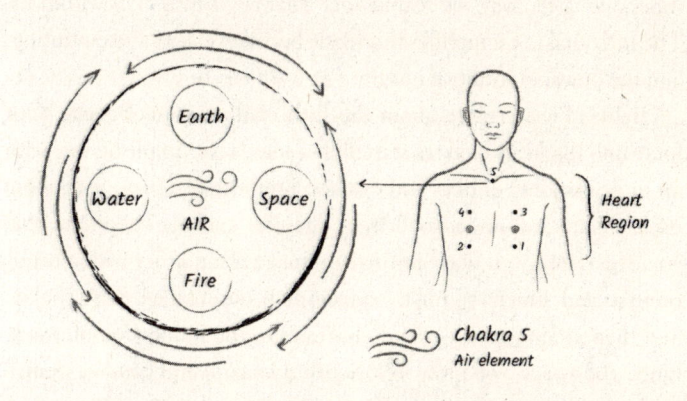

Chakra 5
Air element

Name	Air Chakra, Visuddha, Fifth Chakra
Prominent Element	Air
Color	Green
Location	Throat
Defining Quality	Clarity
Main Feelings	Clarity, discernment, certainty Confusion, chaos, delusion
Similar Vibrations	10
Direction	Clockwise and counterclockwise

Paulo Coelho's bestseller *The Alchemist* tells the story of a Spanish shepherd boy, Santiago, whose recurring dreams of treasure set him on a quest to Egypt to find it. On the way, he is robbed, takes on petty jobs, befriends an Englishman, falls in love, finds a teacher, and finally reaches the pyramids and starts digging. Only then does

MEDITATE AND TRANSCEND

Santiago realize that the treasure he sought all along was not in Egypt but back home in Spain, in the ruined village church where he first had the dream.

Santiago's story strikes a chord in our hearts. Often, in the pursuit of our goals, we jump through hoops and lunge at mirages. Sometimes, along the way, we realize that what we truly seek is within us. The fifth chakra exemplifies this tussle between clarity and confusion, and the power of intuitive insight.

Before I share more about the fifth chakra, a quick recap. Our foray into the heart chakras started in a somewhat simplistic way with an understanding of likes and dislikes. From there, as you read about each chakra and understood their qualities and the conditions that you experience, you likely formed an image of a journey with a neatly orchestrated itinerary: First, you develop acceptance (first chakra) and then attain peace (second chakra). On the foundation of acceptance and peace, you grow in love (third chakra) and courage (fourth chakra). Having developed acceptance, peace, love, and courage in the lower chakras, you then arrive at the fifth chakra, where you can begin to develop clarity.

But while the chapters in this book are necessarily sequential, the journey to the Center is not so linear. At each chakra, there are whirlpools and curvatures. There is the interplay of samskaras. Then there are the traps of ego that ambush you. Like the ups and downs we face in life, the inner journey also has its own flavor of ups and downs.

Here is a mundane example, but it helps make the point. A summary graph of the Dow Jones Industrial Average from the 1900s to 2023 would look like an unstoppable ascent to greater heights. But when you zoom in on the graph, you will see that scattered across that growth are ravines and valleys of financial crises, wars, political turmoil, civil unrest, and more. Zoom in further, and you find that every day, it's the same story: rising up, falling, cratering, coasting—and repeat.

The Fifth Chakra: Clarity

Our inner journey is similar. The ascent of consciousness is the transformation of imperfection into perfection, impurity into purity, and complexity into simplicity. Each day you are waging war with your tendencies and shortcomings. You try to gain new ground while holding the line and preventing losses.

Then there are times when you avoid the fight. You can take a defensive approach and tackle some of the battles indirectly. It's the smart way because a head-on confrontation would drain you. Think of it like pacifying a toddler's tantrum by distraction instead of discipline. The cranky toddler isn't receptive to guidance, so distraction works much better and is easier for the parent, too.

At the fifth chakra, and again at the sixth, we avoid the fight and do not undergo the four stages of opening at these chakras in the same sequence we did with the previous chakras. From the fourth chakra, our consciousness shifts to the periphery of the seventh chakra. The turbulence of the air element present at the fifth chakra makes it wiser for us to approach from a higher state of consciousness. Let me explain.

Clarity, Confusion, and the Onward Journey

The fifth chakra is the air element, and its nature is to be in flux. Whether it's the gusts and gales above the ocean, the zephyr in the meadow, or the rhythmic pulse of breath going in and out, the air is never static. There is always some movement, some churn. In chapter 7, I mentioned there is one moody chakra whose rotation is not fixed. It's the fifth chakra. True to its element, its vacillating nature shows up in both clockwise and counterclockwise motions—always in flux.

In our minds and spirits, the turbulent nature of the air element is reflected in intense swings between opposing feelings. In one moment, you may feel a wave of sadness and tears welling up for no specific reason. In the next, you are laughing at someone's joke so hard that you begin to cry. Both these conditions are an extreme spike in emotions.

MEDITATE AND TRANSCEND

Any samskaras at the fifth chakra cause additional vacillations of the mind, blurring clarity and confusion. Let me give you an example. When you have no one with you, you want company, and when you have company, you want to be left alone. Anyone who has spent a holiday with their extended family knows what I am talking about.

Here is one more example: After working for some years, people sometimes wish to restart their careers. They want to take a sabbatical and use that time to reorient their career. Now, consider this. One fine day, the company you work for suddenly announces layoffs, and your position is eliminated. As bad as it sounds, the abrupt change gave you the opportunity you always wanted: to reset and restart your career.

How would you react?

Chances are that you would feel sour about being laid off. Just because something does not happen on your terms doesn't diminish the fact that it is still what you wanted. But when you get it, you don't value it anymore. The grapes are sour when you can't reach them. The grapes are sour even *when* you reach them. Such is the dilemma unleashed by the samskaras at the fifth chakra.

In order to shield the aspirant from the emotional swings and from the effects of visions or illusions, in the Heartfulness Way, this chakra is worked on in a cascade fashion. The subtler energy from the higher chakras flows down through the fifth chakra, allowing for clarity to develop while avoiding all the other noise. As the aspirant, you don't have to do anything to facilitate this work consciously. Your heart's intuitive intelligence takes care of this.

What you experience will also guide you. For example, if our thought power touches this chakra, we may enter a dreamlike state in meditation. When we try to recollect the experience afterward, we have a hazy memory of it, like a dream. This is a sign that the fifth chakra may have been touched upon during meditation. Aspirants also observe green light when work is done on this chakra.

The Fifth Chakra: Clarity

> **ASK DAAJI**
>
> Daaji, I would like to make better decisions faster. How can meditation help me?
>
> "Compound interest is the eighth wonder of the world. He who understands it, earns it; he who doesn't, pays it." Sometimes, I think about this quote (often attributed to Einstein) in a different context: Making good decisions. On average, we make hundreds of decisions every day. When we make good decisions, they have a compounding positive effect on our lives, and when we don't, we suffer the consequences.
>
> One very important gift of a meditation practice is discernment. A meditative mind can quickly discern, *What is good for me? What will help me evolve? What is ennobling for me?* When such clarity exists, decisions are made faster, even with less information. As we progress in the Heart Region, discernment keeps getting refined and we experience greater clarity, the quality of the air element.
>
> Often, we think it's the big decisions that matter most. For example, whom to marry, which career to choose, and so on. But decision-making is not a one-and-done deal. Decisions form a continuum, where many smaller decisions come before and after the bigger ones. When we steadily improve our batting average in making good decisions, we will become better in achieving our goals.
>
> Meditation will help you improve your batting average. It clears the way for the impulses of the heart to surface unobstructed. When we listen to those impulses and act, the decisions we make are good for us.

In our journey to the Center, mastery over the Heart Region symbolizes an awakening of inner wisdom. At the start of our journey, we struggle with the ups and downs of life, the opposites that are part of human existence. As we grow in wisdom, we learn to make peace with the opposites. Over time, we move beyond the limited idea of making peace to accepting life with a cheerful heart. As we continue to grow, the heart's wisdom transforms cheerful acceptance into unprecedented spiritual openness, where we accept everything as a gift from the higher self to help us transform. We become like the blooming lotus that thrives in the pond water. Others may think the water is muddy or dirty. But the lotus, in its wisdom, embraced the same water and transformed into something beautiful and graceful. Such wisdom makes one eligible for the gift of liberation.

> ### SELF-REFLECTION
>
> *Call to mind a time when you responded to a situation with clarity without any need for the drama of your emotions getting in your way. What helped you act with such clarity? How did this make you feel?*
>
> *Think of a time when you felt guided within, when you just knew what was needed in that moment. Did you trust that feeling?*

18.

Freedom from Freedom: The Gift of the Heart

Picture this. It's evening and you are in your study, absorbed in a book, when you remember that it's recycling day tomorrow. You speed through a few more pages to get to the end of the chapter, then head out to get the recycling ready. Just then, the dryer beeps, indicating the laundry is done. It's also time for your tea, so you put the kettle on and head to the laundry. By the time you finish unloading the warm clothes from the dryer, the kettle whistles for your attention. You pour the hot water into your mug and let it saturate the tea bag, watching the brown currents diffuse into the water as you walk back to the study. You settle back into the book and a few pages in, you realize: "The recycling!"

We are all familiar with such a situation. You leave what you are doing to do something else. On the way, you get sidetracked by another task and forget what you originally set out to do. You might brush off the episode as a side effect of multitasking, but a team of researchers at Notre Dame has a more sympathetic view. In their fittingly titled paper "Walking Through Doorways Causes Forgetting,"[17] the researchers coined the phrase *doorway effect*.

The doorway effect refers to the phenomenon of people forgetting things when they walk through a doorway. This can occur because the doorway acts as an "event boundary" in memory. As you move from one doorway to another, your mind discards information that is not immediately necessary, often resulting in forgetfulness.

Why are we discussing the doorway effect? Wait a minute. I've forgotten.... Joking aside, think of levels of consciousness as doorways; our descent from the Center to the current level had us moving through many doorways. The change in event boundaries made us forget the original home. We have forgotten why we are here, what is real and what is an illusion, what is permanent and what is temporary.

Your spiritual anatomy project creates a reverse doorway effect, whereby when you ascend through each chakra, a doorway of consciousness, the memory of the original home becomes stronger. As you master the heart chakras, you raise your consciousness to a level where you start remembering what was forgotten. It's as if you were asleep for a long time and woke up to a new life, a liberated life.

What Is Liberation?

After crossing the Heart Region, your consciousness is mostly free from the weight of samskaras. You have lightened the load to a level where you attain the freedom to choose your next life. This is what liberation means. You could think of liberation as passing from high school to college. Your life here on earth, this dimension, is like a school where you learn the lessons needed to progress onward. Liberation implies that you learned what was needed, and now you can move to a higher level of consciousness, the next dimension that awaits you. While liberation doesn't preclude the possibility of returning to this dimension, it transforms the experience from a mandatory cycle into a voluntary journey.

Achieving liberation allows you to reach greater heights of consciousness in this life. In the journey, at the second chakra, you start feeling the pleasant effects of liberation, and you attain liberation only after you cross the fifth chakra. But there are many more chakras to cross and regions to cover beyond the fifth chakra. Once liberated, you have the opportunity to keep going and complete the journey.

What happens if you don't attain liberation? Whatever good deeds you do in your life grant salvation to the soul, which is much different from liberation. Salvation is a respite for some time from the cycle of life and death. It is a period of rest for the soul during which the soul receives help from the spirit guides (the wise ones who train and guide souls) on working through the areas that need improvement. The soul contemplates these lessons and prepares the blueprint for the next life. Once the period of rest ends, the soul incarnates and the cycle resumes. Liberation, on the other hand, confers total freedom to *choose* when and where you want to be born if you choose to.

What Does It Feel Like to Be Liberated?

You feel free, so free that you're beyond even the idea of freedom. The recollection of what was forgotten, your real purpose, helps you appreciate life more. By "the recollection of purpose," I don't mean that your purpose is as clear to you as spring water, but it's a feeling of certainty in the heart; you know that an evolution awaits you beyond the objective world. You are in this world, of this world, and aware that the real home lies elsewhere. You start preparing for that home with great enthusiasm.

Think of it this way. There are companies where young management graduates start as interns. They spend a couple of months in each department and learn. The interns are an enthusiastic bunch. They brainstorm, challenge the old ways of doing things, and absorb knowledge rapidly. What makes the interns enthusiastic is that their end goal is clear: *Learn as much as I can so I can succeed in the real job*. Life on earth is an internship, and a liberated soul recognizes this opportunity in the depths of their heart. They use their time wisely and keep their eyes on the goal.

In the liberated state, one is free from the sways of opposites. You arrive at a state called the undifferentiated state (*avyakta gati*). In this state, the opposites don't manifest, and pushes and pulls from the five Cs and five Ds are transcended. They now give you guidance on whether you should act or pause. You know that all the guidance you receive is for your evolution, and this understanding makes you generous.

Generosity is the hallmark of liberation. In all facets of your behavior, generosity shows itself. As I mentioned earlier, true generosity lies in accepting others as they are. There is no judgment about or preconditions for how someone needs to be to deserve your courtesy and compassion. Those who are liberated exhibit generosity of the highest order: the generosity of the soul. By accepting others as they are, they allow the qualities of the soul to flow through their actions and words. Their hearts are open and pure, and they begin to understand the raison d'être of life and everything it brings our way.

Their mastery of the five elements endows them with acceptance, peace, love, courage, and clarity. There is no limit to how much these qualities can grow and how generous you can be. And the biggest beneficiary of all this generosity? You. In fact, the latest research shows a clear neural link between acts of altruism, generosity, and kindness and an increase in happiness and well-being. The increase is greatest when the acts of kindness are toward a stranger, which makes sense from an evolutionary perspective. Researchers studying kindness have found that "our brains are wired to operate better when we demonstrate support to others."[18] Because generosity makes us feel good, it becomes a self-reinforcing habit, which requires less effort. Demonstrating kindness consistently creates new neural connections. It changes our brain.[19] As a result, we are kinder, more generous, more compassionate, more connected with others, and happier.

Often when one reads yogic philosophy, one reads statements like "This world is unreal. It's all a dream," and so on. You may think they are identifying with a reality that lies beyond this life, but a dream is real to the one dreaming. During the dream, our reality is influenced by the dream. We feel fear, anger, joy, sorrow, confusion, and so many other emotions. When we have a nightmare, we sweat, the heart trembles, and when we wake up, we are shaken up. It was only a dream but the effect was real. So how can something that has a real effect on you be unreal? Next day you have a dream again, and when you wake up, you realize that it was a dream. Same goes for life, which is a reality that you are living.

Something profound occurs when you cross the fifth chakra. You wake up once and for all and break the cycle of dreaming and waking up, which is referred to in yoga as breaking free from *maya*, or illusion. The maya is the sensory, objective world. In our waking state we are in this world and of this world. As you progress through the heart chakras, your consciousness transcends the narrow event boundary of the objective world and draws nearer to the Center.

Think of a lamp. The burning point of the lamp is the First Mind, the creator, and the shedding light is all creation. As we keep moving away from the lamp, the darkness increases. And the darkness represents the heavier or denser states of creation. In your journey, crossing the various circles represents your swim toward the lamp (First Mind), and you go beyond it toward the Center. To make the journey possible, you needed this world. This creation, which is an illusion you transcend, was part of the plan to help you remember what you had forgotten. So, the question of whether this world is real does not bother you anymore. It is replaced with the grateful feeling that this station enabled your journey onward.

Liberation and Detachment

Some people worry that attainments like liberation might make a person detached from friends and family. They are concerned that a liberated person might not participate in the joys and sorrows of life. This is a misunderstanding. The heart of a liberated person is ennobled with generosity. They live an authentic life guided by the wisdom of the heart.

Let me illustrate this with a story: Lalaji, the founding teacher of Heartfulness, was once conducting a group meditation when the news reached him that one of his daughters, who had been unwell for some

MEDITATE AND TRANSCEND

time, had passed away. Upon hearing the news, he sat in stoic silence, and a few moments later, tears rolled down his cheeks. One ascetic, also sitting there, commented, "How can a saint in the best condition mourn? How can he shed tears of attachment?"

Lalaji continued to sit in silence for some more time. Then he picked up a few dry leaves lying nearby and crumpled them. As he did so, the leaves crackled. Then he said, "Even dead leaves make a sound when crushed. I am a living human being with a heart. When combined elements are separated, there is bound to be a sound. Such a reaction is natural." Feelings of love, care, and attachment are natural to a human being—liberated or not. Our journey is moving from human to humane to divine and beyond. In this evolution, you do not transcend the innate realities of creation—you become one with them.

Don't Seek Liberation as an Escape

Some pursue liberation because they feel tormented by life. Bad relationships, betrayal, too much suffering, war, disease, and other near-intolerable conditions. Some people I meet express their disgust with life and never want to return. They crave liberation out of aversion to this life. I sympathize with that feeling. When you see the worst of humanity, why would you want to be here anymore? When your life feels intolerable to you, why would you want another? But liberation is not an escape. It is a broadening of horizon, where you get a much deeper understanding of life.

Think of it this way. You put in all the hard work, evolve, and at the end of life you are liberated. Then from up above, you see all of humanity suffering. How can your heart, which is now sensitized to the suffering of others, watch and not act? You will strive to jump back into the fray and help your fellow beings. Liberation confers on you the freedom to choose when and how. It also gives you the wisdom that we all rise together. We all grow together.

Freedom from Freedom: The Gift of the Heart

Liberation also confers you with the escape velocity to move farther and plunge into the next big frontier of the journey, the Mind Region. Resolving the opposites of life frees the soul from the burden of samskaras. With this lightness and purity, the soul now readies itself for the journey onward to becoming one with the Center.

ASK DAAJI

What is the best quality a human being can have?

Many people asked me this question: "Kamlesh, what is the best quality a human being should have?" Three things stand out in my heart: simplicity, purity, and humility. We are all aware of simplicity and purity and how important they are. Rarely do people understand the significance of humility.

In the summertime, when mangoes come up in the branches of the tree, you will see that under the heavy weight of the mangoes, the entire branch touches the soil. If it doesn't and tries to remain erect, it will break all the branches, and the weight of these fruits will destroy the tree itself.

So, we bow down with the weight of growth, with the weight of progress. We should not become so erect and arrogant. If you lack humility, you cannot be labeled as a human being.

What else do we learn from nature? Take cows, for example. What do they return after taking grass, water, and some nutrients? They give you milk, and even sacrifice their lives. But in contrast to everything they give us, all that the cows take from us is grass and water.

Nature is magnanimous. Everything around us in nature takes the minimum. The input is minimum, and the output is maximum. What about us? We take the best from nature. Our intake is always the best. What should be our output? I will leave you with that question.

PART 7

THE MIND REGION

19.

The Mind Region: A Journey to Humility

When someone asks where we feel things, we point to the heart. If someone asks where we think, we point to the head. But where does your sense of self, your ego, live? You can't pinpoint a location. That's because the ego is an illusion. But it's necessary because it endows the soul with identity.

To appreciate the need for ego, imagine the soul at the moment of creation. It is now separate from the Source. All around it is the celestial boom of creation and the Universe in a state of frenzied expansion. In such a setting, the soul was gripped with fear and the illusion of estrangement. It needed an anchor. So it looked hither and thither and said, "I am." The feeling of "I" created from that time onward took the form of ego. And in its purest form, the ego gave the soul the support it needed in finding meaning and purpose.

For this, we should be grateful to the ego. But instead, we see the ego is railed against in the harshest terms as the enemy of the soul and the reason for the downfall of a human being. The ego is blamed as the root cause for prejudice, greed, jealousy, dominance, and everything else horrible that humans inflict upon each other and on nature.

But it's not a fair assessment. Brashness, arrogance, and hubris are all adulterations of the ego. As it happens, the ego can be your best friend or your worst enemy. I find it ennobling to refer to the ego as a dear friend who has unconditionally offered us limitless resources to help us on the march through the Mind Region and toward the Center.

In the coming chapters, as we learn more about the Mind Region, We will clarify the pivotal role of ego in making our spiritual journey a

MEDITATE AND TRANSCEND

success. For now, I request that you be sympathetic to the idea of ego. Don't judge it as good or bad. Instead, appreciate the necessity of ego in self-development.

The Trap of Egoism

After the five chakras of the heart, the next seven chakras are all the realm of ego. Having now transcended our earthly opposites (the five Cs and five Ds) and liberated ourselves from samskaras, we are ready to confront just one pair of opposites: Soul versus Source.

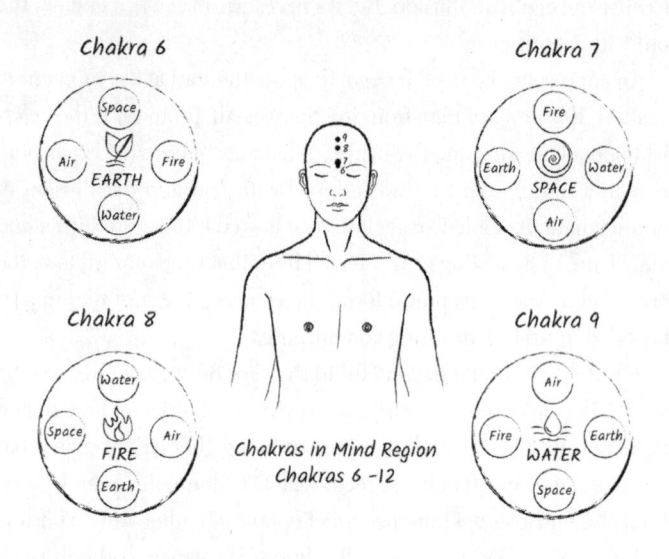

Chakras in Mind Region
Chakras 6 -12

This is a vast area of consciousness and is called the *Mind Region*. As you move in the Mind Region, "I-ness" or "I am-ness" begins to recede, and we anchor ourselves in the Center. Up to this point, our life was centered around *I*, and the *Thou*, the higher self, was in the periphery. Now, we are recentering around *Thou*, and the *I* is dissolving away, even from the periphery.

The Mind Region: A Journey to Humility

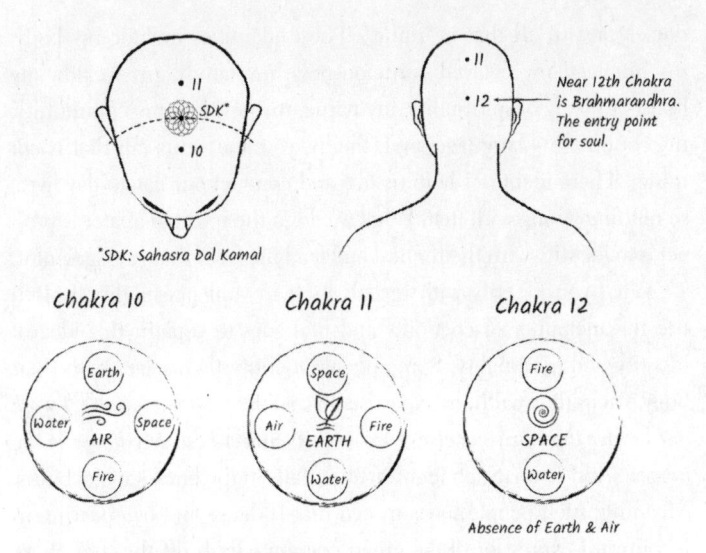

Near 12th Chakra is Brahmarandhra. The entry point for soul.

SDK: Sahasra Dal Kamal

Chakra 10 — Earth, Water, Space, Fire, AIR

Chakra 11 — Space, Air, Fire, Water, EARTH

Chakra 12 — Fire, Water, SPACE

Absence of Earth & Air

Chakras in Mind Region - Chakras 6 -12

What is the higher self, or Thou? It is the possibility of all that you could be, the highest potentiality that your soul can ascend to. Remember that merger is between two like entities, infinity merging into infinity. Your higher self represents the highest possibility that you embody, and your yatra is the journey to actualize that possibility.

The journey through the Mind Region asks us to sublimate the ego to its purest form. In this context, *sublimate* means "to make nobler and purer." We are not pushing down or dominating our egos, but rather refining them to a higher status. All of our efforts are directed at changing the form, not the essence. When we work on ourselves to sublimate the ego, we preserve its essence of humility and allow it to manifest in our lives.

The ego creates I-ness, which is your sense of self. Without the sense of self could you imagine *I*, *me*, and *mine*? These "I, me, and mine" tendencies add up in a subtle way, where we start identifying

MEDITATE AND TRANSCEND

ourselves with all that is "mine." These identities include my body, my intellect, my evolved consciousness, my family, my wealth, my house, my way of spirituality, my name, my position, my community, my country, my language, and, finally, you and yours (all that is *not* mine). These identities help us live and conduct our day-to-day lives, so nothing wrong with that. What we do in the spiritual anatomy project is to identify with the highest and lead life from that vantage point.

What you identify with reveals itself in your personality. I often use the metaphor of coconuts and mangoes to explain this idea of identity and personality. Some people identify themselves with their body, strength, wealth, or expertise on a subject: *I am so strong. I work out harder than anyone else. I know this subject best. My house is the biggest.* And so on. Such identification falls in the bucket of coconuts. Meaning, such people have an ego that is dense and overbearing in its outward expression. Like green coconuts fresh off the tree, these people have tough exteriors. But once you break through the exterior, they are soft on the inside.

Then there are the ripe mangoes. Such people identify with softer aspects of themselves: *I am so humble. I am so soft. I am so generous. I am so spiritual.* And on it goes. Their outward expression is civil and considered. But on the inside, there is strong resistance to change. Their attachment to how good they are blocks their hearts. It takes considerable effort to dissolve the blocks in such cases. (In a lighter vein, my associates have extended the coconut-mango scientific personality model to include kiwis, peaches, and even pumpkins. I will let your creativity figure out the traits of these categories.)

What's important to understand is that egoism is a consequence of moving away from the feeling that *everything* is of the Source. As the feeling that the *entire existence is one* takes root in the heart, the separation begins to dissolve, starting with the feeling *I am a part of this existence*, which evolves into *We all belong to the same* and culminating in *We are all one*. The latter realization sublimates ego in one go!

The Mind Region: A Journey to Humility

The Spectrum of Ego and Its Role

The interplay between your soul and the Source can be described as the space outside a room and the space inside a room. How would you describe that space if the walls were removed and the inside and outside no longer existed? Those walls are our identity—our self-awareness, also called ego. Just as the existence of a room separates outside and inside, the dominance of the ego separates you and the Source.

During meditation, you enter into deeper and deeper levels of *samadhi*, or the original state, becoming absorbed in its depths. Each time you surface, your consciousness returns with an incremental awareness of your higher self. Over time your awareness can reach a level of soul consciousness, where only the barest identities of the Source and the soul remain. This state represents a threshold that can never be crossed as long as the soul retains its ego-awareness. When ego-awareness is lost, the differences between the Source and the individual soul are also resolved. At this most refined state, the ego constitutes your basic identity. In this state, ego is humility personified.

But in an unrefined state, the ego wreaks havoc by creating fear, insecurity, anger, and so on. But it's important to recognize that without the ego, we can't even lift a pin. Our willpower comes from the ego. Confidence comes from the ego. The idea of self-improvement comes from the ego. Our sense of self comes from the ego.

But for all this good, we allow the ego to blow up and take over our lives. That's where it becomes a problem. A dominant ego becomes unreceptive to the mind's inspirations. It's as if the mind is shut out from providing any guidance. The powerful discriminatory ability of the intellect remains unused. Thinking becomes biased and unclear. In such a state where ego has taken over, it assumes the form of arrogance and it decays self-improvement.

Arrogance puts you in a make-believe world where you believe yourself to be perfect, thereby not acknowledging any weakness. Arrogance

MEDITATE AND TRANSCEND

prevents self-introspection, and you remain deaf to the voice of the conscience. How can you improve then? Think of an argument where all you wanted was to dominate the other person. In such interactions, the ego shuts down all other faculties. All the ego wants is dominance, no matter what the cost. The mind is no longer relevant, and the intellect is used for devious means. In such a state, your consciousness contracts, and the entire system feels heavy. Not to mention the samskara chain reaction triggered across the heart chakras.

However, if properly used, the ego becomes an alchemic ingredient in your evolution. After all, it is the ego that entices us to succeed in our work. By competing against others, you fall victim to insecurity and arrogance. By competing with yourself, you avoid these pitfalls and improve. Without the motivation of the ego, we would timidly accept our imperfections and weaknesses and give up on the goal of self-improvement entirely.

Pursuit of excellence initially because of ego and later because of love endows you with the clarity to take stock of where you are and benchmark yourself against your highest ideal. The ego falls into its right place when you experience something higher and when you have the discernment to recognize it as such. Then the power of ego works to uplift you toward the higher.

When the ego no longer serves itself, it starts applying itself to the work at hand. Let us look at the ego as a spectrum. To brush your teeth, maybe your ego needs to be at 3 percent. To give a speech in front of ten thousand people, perhaps you need your ego to be at 80 percent. But if your ego stays at 80 percent after the speech, it's now a problem because your ego no longer matches your level of activity. We say that such a person has a bloated ego.[20] Or, if your ego stays at 3 percent when you need to give a speech in front of ten thousand people, you'll fail in your task. What is necessary is a flexible ego, an ego that can rise up to meet the task at hand, and subside to a state of total humility when it is no longer needed, working always in the service

The Mind Region: A Journey to Humility

of a higher self. There are five words to represent the main shades of the ego spectrum: *arrogance, pride, confidence, presence,* and *humility.* These words are self-explanatory except for *humility.*

Humility is the noblest form of ego expression. It's a state of total confidence in something far greater than oneself. Humility is often confused for servility and lack of confidence, but it is, in fact, your greatest strength. When you are humble, you acknowledge that you are not the doer, but an instrument that allows a greater power to manifest. A humble heart is like fertile soil, where inspirations bloom effortlessly and without resistance. Our actions become evolutionary, and we perform them automatically, lacking any feeling of being the doer. Forgetting ourselves, we march toward perfection.

To ensure the ego stays in a humble state, interiorize in the heart and melt away in its love. When we open ourselves to love, it creates a beautiful world within our hearts, where we are filled with a sense of lightness and joy. We march confidently toward our goal of perfection. "Know thyself" becomes "Forget thyself," and in that process, the higher self is revealed. You arrive at the state of yoga, defined as "skill in action."* In this state, your actions become natural, effortless, and free from deliberation. You derive the best possible results and achieve excellence.

The journey to humility is a steep one. The ego needs something to identify with, and in that process, we hold fast to many of the labels we've been tagged with. The journey in the Mind Region is a peeling away of identities that are not real, so we end up with one identity, that which is our authentic self.

---

* Bhagavad Gita, Chapter 2, 2:50.

20.

The Sixth Chakra: Selflessness

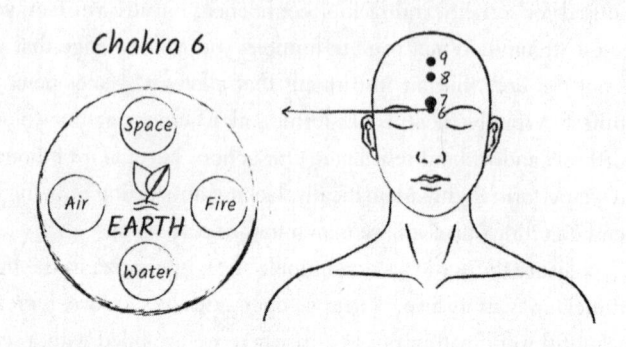

Name	*Ajna* Chakra, Sixth Chakra
Prominent Element	Earth
Color	Mild yellow
Location	Between the eyebrows
Defining Quality	Responsiveness of the heart
Main Feelings	Expansion, relief, empathy, confidence
Similar Vibrations	1 and 11
Region	Cosmic, *Brahmand*

In January 1987, I traveled to India to attend the 114th birth anniversary celebrations of Lalaji, the founding teacher of Heartfulness. A few nights before my travel, I had a dream in which Babuji appeared before me and gave me a sitting. While asleep, I adjusted my awareness and tuned into the meditation. Within minutes, I slipped into deep meditation. When I woke up the next morning, I wrote down my experience in my journal: "In the dream there was gripping absorbency in

The Sixth Chakra: Selflessness

the pin-pointed ray of transmission directed at my heart. Some work was initiated but remained unfinished."

After reaching India, I had an audience with Chariji. After the small talk, in a somewhat gruff tone, he asked me why I hadn't come earlier to India. I was not sure how to answer this question. The celebrations were still a few days out. Also, Chariji and I communicated often. If he needed me for some work, he called or sent a fax (a fax machine was the in thing in those days). Unsure of how to respond, I kept quiet. After some time, I took his leave, still pondering.

The next few days went by blissfully. Thousands of people from all over the world gathered in the coastal city of Mumbai, where the celebrations took place. The meditations during these special events are one of a kind. It's as if Mother Nature envelops the venue with a blanket of special grace.

After the celebrations, Chariji asked me to travel with him to Bangalore. There, one evening, he was leading a group meditation. There were many people around him. I was standing at a distance, maybe around a hundred feet. When I saw Chariji, I felt waves of grace engulf me. It was such a vivid feeling that I sat down where I was and started meditating.

As soon as I closed my eyes, I felt the waves carry me. This meditation started right where the meditation with Babuji in the dream had ended. It was an unmistakable feeling of continuity, and I knew it was a sign of something important. After meditation, Chariji walked straight to me, and said, "Come tomorrow. I will give you a sitting." The following morning, a brisk wintry dawn, I meditated with Chariji. As I observed my condition, I realized that I had crossed the sixth chakra (also called the Cosmic Region) and landed at the seventh chakra.

I am sharing this experience not to celebrate my own progress, but to shed light on an important aspect of the guru's work in Heartfulness. The guru is ever eager to raise the aspirant to higher levels.

Even if there is an inkling of an opportunity, the guru will use it to push the student onward. Chariji was eager to take up my case and was hoping to do it in advance of the celebrations. I have seen many instances, over a meal, in an informal conversation, or during a walk, when Chariji would silently elevate individuals and entire groups of people to higher levels. Such work is above and beyond the work that a guru does in anonymity.

When you read the life stories of great teachers, you will find similar examples everywhere. Buddha blessing someone with a mere glance, Saint Therese of Lisieux elevating souls through her words of love, Vivekananda granting liberation to a thirsty soul while taking a walk on the beach, and so on. These stories all emphasize the importance of preparing oneself and being ready to receive the gift of inner change. These stories all make the same point: Enter the field of spirituality with grand ambitions. Come with the thirst to drink the ocean itself. Think big and bold, and, with a heart full of love, proceed on this inventure.

From Movement to Expansion: Hallmark of the Sixth Chakra

In the human frame, if you draw a line connecting the two eyebrows, the sixth chakra is slightly above that line.

As with the fifth chakra, the sixth chakra blooms as a result of work done on higher chakras. We do not progress linearly through the four stages of merger here; the downward flow of power is too intense to permit us to linger. It would be like trying to float leisurely in a rapid. Not only will you not succeed, but you're very likely to slip down with the current. Instead, the energy we have built opening the first, second, third, and fourth chakras and the support of the guru catapults us straight to the periphery of the seventh chakra.

The Sixth Chakra: Selflessness

What this means is that we experience the conditions at the sixth chakra from a higher vantage point. We feel the weather of this unique position while avoiding the inclement conditions that might otherwise create discomfort in our consciousness. Once we cross the Heart Region, the distinct feeling one has is the expansion of consciousness. The journey in the Heart Region is characterized by movement from one chakra to another. Once we cross the Heart Region, movement changes into expansion. Whereas movement is linear and two-dimensional, the nature of expansion is infinitely multidimensional.

It's the difference between owning a boutique chain of stores and opening a factory to manufacture the products you sell, and a logistics company to operate the warehouses. All of a sudden, you're operating on a different order of magnitude.

ASK DAAJI

Daaji, I have seen systems and scriptures recommend meditation specifically on the sixth chakra. Should I do so?

It's true that some scriptures recommend meditating specifically on the sixth chakra. For example, in the Bhagavad Gita, Lord Krishna advises Arjuna to meditate at the sixth chakra. Arjuna was a warrior who fought in the Mahabharat war, which is said to have taken place in 3137 BCE. The sixth chakra is the distribution center of power to all the chakras below it. Arjuna was wavering on the battlefield. He was asked to meditate at the sixth chakra to boost his drive and prepare him for battle. Similarly, other systems that advocate the pursuit of psychic powers suggest meditating at this chakra. I am sure they have their reasons.

> My view is this: We are not going into any wars or seeking powers. We are leading normal lives that, though they may sometimes feel like battlefields, require love, not weapons, to win our daily battles. For thousands of years, the great sages have said the heart is the way to God. Lord Jesus said, "Blessed are the pure in heart, for they will see God."[21] Lord Buddha said, "So with a boundless heart should one cherish all living beings; radiating kindness over the entire world."[22] The need of the hour is to meditate on the heart. We don't need powers on this path. Power is not what makes a master. An ordinary person requires power to work, but it takes a master to work with no power.

Conditions Experienced Once You Cross the Heart Region

As you journey in the Mind Region, the grip of the ego loosens. As a result, the reactiveness in one's nature subsides, and the responsiveness of the heart increases. Your humane nature leads you to the portals of the angelic realm, and your soul begins to amplify in potency in a variety of ways.

Generosity Transforms to Selflessness

What distinguishes human, humane, and divine life? To move from human to humane requires generosity, while to move from humane to angelic necessitates selflessness and sacrifice. Generosity is sharing what you have, while sacrifice is giving even when you don't have. Generosity accepts people as they are, but selflessness dissolves the distinction between people, we are all one.

People with angelic qualities sacrifice without hesitation. That's why people say, "I prayed, and an angel helped me." While we can

The Sixth Chakra: Selflessness

take inspiration from the benevolent actions of Michael, Gabriel, Raphael, and other angels, I am not talking about them. Angels don't know you, and need nothing from you, yet they help you because that's what they do.

Crossing the Heart Region can bring about a heightened sense of empathy and compassion, cultivating angelic qualities within you. If you notice a pregnant woman while walking down the street, your heart automatically sends a prayer of well-being for the mother, child, and family. Seeing a homeless person on the street, you feel their cold and pain, and you share the soup you bought for lunch. During meditation, when someone comes to mind, your heart sends thoughts of love their way. None of this behavior is premeditated; your heart is in a state of flow where you do what it says and move on. Progress in the higher realms depends on the selflessness you cultivate in your heart and the sacrifice that flows in your actions.

Relief and Renunciation

One of the most pronounced feelings you experience upon crossing the Heart Region is a sense of relief. For perhaps the first time in your life, the pinpricks of likes and dislikes have dwindled to almost nothing, and the emotional turmoil that used to bother you has settled. Your devotion has matured to a level where you sail through storms with poise because you are assured of a higher power guiding the helm. The words *God*, *divine*, and *Source*, which had been intellectual concepts until this point, now become feelings in your heart. Such a new flavor of consciousness brings real relief. Spiritual restlessness is present, but it is subtler and more potent.

The other change one can notice is the refinement in one's renunciation. As you may recall from all the way back at the first chakra, renunciation is the feeling of loving detachment where you are involved but not ensnared. It starts developing the Heart Region and becomes more refined as you travel the Mind Region. At this stage, the opposites of the five Cs and five Ds no longer sway you, and you are freed from ulterior motives and personal prejudices.

Sacred Sounds of the Heart: Anahat Ajapa

When the first chakra becomes active, it emits vibrations corresponding to the sacred word *Aum*. Aum is often associated with Hinduism, but it is more than a Hindu symbol—it's a primordial vibration of space that has been heard by saints and mystics. The arousal of Aum in the heart happens naturally and shouldn't be forced through mental techniques. As the journey progresses beyond the sixth chakra, the vibrations of Aum spread throughout the body. It is called *anahat ajapa*, meaning "natural vibration of the heart."

Shadowy Darkness and Pressure at the Temples

As one approaches the Cosmic Region, some abhyasis, after their meditation, may experience a sense of shadowy darkness. After meditation, when they open their eyes and look at objects, say a chair or a vase, for a few seconds, they seem as though they're dark. This hints that one is moving away from materiality toward energy. Furthermore, as one crosses the cosmic region, abhyasis may also experience a gentle and soothing pressure on the temples, like a comforting touch.

※

Again, a word of caution: Don't try to create any of these conditions mentally. You have nothing to prove to anyone. If you experience any of these conditions on their own, make an entry in your journal and move on. If you do not, that is okay, too. Measuring spiritual progress is not as cut-and-dried as taking your blood pressure and comparing it to last week's number. Its more nuanced and multifaceted. As you become more sensitive, you're better able to observe the changes in your inner conditions, attitudes, and reactions.

The Sixth Chakra: Selflessness

One more aspect to appreciate when it comes to inner progress is that the more you grow, the humbler you become. Humility, an essential characteristic of a spiritually growing person, helps you compare yourself to a higher ideal and strive to continue growing. Our journey is toward infinity, and the progress we attain is making us akin to infinity.

> **SELF-REFLECTION**
>
> *Can you give an example of a situation involving others where you responded with poise, confidence, and the delicacy that the situation required to provide a favorable outcome for those others?*
>
> *What have you learned about yourself from these situations?*

21.

The Seventh Chakra: Stillness

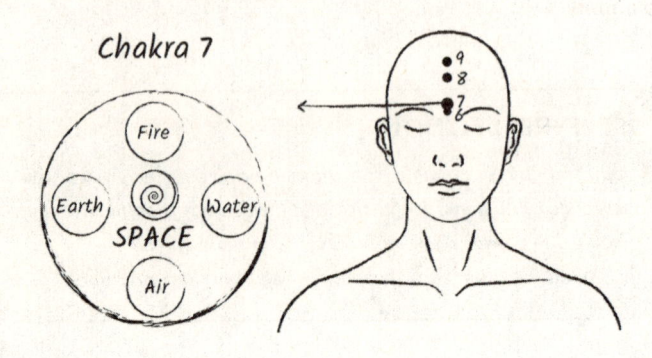

Name	Seventh Chakra
Prominent Element	Space
Color	Mild red / pink
Location	Above the sixth chakra, behind it
Defining Quality	Stillness
Main Feelings	Power, ecstasy
Similar Vibrations	2 and 12
Region	Paracosmic, *Parabrahmand*

There is a parable attributed to Buddha that goes like this: One day, Buddha asked his disciples to bring him a cup of water from a nearby pond. When they returned with the water, Buddha asked them to drink it. However, the water was dirty and murky, and the disciples couldn't drink it. Buddha then told them to set the cup aside and wait.

The Seventh Chakra: Stillness

After some time, the dirt settled to the bottom, and the water became clear and drinkable.

Stillness creates clarity. It creates the space for inspiration to be transformed into insight. Famous people like Archimedes, August Kekulé, and Marie Curie all made discoveries in moments of relaxed awareness where the mind was still and essential, invisible truths revealed themselves.

In today's fast-paced world, stillness is vital. Otherwise, we miss out on the beauty of life. Imagine a vibrant, velvety rose unfolding its petals and releasing its sweet fragrance into the air. If you are on a flight, you won't notice a thing. Even when you're in a car or running at a fast pace, you may not notice it. But if you stand still in front of the flower, you can appreciate its entire beauty. Mind is the fastest thing in the Universe. If the mind is in a storm of restlessness, can you appreciate the beauty blooming in your heart?

Your spiritual anatomy project invokes inner stillness from day one. Meditation infuses your consciousness with a stillness that helps anchor the mind. By the time we arrive at the seventh chakra, the dimension of stillness that reveals itself leaves us spellbound. This region is also called the Paracosmic Region, meaning something that's vaster than the cosmos. It's an immense region of consciousness.

Conditions Experienced at the Seventh Chakra

Lifetimes can be spent exploring this region. It's like stepping into a different dimension where one feels as if they are standing on the edge of a vast, limitless expanse of stillness, power, and beauty. In Heartfulness, the journey is such that one gets a rich experience of this region, especially its stillness and immensity.

MEDITATE AND TRANSCEND

Absolute Stillness and Infinite Movement: Consciousness at the Seventh Chakra

At the seventh chakra, one calms in the eye of the storm. Around you, there could be unpredictability, chaos, stress, and everything else that can disturb the inner peace, but you remain centered in stillness. There is a specific reason why this occurs. See, when you settle down at the seventh chakra, the stillness of the soul resonates with the stillness of the mind. It's as though they click into place: This is the exact moment when you realize the existence of the higher entity within.

Once the resonance between the soul and mind is harmonized, nothing can shake the stillness of your mind. No matter what happens in the world around you, you are centered. You appreciate the immense beauty of the soul blooming within, and your stillness radiates in peace and moderation.

Stillness does not mean that you are stationary. Think about a wooden top that kids spin with twine or the fidget spinners they play with. When the top is spinning at a high speed, it looks stationary. Only when it begins to lose speed do you realize it's moving. It's exactly the same for your consciousness: It is moving so quickly that you seem still to the eyes of the Universe. This is the quality of consciousness at the seventh chakra: absolute stillness and infinite movement.

When one merges with this chakra, they become unshakable. Be it a subject to study, a business deal to close, things in the family to attend to, or working on behalf of nature's commands, they can steady the mind in all these areas simultaneously. Even their agitation will have a stillness, indicating the enormous poise that reigns within. If you are in the company of someone in this condition, you imbibe that essence and benefit from it. You feel their peace and stillness in your heart.

Such a condition and many other higher conditions result from mastery of consciousness. The integrated development in the spiritual anatomy project brings you face-to-face with such conditions in

The Seventh Chakra: Stillness

a natural way. We don't hanker for conditions or try hacks to access altered states of consciousness. We seek mastery that brings us to a level where states of consciousness descend on demand.

The Paracosmic Region: A Powerhouse

Besides stillness, power and expansion take on a new meaning at the seventh chakra. This chakra is the storehouse of inexhaustible energy, and power descends from here to the sixth chakra; from there, it is distributed to the lower regions. When you merge in this chakra, you feel all the lower chakras are also energized with power. It's as if a bolt of lightning is discharged from the seventh chakra, which continues to support the expansion of lower chakras.

In some of your meditations while at the seventh chakra, you feel as if the field of your meditation is expanding from your heart and growing outward. When you come out of meditation, you have a distinct feeling of expansion within and without. Some also feel the expansion as ascension, where they soar to a higher level, riding waves of energy higher and higher. Consciousness becomes so liberated that you can sense it projected in all directions. Some sensitive practitioners feel that they are expanded all over, and the distance no longer feels like a barrier. To some, even the Universe seems small.

THE TRAPPINGS OF POWER: CURVATURE AND UNLEASHING DOMINANCE

This chakra is an ocean of power and ecstasy replete with curvatures. One may feel ecstatic when passing through this region. The feeling of ecstasy created by power is the sign of an ecstatic ego. The effects of such ecstasy are countered by the spiritual restlessness within, which helps one move onward. Additionally, if one can remain vigilant to such conditions, then the journey becomes faster.

Besides ecstasy, some may enjoy the charming effects of power and feel invincible. And upon whom do we unleash our so-called invincibility? Mostly our loved ones bear the brunt.

There once lived a sage named Durvasa in India during the Vedic times. He was notorious for his power and harshness. His every word would upset others to tears, and people froze around him. His life was a saga of unleashing fear and discomfort in others. Instead of receiving love and warmth from those around him, Durvasa created an aura of wrath and fear, estranging himself from what he most sought. I bring up this example to remind you that we are all on this path to become one with the Source. We are here to become love.

As we progress in our spiritual journey, it's important that our etiquette, especially our words and actions, reflect the loving tenderness of the heart. The words we use can either serve as a bridge to connect with someone's heart, or they can be like barbs that hurt the feelings of others. At the seventh chakra, it's particularly important to counter any feelings of power or superiority with humility and kindness. This means being mindful of our words and speaking with compassion and respect.

Powers for Nature's Work

At the seventh chakra, there are many powers that highly elevated yogis can harness to carry out nature's work. The powers are of an order that can shake up galaxies and planetary systems. The seventh chakra is also home to the mightiest instrument of power, the Wheel of the Supreme (or the *Maha-Kal-Chakra*), which is utilized to cleanse the Universe of negative elements and restore order.

The Seventh Chakra: Stillness

It's important to note that these powers are not meant for pleasure, showboating, or dominating others. They are meant for the betterment of humanity and are used by evolved souls working under the orders of nature. Heartfulness is the path of love and not power. The system is designed such that practitioners are insulated from any powers along the way. Also, any effects of power that come our way are channeled into creating onward momentum for the journey.

> **ASK DAAJI**
>
> Daaji, I often hear about the mystical powers of the yogis, especially astral travel. Can you talk more about this?
>
> Astral travel has been a popular subject in pop culture books and movies, including *Star Wars: The Last Jedi*, in which Luke Skywalker projects his avatar across the galaxy to confront Kylo Ren and his army. While these creative depictions are entertaining, astral travel is meant for spiritual work.
>
> When you are at the seventh chakra, astral travel becomes a possibility. Astral travel enables a yogi to go wherever the work demands. The subtle body is sent to the area of work with the intention of completing the work and returning. The yogi can also send the subtle body to many locations at the same time. In the world outside, we travel from one place to another. In the inner world, the journey is such that you go nowhere and yet your presence is there where you will it.

Development of Intuitive Capacity

Intuition is inner guidance in the form of inspiration. These inspirations can come during meditation or when you are in a meditative state, or sometimes even in dreams. Simplicity, purity and selflessness create the conditions for intuition to arise.

MEDITATE AND TRANSCEND

The seventh chakra is the astral realm, and the intuitive capacity of the finest type starts developing from here. To help accelerate the inner transformation, the abhyasi gets inspirations about what to do, what not to do, how to act, what decision to make, what lifestyle to adopt, and so on. The astral realm gives indications and suggestions. They are like ideas filled with potential. It is for us to actualize them. We can either further develop it, delay it, or kill it. It's up to us.

You can think of intuitive guidance like friendly advice from a caring elder. They come from a place of your well-being and growth. The more you adopt and implement and realize, *Yes, this works*, the more guidance flows toward you.

Aham Brahmasmi: I Am the Source

A feeling of inseparableness from the Absolute is felt as one journeys across chakras. This feeling grows finer and finer as one advances toward higher chakras. The inseparableness with the Absolute is felt on three levels.

At the lowest level, it appears in the form of feeling *I am the Source*—that is, there is no separation between me and the Source. Next, it turns into the feeling *All is the Source*, conveying a sense of universal inseparableness. Everything in creation has a connection with the Source. Last of all, it assumes the feeling *All from the Source*. This feeling conveys a sense of extinction of every view leading to a state of non-beingness. At each chakra, these three feelings are felt, but at the seventh chakra, the abhyasi's mind harmonizes well with these feelings, and the condition is felt in the most vivid way.

Albert Einstein once said, "He who can no longer pause to wonder and stand rapt in awe, is as good as dead; his eyes are closed." Our journey

The Seventh Chakra: Stillness

at the seventh chakra infuses us with stillness of a most refined quality. The stillness within gives birth to awe, igniting the journey of the next chakra.

> **SELF-REFLECTION**
>
> *Have you had experiences of intuition when the chatter in your mind is silent?*
>
> *How do you think your life might change the more you listen in silence to your heart?*

22.

The Eighth Chakra: Surrender

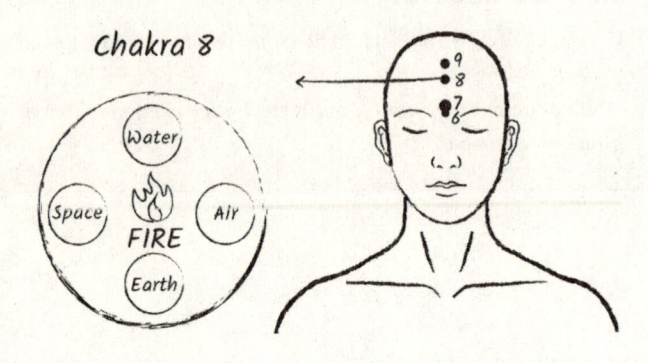

chakra 8

Name	Eighth Chakra
Prominent Element	Fire
Color	White
Location	Three finger-widths above sixth chakra
Defining Quality	Peace
Main Feelings	Wonder, peace, surrender
Similar Vibrations	Third chakra
Points Nearby	Chit Lake, Passion, and Saraswati
Region	Surrender, *Prapanna*

In the jagged wilderness of the Jalini Forest in the kingdom of Kosala, there lived a dacoit who killed travelers and collected their right-hand pinky fingers as souvenirs.[23] He wove these fingers into a garland, which he wore around his neck. The morbid display of his kills earned him

The Eighth Chakra: Surrender

the name *Angulimala*, meaning "the one who wears a garland (*mala*) of fingers (*anguli*)." The legend goes that he had slain 999 people and was awaiting the one thousandth victim to complete his garland.

One fateful day as he prowled the forest for his next victim, he saw a monk strolling alone. By that point, everyone in the kingdom knew of the dacoit's viciousness, and no one dared walk the forest alone. Yet here was a monk, enjoying his walk alone. Angulimala bolted to pin down the monk. But as he lunged for the monk, the monk seemed to float farther away.

After a few failed attempts, frustrated, he roared, "Monk! Stop now!"

The monk, none other than the Buddha, turned around, and his eyes met Angulimala's. In those moments, the dacoit saw the unending depths of the Buddha's eyes.

"I have stopped," the Buddha whispered. "When will you stop?"

The Buddha's kindness and loving sympathy dissolved Angulimala's hate and rage. A mere glance and a few words transformed Angulimala. He fell at the feet of the Buddha and sought redemption. It is said that Angulimala became a disciple of Buddha and even composed scriptures.

What Angulimala experienced was *awe*. A profound moment where you come across something so surreal, majestic, and limitless that all your ideas, conditioning, and frameworks dissolve. In these moments of awe, the human spirit transforms.

Modern-day psychologists studying awe describe it as a spiritual, moral, and aesthetic emotion.[24] The towering granite cliffs of Yosemite, the limitlessness of the Pacific Ocean, the moving beauty of a Vermeer, the profound depth of a meditation—such experiences fill you with awe. In such transcendent moments, you rejoice in your smallness. Toward the end of your journey in the Paracosmic Region (the seventh chakra), you begin to experience awe, which comes to its zenith in the eighth chakra. You witness a shift in your consciousness that creates quietude in your heart. Quietude is an attitude of

MEDITATE AND TRANSCEND

enrapture where, in silence, you are drawn toward something far greater than you.

Such awe from spiritual experiences helps sublimate the ego. Overcoming the ego by forced subservience to a grander ideal is artificial, and it does not work. But when you experience something greater and feel your connection with it, the resulting awe helps you focus on that greater ideal. In this way, the ego shifts focus from *I*, *me*, and *myself* and looks up to *thee*, *thou*, and *thine*.

From Awe to Surrender

This shift in focus from the lower self (I) to the higher self (Thee) is the beginning of surrender. It's a grand epoch in your consciousness and a worthy goal to strive for. I use the word *surrender*, but in the yogic tradition, the actual word is *Saranagati*, or *Prapatti*. It is a state of loving dependence and a reverential and joyful acceptance of all that comes your way in life. You can think of surrender as *letting go* of the limited self and its bondage.

From the eighth chakra on, your journey is one of letting go. To climb a ladder, you let go of the lower step so you can go higher. The trees let go of leaves to make way for new ones. The flowers let go of the seeds and, in turn, create meadows filled with blossoms. You, too, arrive at more sublime states of consciousness only because you have let go of previous ones.

Letting go means making decisions in favor of growth and implementing those decisions with love. As you evolve, you let go of all the baggage you are carrying. By *baggage*, I mean the emotional baggage of prejudices, anger, jealousy, guilt, likes and dislikes, and anything else that burdens the soul. Some baggage you let go of through the cleaning process. The rest, you hand over to the guru and you move onward. In the yatra, the guru takes over the baggage, provided you

The Eighth Chakra: Surrender

allow it. Surrender is nothing but handing over the baggage to the guru so you can travel light on the journey.

Prior to the eighth chakra, there was a lot of pushing and pulling to surrender. This is understandable, since the ego needs to latch on to something for its survival. But as you refine and sublimate the ego, the process of letting go unfolds naturally. Religions have used symbolism to indicate this idea: Lord Krishna surrounded by cows. The cows are content letting go of their worries of sustenance and survival. They know the cowherd who led them to the pasture will lead them back to the stable. Lord Jesus holding the lamb in his arms depicts a similar vision of a good shepherd, protecting the flock now settled in the caring embrace of God.

That becomes our state, too. Everything seems just as it should be. There is decreasing separation between the soul and the Source. Your single-minded attention is now set on the goal, the Center. So far, your devotion, your effort, and your strength moved you forward. But awe makes you realize, *Why struggle when I am being lovingly carried?* Awe leads to surrender, which leads you to wisdom.

Conditions Experienced at the Eighth Chakra

By the time you are at the eighth chakra, many noticeable changes occur. Some of the most important are:

Synchronicity Becomes Routine

Some of you may notice deeper synchronicity with your surroundings. You may be pondering a question, and the answer appears in the book you're reading. You think of someone from the distant past, and they drop you a note. You wish something well for a family, and it happens. Such synchronicities have occurred before, too, but now they occur so often that you stop wondering about them. They become such a routine affair that you rely on them. You get into a rhythm of waiting for a hint or a sign, and sure enough, it shows up. It's one of the ways that surrender expresses itself in your behavior. A lot more can be said about this topic, but it would be better to experience how synchronicity manifests in daily life and guides you.

Relationship with the Guru

I have observed that in Asian countries and other parts of the East, it is common for families to have a spiritual teacher. They may have a photo of the teacher in their household and follow their teachings. The main focus is on the teacher. On the other hand, in the West, there is a greater emphasis on the teaching itself, with the Western mind evaluating and assessing the teachings before focusing on the teacher. Despite these differences, the goal remains the same: spiritual growth.

In the Heartfulness Way, by the time you arrive at the eighth chakra, you may have spent years, possibly decades, with the practice. By now, the spiritual anatomy project becomes a top priority for you. You also develop an authentic curiosity about the guru.

Beyond the person and the physical presence, you are keen to comprehend the guru as a principle. This idea helps one think of the guru as a guiding energy or an inspiration. In that sense, the guru is not necessarily a specific person, but a concept or an idea that represents the highest potential of human consciousness. Such shift in thinking encourages aspirants to look within, to connect with their inner wisdom and cultivate a richer understanding of their place in the Universe. It leads to soulful inquiries like *How do I deepen the heart-to-heart connection? How do I experience what the guru experienced? What is my real identity?*

The Eighth Chakra: Surrender

A Refined Flavor of Peace

In contrast to the seventh chakra, at the eighth chakra power loses its charm. One realizes the difference between power and the source of the power. With the greatness of the Source imprinted in one's heart, it brings one to a special flavor of peace. Think of the freshness a person walking in the blazing sun would feel after a bath in the cool waters of a river. The flavor of peace at the eighth chakra rejuvenates you with its freshness.

All through the journey, you experience peace at regular intervals. After the journey at the first chakra, you enjoy peace when you land at the second. Similarly, tired from the aftermath of emotions at the third chakra, you feel refreshing peace when you enter the fourth, the water chakra. Now again, after the ecstasy of power of the seventh chakra, you hit a high pitch of peace at the eighth chakra. It's as if nature designed the journey with pit stops. Besides rest and rejuvenation, is there any special reason why the journey is designed this way?

You see, the yogic traditions have a special name for inner peace, and it's called *atma shanti*, where your atma (soul) finds peace. Such peace is an outcome of the soul's confidence that the means chosen for the goal are proper. If they were not, you would not find atma shanti. So that's why at regular intervals the soul conveys a message of peace, seeing the assurance of the path.

By the time you come to the eighth chakra, the peace has actualized. You can say that the soul is now at reasonable height from where it can see and be reassured, *Yes, now I have made my way up.* It's an extraordinary condition to have.

The Matrix Moment: Renunciation Evolves

Do you remember the ending sequence in the movie *The Matrix* when Neo deciphers the green screen of flowing numbers? It's when he unravels the Matrix and sees it for what it is. At the eighth chakra, something similar happens, but it's even more exhilarating. (Sorry, Neo, the yogis got there long before you.)

When you access the eighth chakra, you develop an inner condition where the deeper meaning and purpose of life become clear. You comprehend the reason for likes and dislikes, the role of desires, the need for generosity, the value of sacrifice, the importance of humility, and many other concepts finally fall into place. You recognize their necessity, and this recognition refines renunciation (*Vairagya*).

So far, renunciation has grown at each level of your journey, becoming more refined as you move from one chakra to another. Renunciation is not the nonpossession of things but nonattachment to them, a loving detachment where you are involved but not ensnared. But the renunciation developed up to this point has a subtle aversion to the world. There is a feeling of avoidance.

At the eighth chakra, renunciation evolves into another state called self-withdrawal (*Uparati* in Sanskrit). In self-withdrawal, you are free of all desires, even those pertaining to the next world. Your mind is centered on the Absolute, and your senses are completely purified. You use them for the purposes they were meant for: eyes to see and not compare, tongue to speak with kindness and not gossip, ears to hear only that which is ennobling, and touch that connects and not repels.

In self-withdrawal, whatever work you do, there is a balance in all senses and faculties. You experience peace and settledness where activity does not cast the slightest impression on your mind. You feel as if the whole world is like a dream. Modern-day psychologists studying the flow state often described as a feeling of effortless concentration and enjoyment in what you are doing. Self-withdrawal is like a superlative flow state.

To allow self-withdrawal to mature, we all must cultivate moderation. Moderation means balance in all senses and faculties, nothing more or less than what is naturally required at the time for any specific purpose without its slightest impression on the mind. Moderation is a characteristic of nature and the essence of spirituality. Practicing gentle and polite language, courteous dealings with others, sympathy and love for fellow beings, reverence toward elders, and an unrevengeful nature is greatly helpful in allowing the state of self-withdrawal to settle in your being.

> **POINTS NEAR THE EIGHTH CHAKRA: CHIT LAKE, POINTS OF PASSION, AND KNOWLEDGE**
>
> There are three other points near the eighth chakra: Chit Lake, Points of Passion, and Knowledge. These points play a vital role in contributing to inner peace. I describe these points while we are at the eighth chakra because of their physical proximity; however, the work at these points has been occurring from the very start of your practice. The essential practices of Heartfulness meditation and sittings facilitate the work at these points—the flowering of which contributes to inner peace.
>
> If you were to draw one-inch lines from the seventh and eighth chakras toward the inside of your head, forming a triangle, the meeting point of those lines is where you'll find there three points: Chit Lake, Knowledge Point, and Passion Point, bunched together like grapes.

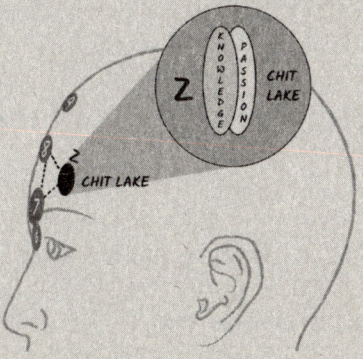

MEDITATE AND TRANSCEND

Chit Lake

The constant flow of thoughts that descends from the mind is generated by a chakra called *chit lake*. The word *chit* means "consciousness," and Chit Lake conveys the source from which thoughts descend. The current, or thought flow, from the Chit Lake descends, passes through the fifth chakra, and divides into three branches—two of them flow toward the first chakra, and the third branch flows toward the second chakra.

During meditation, the Chit Lake gets cleaned, and as a result the flow from the Chit Lake is also clean. The excessive thoughts that bother us during meditation are also calmed as the Chit Lake is purified. In the early days of your practice, the perceived color of the Chit Lake is grayish. As you advance, you perceive a brilliant ruby red color at this chakra.

The Point of Knowledge and the Point of Passion

Near the Chit Lake are the twin Points of Knowledge and Passion. These two Points, which almost touch each other, are inseparable. If you work on one, the other is also worked on.

Knowledge Point is all about the knowledge you need. This point is very active in intellectuals, but don't confuse the opening of the Knowledge Point with becoming all-knowing in one fell swoop. It is more that whatever knowledge is needed comes to you effortlessly. For example, any confusion you may feel in the early days of practice is replaced with the assurance that whatever knowledge is necessary will descend.

The Passion Point is all about stirring of passion. It's likely that as you cross the eighth chakra, the passion you feel surpasses even what you may have felt during your teenage years as, out of nowhere, the mind is overwhelmed with sexual thoughts. (This can come as a distressing surprise to anyone who arrives at the eighth

The Eighth Chakra: Surrender

> chakra in their old age; often, at some level we like to believe that passions have left us behind.)
>
> Many people want to suppress their passion because they think it's not conducive to spiritual growth. But by doing so, they will also suppress knowledge. When Knowledge Point is active, you activate Passion also. When you cut passion, you cut knowledge as well. So, forcefully repressing passion through thoughts is not advisable. A better way is to allow moderation to develop through regular practice and cultivating the right attitudes. Some advanced practices for Point A meditation and cleaning at Point B also help; you can learn these from a preceptor.

As you move forward from the eighth chakra, the state of surrender blossoms to create a new level of openness to life. Even without us being aware, we accept everything that comes our way without judgment. The eye is fixed on the goal, and the feeling of one's insignificance as compared to the grandeur of the Source takes root in the heart.

> ### SELF-REFLECTION
>
> *Can you recall an example of how you let go of a situation in life? What did that teach you about yourself?*
>
> *Would a life not guided by seeing things as good and bad bring you comfort and peace?*

23.

The Ninth Chakra: Insignificance

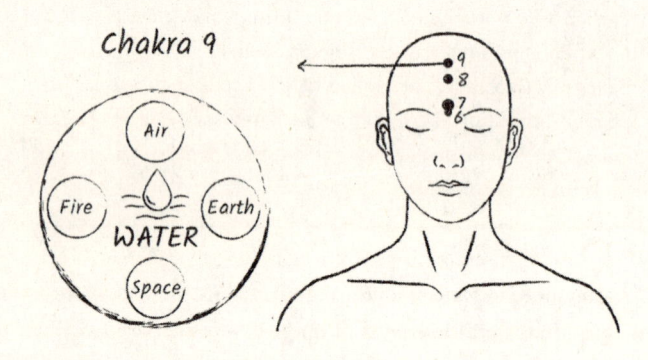

Name	Ninth Chakra
Prominent Element	Water
Color	Gray
Location	Four finger-widths from the tenth chakra, toward the forehead
Defining Quality	Surrender and humility
Main Feelings	Divinity all around
Similar Vibrations	4
Region	Surrender and Absolute, *Prapanna Prabhu*

Once an emperor drew a line on the floor with a piece of chalk. Then, looking at his courtiers, he said, "I want you to shorten this line. But you can't erase the line or break the floor."

When no one could figure out how to shorten the line, the king's favorite minister stepped in. He took a piece of chalk and drew a longer

The Ninth Chakra: Insignificance

line right next to the one the king had drawn. In an instant, the line drawn by the king became shorter.

Drawing a new line changed the perspective. The sublimation of the ego is a similar exercise. If you try to annihilate the ego by force, it doesn't work. But when you change your perspective and look up to something far grander and magnificent, then the heart is filled with appreciation. It longs to become one with the grander idea, and the ego supports this endeavor. Such a life-altering perspective occurs when you enter the ninth chakra. You enter a state where you feel you are born into a new world.

The ninth chakra is the region where the balance tips between you and the Source. Up to this point, our life was centered around I, and the higher self, the Thou, was in the periphery. At the ninth chakra, you are re-centered around Thou, and the I dissolves away even from the periphery. After a considerable ascent, rising above the clouds, for the first time in your spiritual anatomy project, you have a direct view of the Source. The feeling so near, and yet so far, which was a constant companion until now, is gone. Your heart knows that you are in the presence of the Absolute.

This experience leaves such a deep impact on you that an automatic meditative state develops in the heart. You may be running to catch a flight, mowing the lawn, cooking dinner, or even in the middle of an argument, but through all this, within you, the meditative state continues undisturbed. Constant remembrance, which until this point was a practice you cultivated, is now as automatic as breathing.

Radha, the spiritual companion of Lord Krishna, was thinking of Krishna and slipped into meditation. As she meditated, her heart called out *Krishna. Krishna. Krishna....* After a time, the form of Radha changed into that of Krishna. And then, Krishna started thinking of Radha and called out, *Radha. Radha. Radha....*

The story is not about Radha or Krishna. It's about how in the journey you have come to a place where your call echoes in the Center. So far, you were seeking the Center, and now the Center seeks you.

Conditions Experienced at the Ninth Chakra

Extending the analogy of the small line and the big line, your heart now perceives the Source throughout as if every beat is a reminder of its presence. Wherever you look, you feel the radiance of the Source flowing. The birds, flowers, insects, plants, air, water, people—all are from the Source; this feeling is predominant. The heart overflows with feelings of tenderness, and such a tender heart bids farewell to all ill will and prejudice.

From the ninth chakra on, the ego sublimates into humility. The more you allow your heart to yield, the humbler and more loving you become. And is there any limit to how much the heart can yield? We come from infinity, we merge into infinity, and our capacity to love is infinite. The more the heart surrenders, the more love flows through you.

From this region onward, your conscience is clear like spring water, and your weaknesses appear more clearly to you. Any inclination of the ego to dominate others feels torturous. Even the slightest wrong thoughts create whiplash within, and instantly you repent by correcting your thoughts and praying for forgiveness.

The State of Insignificance

Recall the story I shared while writing about the heart chakras, where Babuji complimented my inner condition. My condition in those days was like a dog relaxing in the shade of a tree on a blazing hot afternoon. Babuji read my state and said, "You should be in this condition 24/7." It was the condition of insignificance (abhoodhiyat, or subdued state). When you merge in the ninth chakra, you arrive at that condition of insignificance. In this state one doesn't care about things like

The Ninth Chakra: Insignificance

respect, disrespect, and so on. One is centered in Thou, and that's where the attention rests.*

There is a certain forgetfulness that accompanies this state, where you become less mindful of your abilities. Don't be alarmed. You didn't lose them. Instead you lose the burden of proving to yourself and others how good you are. Your skills become high-performance tools at your disposal. You use them when needed and then put them away.

Freedom from the Choice-Busy Mind

We often underestimate how overwhelming choice can be. Consider these choices we make every day: what to do, how to spend money, whom to spend time with, what to eat, when to get up, when to go to sleep, what to wear, and so on. According to a study by Cornell University researchers, our brains churn through 226.7 decisions a day, just about food alone![25] Not to mention significant life choices like where to live, whom to marry, what to study, which career to pursue, and so on.

The weight of constant decision-making and personal preferences often meld into a potent cocktail of FOMO (fear of missing out) for many individuals. Even before they make a choice, regret sets in for the choice they won't be making. They keep brooding over the decisions they did not make and spoil the good thing they may have going.

At the ninth chakra, you are freed from the cognitive and emotional burden that comes from thinking and choosing. A choice-free mind intuitively guides you to cut through the clutter. You don't have to think for long; the answer is readily felt in your heart. This

---

* In Indian mythology, Hanumaan was a devotee of Lord Rama. He exemplifies the state of insignificance. *Hanu* means "without" and *maan* means "respect." *Hanumaan* means "one who doesn't care for one's own *maan* or *apmaan* (respect or disrepect)." One's attention is fully centered in the ideal taken up for devotion.

heart-based decision-making is a shift in behavior from thinking to feeling, and you can experience this shift yourself. You don't have to wait until you reach the ninth chakra. The shift from thinking to feeling begins much earlier, where your heart becomes more vocal and guides you in decision-making by inspiring you and alerting you when you may be steering off course.

At the ninth chakra, heart-based decision-making becomes the norm. You have an innate ability to face circumstances with courage, respect, and reverence (*dheerata*) because the heart-mind field is in resonance. Your intentions, thoughts, and choices are aligned with your evolution. The energy of desire is transformed into energy for evolution. There is clarity in thinking, humanity in execution, and contentment in the results that follow.

The Guru and Abhyasi Relationship Hits a High Note

By the time you arrive at the ninth chakra, your relationship with the guru has matured to a level of mutual trust and adoration. As an abhyasi, you are grateful to the teacher for the conditions and the experiences that helped you progress. Your heart appreciates what you have achieved, and that appreciation cultivates trust. This trust solidifies into faith: *Yes, here is someone who can help me reach my goal.* In your heart, when you feel this faith irrevocably, then the heart-to-heart connection becomes permanent.

Arriving at this level of heart-to-heart connection is extremely special. Not everyone reaches this level, not because the guru doesn't want you to or because nature is filtering people out. Rather, achieving spiritual or worldly goals hinges on aligning priorities with one's goals. When your goals and priorities are aligned, then you progress fast, and if they diverge, progress slows. If your goal is to achieve peak

The Ninth Chakra: Insignificance

fitness, then exercise should be a top priority. If you want financial freedom, then creating wealth should be a top priority. If you want to achieve the Absolute, then practice with the right attitude must be a top priority.

An aspirant whose goals and priorities merge forges a unique connection with the guru. The sincerity, discipline, and eagerness of the aspirant to reach the goal move the guru's heart. At this stage, the aspirant can be called a disciple in a nod to the self-discipline that has developed. The guru ensures that the heart-to-heart connection they share becomes permanent.

Like a mother carrying a child in her womb, the guru at this stage of the journey ensconces the remembrance of the disciple in their mental womb for seven months. The togetherness of thought during seven months allows the guru to create a *spiritual entity* of the disciple. At the end of this period, the guru delivers the spiritual entity of the disciple into a higher dimension of existence.

Think for a moment about backing up your hard drive to the cloud, where the backup is an exact replica of your hard drive. You can think of a spiritual entity in similar terms—a replica of the soul—although, unlike clicking a button to back up your drive, it's not a simple achievement at all. The soul replication is a great spiritual milestone, which the guru eagerly awaits all to arrive at.

The condition of insignificance makes all this possible. It's not a comparative state where one thinks of themselves as insignificant by beating down one's ego. The inner softness of the heart is such that the idea of any form of comparison is lost. Such a soul grows in potency because of the inner pliability. In chapter 2, I gave the example of a block of ice, water, and water vapor. Between the three, it's water vapor, the subtlest, that has the maximum potential to expand. Likewise, a soul at the ninth chakra has such a level of subtlety that it can grow further by replication.

MEDITATE AND TRANSCEND

Soul Replication Explained

To understand the idea of soul replication, think about the life force and how it divides and grows. There are plants such as rose, lavender, and banyan, from which you can cut a small branch and plant it in the soil, and in a few days it takes root. Other plants, like the acacia, disperse seeds that carry the life force. So, depending on the level of consciousness, the life force propagates in different ways.

In the case of human beings, physical birth aside, there is the possibility of spiritual birth within a person's lifetime. Soul replication is the mechanism for achieving spiritual birth. Souls that achieve a certain level of potency can replicate. For souls with lower potency, replication is not possible. But higher-potency souls give birth to what we can call the *spiritual entity*, a replica of your soul. It has the same level of potency as your soul does.

The spiritual entity takes birth in a dimension that can support the vibratory lightness that it needs. Under the watchful guidance of the guru, the spiritual entity is born in a dimension of consciousness corresponding to the ninth chakra. In this dimension, the spiritual entity is welcomed by the hierarchy of spiritual guides who receive it with warmth and care.

The spiritual entity is at home here, but it gets its nourishment through you. The actions that you take here in this world affect its growth. It's as if an umbilical cord is connecting you and your spiritual entity. When you meditate, the enriching vibrations travel to your spiritual entity and help it grow. When you are drowned in constant remembrance, the spiritual energy that charges you also enriches your spiritual entity. When you develop simplicity and purity, the spiritual entity feels the lightness you exude. A life of acceptance, generosity, and sacrifice helps you here in this life, and it also helps you in the beyond by enriching your spiritual entity.

While nurturing is possible, so is neglect.

The Ninth Chakra: Insignificance

If one ends up falling victim to prejudice, hatred, and other negative traits while being stationed at the ninth chakra or the higher chakras, then the spiritual entity also suffers. What height one falls from decides how much it hurts. If we slip while walking on the road, we might get away with a bruise or a sprain. But the consequences can be catastrophic if one falls from a great height.

Similarly, if the inner compass gets misdirected while you are in the higher regions, the spiritual entity shrivels. It quivers with the pain inflicted by heavier vibrations and is tormented in the other dimension. In some extreme cases, the spiritual entity can even wither away. This is a spiritual tragedy.

Does this mean we keep worrying about mistakes we might make? Living in fear of making mistakes that might cause downfall is not a positive way to approach the goal. Also, if we keep worrying about mistakes, we will make one sooner or later. We should remind ourselves of what brought us here. It's our devotion. Loving devotion to the goal made our ascent possible. We take refuge in devotion and allow that force to continue propelling our progress.

We must be mindful of the banks that allow the river of devotion to flow serenely. Those banks are humility and purity. The famous line that Clint Eastwood's character, Dirty Harry, speaks in the movie *Magnum Force*, "A man's got to know his limitations," rings true here. Humility and purity create awareness of limits. The heart is sensitized, and any slight indication of older conditioning kicking in triggers warning signs in your heart. Thoughts like *Is this the right way to think? How should I amend my actions? Am I conducting myself with the right softness of heart?* and *How will my family or my guru feel about such actions?* help you to course-correct.

The spiritual entity's primary role is to enhance the potency of your soul. Instead of one working alone, you now have a force multiplier. There are two of you working in tandem and growing faster.

One more thing to remember: Even if it is billions of years away, at

MEDITATE AND TRANSCEND

the time of the final dissolution of the Universe, when everything in creation will merge back into the Center, the evolved souls with spiritual entities will affect the level of consciousness of the next creation.

> **ASK DAAJI**
> What happens to my soul after I die?
>
> At the time of death, your soul ascends to a dimension that resonates with the vibration of your soul. There are infinite dimensions, so the soul will always find its exact vibratory match. It's a perfect fit like a lock and key.
>
> If the consciousness has evolved beyond the fifth chakra, then the soul attains liberation. For such a soul, there is no rebirth (unless it chooses to take birth). The journey of a liberated soul is guided by the spirit guides in those dimensions. If the soul does not attain liberation, then depending on its karma, the soul enjoys a period of salvation and then takes birth.
>
> At each dimension there are spirit guides. Some spirit guides travel back and forth, visiting many dimensions. But there is always a designated spirit guide or a team of spirit guides to look after our spiritual progress. There, too, a spirit guide who is fixed at a certain dimension has no liberty to move up. But there are spirit guides who can go to any dimension, up or down. The spirit guides who have the freedom to travel across dimensions are highly elevated ones.

The journey at the ninth chakra shows how insignificance helps us rise to great heights of consciousness. It shows the beauty of nature's design where the humbler we become the higher we rise, and the lighter our ego becomes, the grander the states of consciousness that descend into our heart.

The Ninth Chakra: Insignificance

SELF-REFLECTION

Have you experienced a feeling of overwhelm brought on by too many choices? How did you overcome this feeling?

What are your thoughts at this point about the importance of humility in order for you to grow further spiritually?

24.

The Tenth Chakra: Belongingness

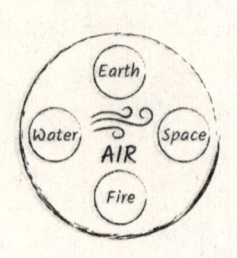

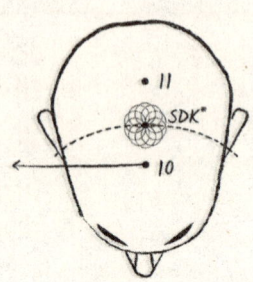

Chakra 10

*SDK: Sahasra Dal Kamal

Name	Tenth Chakra
Prominent Element	Air
Color	Medium green
Location	Two finger-widths from the crown chakra toward the forehead
Defining Quality	Belongingness
Main Feelings	Oneness with the Absolute
Similar Vibrations	5
Region	Absolute, *Prabhu*

A sensei was walking on the monastery grounds, preoccupied with thoughts about finding his successor. As he walked around, he inspected a wall that was being constructed around the monastery. He saw one of the monks who had been in the monastery for a long time, working on a section of the wall. He asked the monk what he was doing.

The Tenth Chakra: Belongingness

The monk politely replied, "Laying bricks, Master."

The sensei continued his walk and saw one more monk working on another section of the wall, and he asked him the same question.

"Building a wall to protect the monastery," replied the monk.

Toward the end of his walk, the master saw a young monk whistling away and laying bricks. The lightness and joy of the young monk touched the master. The young monk was new to the monastery, and he had never seen the master before. The master approached him and asked, "Young man, what are you doing?"

"I am building a part of my master's vision. I am laying bricks, but it's the beginning of something exquisite. You will see, sir, in the coming years this monastery will grow into a beacon of light."

A sense of belongingness made the young monk one with the sensei's vision. Such belongingness comes when hearts beat as one for a higher purpose. It reflects the deep spiritual connection that unites all beings, where the vision of one is the vision of all.

Such a condition begins to emerge when one enters the tenth chakra. The entry into the tenth chakra marks the beginning of your journey in the Region of the Absolute, also called the First Mind, or the Godly Region. This is a vast region that spans the tenth, eleventh, and twelfth chakras. Entry into the Region of the Absolute marks a high point in the journey, where one has transcended human and humane levels and now swims in the divine realms to go toward the Source.

Conditions Experienced at the Tenth Chakra

At the ninth chakra, there were two entities: you and the Source. Your prayerful calls from the ninth chakra echoed in the Source. Up to that moment, you were seeking the Source, and at the ninth chakra, the Source seeks you. That game of the seeker and the sought that started at the ninth chakra is now in full swing at the tenth chakra. And, as the name of the region suggests, by the time your journey through this region ends, only one entity remains: the Absolute. You have succeeded in sublimating your ego by the time your journey in the Mind Region ends.

Belongingness

The intimacy with which the Absolute becomes everything and one's ego sublimates totally is something to behold. This is not a conquest of dominance and authority. It's a story of melting away in love. While at the ninth chakra, you had a view of the Source; once you enter the tenth chakra, you feel the proximity to the Source. The proximity makes you feel *I and the Absolute are now one. There is no difference between us. Everything that is of the Absolute is also mine.*

When this sense of "mine-ness" grows, it spills over into all aspects of life. At work, home, in the community, anywhere you may be, the openness of your heart and your very presence inspires others. The usual motivations like more money, more power, better visibility, and so on are all superseded when belongingness takes center stage.

Think of this example: A storm is coming. A window in your home is broken. The glass is shattered, and you don't have money to fix it. What would you do? Likely, you would borrow money, call in a favor, or get creative with some other materials to fix the window. Whatever it takes, you would fix the window. Why? Because you have the sense that you must take care of your family. The sense of belonging creates the urgency to care, to protect, to nurture, to nourish, and, most important of all, to love.

Reverence for the Self

In such a state, the reverence for the Absolute is the reverence for the self. Why? Because the Absolute is in you, and you realize this

The Tenth Chakra: Belongingness

irrefutably. The space outside and the space inside were an illusion created by the walls of ego. When the walls are taken down, the outside and inside become one. As the ego dissolves, you feel the oneness all around and within you.

The metaphorical separation between you and the Absolute has disappeared. You see the world through the eyes of the Absolute. When you speak, you feel it's the Absolute speaking through you. In the past, to enjoy the fragrance of roses, you walked all the way to the garden. Now the scent of roses is always with you.

For this reason, you treat the body as a sacred place. You take care of the body as the abode of the Absolute. You refrain from any acts that would diminish the sanctity of your body, mind, and soul, aware of the communion you now have with the Absolute.

Sameness

Belongingness matures into sameness. There is an old wives' tale that couples who age together start resembling each other. While that tale, like many others, is debatable, what isn't debatable is that by the time you arrive at the tenth chakra, you have spent years loving, revering, thinking, feeling, and becoming like the Absolute. The purity and simplicity of your heart, the humility of ego, and the fervent song of prayer have all created a likeness between you and the Absolute. After all, what is the Absolute? It is you in the purest, simplest state.

Starting at the tenth chakra, sameness develops, and it continues as you go onward in this region. The idea of a creator and the creation starts to lose its hold on you in this chakra because you don't see that separation as vividly anymore. Your gaze shifts higher, and you are looking at the horizon toward the origins of the First Mind.

ESCAPING THE TRAP OF BLISS: THE CROWN CHAKRA

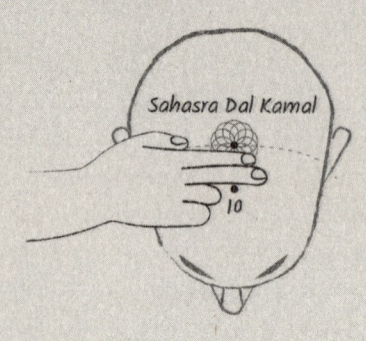

Sahasra Dal Kamal

Toward the end of the journey at the tenth chakra one comes face-to-face with the SDK (crown chakra, Sahasra Dal Kamal, Sahasrara). Located between the tenth and the eleventh chakras, SDK is the chakra for bliss. Yogic literature makes a big to-do about this chakra, and it is commonly regarded as the ultimate state. It's understandable: After all, who doesn't want bliss?

Yet, if you recall, at various parts of the journey, chakras can cast curvatures of consciousness. These are labyrinths in which consciousness gets trapped, and the journey stalls. The curvatures can appear in various forms. At the second chakra, it was peace. At the seventh chakra, it was power and ecstasy, and between the tenth and eleventh chakras, the SDK can trap you with bliss.

What we are seeking is merger with the Center, the highest approach available to us. Bliss at the SDK is like a scenic overlook on the freeway and not the destination. Also, when there is bliss, who is enjoying it? *You* are the one enjoying it, which means the ego is still there, and the goal is far away.

The elders offered us a coded word to remind us that the real goal is far beyond bliss. The coded word is *sat-chit-anand*, existence, consciousness, bliss. *Sat-chit-anand* is a mantra or a coded word for

The Tenth Chakra: Belongingness

humanity to map our trajectory from human, to humane, to divine and beyond. It is a sacred formula: "Our existence (*sat*) can become worthwhile, enjoyable, successful, and purposeful (*anand*) only if our consciousness (*chit*) is allowed to evolve. When this happens, then we will experience *real* bliss."

In the Heartfulness journey, while we move to the eleventh chakra, we do feel some effects of the SDK. If you are wearing white, no matter how fast you run through a coal mine, you will gather coal dust. It's inevitable. Similarly, the SDK is the powerhouse of bliss, and some of the bliss rubs off on you. You enjoy this bliss as a restful supplement. And you need it for what comes next at the eleventh chakra.

SELF-REFLECTION

Can you recall examples of paying careful attention to the thoughts arising in your mind because you realize the impact of your thoughts and intentions on others?

What do you imagine it might feel like if you see yourself as part of everything in the Universe? How might that awareness expand your consciousness?

25.

The Eleventh Chakra: Restlessness

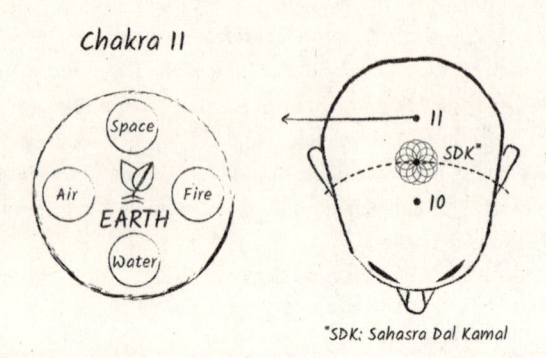

Chakra 11

*SDK: Sahasra Dal Kamal

Name	Eleventh Chakra
Prominent Element	Earth
Color	Pale yellow
Location	Two finger-widths from the crown chakra toward the back
Defining Quality	Vision of reality
Main Feelings	Helplessness, restlessness
Region	Absolute, *Prabhu*
Similar Vibrations	1 and 6

As you begin this chapter, I invite you to meditate for a few minutes on the meaning of these two words: *life* and *existence*. If you have a journal handy, write a sentence or two about the meaning of each word. If it's easier, write down your responses on this page itself and mark the date, so when you revisit, you can see how your answers change over time.

Describing experiences is a tricky affair. It's like describing a rain-

The Eleventh Chakra: Restlessness

bow. Anyone who has seen a rainbow can attest to its beauty and grandeur. But to put it into words is a challenge. Regular journaling helps you to develop the vocabulary to put into words what is felt in the depth of the heart.

In my understanding, existence is eternal. When existence becomes encapsulated in a body, it becomes life. Your life has a beginning and an end. But existence is a continuum. Your body has a life, and your soul has an existence. A hint that you have completed the journey at the tenth chakra is the realization that there is an eternal, universal existence. In your heart, you feel the universal existence and feel its flow from the Center. Whatever shapes, forms, and colors life may take, they all flow in the continuum of existence.

While lives can be many, existence is but one. You knew of this before, but at the tenth chakra, you have the conviction of your experience. You know that you are eternity itself. When this feeling matures, then you are ready to plunge into the eleventh chakra.

The experience of universal existence gives you a vision of the Source from which everything, including you, sprang forth. Home is in sight, the feeling similar to taking the exit for your hometown after a daylong road trip: You're so close you can taste it. With the anticipation of that final step—becoming one with the Absolute—whatever peace and bliss propelled you to this moment evaporates, and you become restless with yearning.

You are now in the wellspring of restlessness. And thankfully so. Restlessness is your best vehicle for growth. Think about it: At each stage, restlessness for the next stop helped you make progress. When you got to that next stop, the result was peace. Thereafter, restlessness kicked in again to propel you further.

Unrelenting restlessness and a sense of urgency is essential for success in material or spiritual realms. In a span of two years, a young Isaac Newton created calculus and offered some foundational ideas about gravitation, and in his quest to understand light and lenses, he

MEDITATE AND TRANSCEND

even ended up sticking a needle in his eye. Many years later, when someone asked him how he worked out gravity, Newton replied, "By thinking continually."[26] Edison, a prolific inventor talking about his light bulb invention, said, "I have not failed. I've just found ten thousand ways that won't work."

Likewise in the spiritual realm, there are so many examples of unrelenting restlessness that led to human flowering. One day, a disciple asked Ramakrishna Paramahamsa, a great saint, why he was so restless in his devotion. Ramakrishna replied, "The restlessness is like a fish swimming in the ocean of devotion. Without restlessness, the fish would become stagnant and die. Similarly, without restlessness, the devotee's spiritual progress would come to a standstill."

In our journey, restlessness is the forerunner, and the condition we experience from all this restlessness is pain. Not intolerable pain, but growing pains akin to the pain of a butterfly breaking free from the shackles of the cocoon. It is pain that makes you a new you. Science shows this, too: When people are afflicted by pain and trauma, those with a strong spiritual core emerge resilient. They use the pain to create a new version of themselves.[27]

But remember, we don't go around seeking restlessness and pain. The Heartfulness Way is the natural way. Whatever comes, we take it and use it for progress. Also important to understand is that the restlessness I am describing here is spiritual restlessness. Unlike the restlessness triggered because of an ailment or some other inconvenience, spiritual restlessness thrives as an undercurrent in the heart inspiring you to keep moving. There is great joy and fervor in this silent undercurrent that keeps propelling you onward.

At the tenth chakra, the restlessness and pain trigger a condition that can be described as "nonpeace peace." Try to imagine a lump of salt without saltiness. It looks the part, feels the part, but its key essence—its saltiness—isn't there. Something similar happens with peace at the eleventh chakra. It feels like peace, but there is no

The Eleventh Chakra: Restlessness

peacefulness there, only the agitation to move. Enveloped in this most beautiful restlessness, you continue to progress in the Region of the Absolute.

> **SELF-REFLECTION**
>
> *Does your restlessness for spiritual growth make it easier for you to accept daily challenges at work and in the family? Do you have an example of a recent challenge that you cheerfully accepted?*
>
> *What is the greatest lesson you have learned from something that you have repeatedly struggled with in your life? Has this lesson inspired you to embrace your human foibles with humility?*

26.

The Twelfth Chakra: Settledness

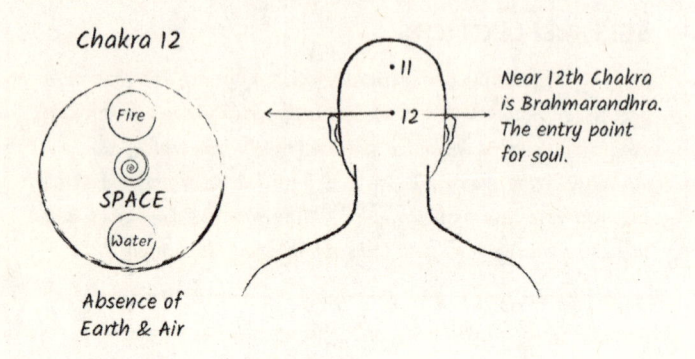

Chakra 12

Fire
SPACE
Water

Absence of Earth & Air

Near 12th Chakra is *Brahmarandhra*. The entry point for soul.

Name	Twelfth Chakra
Prominent Element	Space
Color	Pale pink
Location	Four finger-widths from the eleventh chakra, toward the back
Marquee Quality	Total settledness
Main Feelings	Complete humility and settledness
Points Nearby	*Satyapad, Brahmarandhra*
Similar Vibrations	2 and 7
Region	Absolute, *Prabhu*

The merging of rivers is an evocative metaphor used in spiritual stories and traditions to represent the union of the soul with the Source. When two or more rivers merge, they create a force that is greater than the sum of its parts. In Hindu mythology, the convergence of

The Twelfth Chakra: Settledness

the Ganges, Yamuna, and Saraswati Rivers symbolizes the merging of individual consciousness with universal consciousness. Similarly, the merging of the Missouri River and the Mississippi River in Native American traditions represents the transformative power of unity and the importance of working together toward a common goal.

As you imagine shifting from the eleventh to the twelfth chakra, I want you to envision the energy flow from chakra as a river. There are rivers of acceptance, peace, love, courage, and many more, all flowing toward the ocean, the Source. Some rivers might have started as a trickle, but as you progress, the rivers swell in their flow. The twelfth chakra is the grand junction, where everything you've accrued so far in the journey merges into one majestic river gushing toward the Center. You may recall the four stages of the flowering of a chakra: coexistence, nearness, identicality, and merger. The twelfth chakra mirrors this process at the macro level, as the states from every previous chakra unite to create identicality with the Source.

This is an important aspect to understand. When one embarks on the spiritual anatomy project, it is the first stage of the journey: coexistence. In this first stage, one has a vague understanding of something called the Center, and the journey begins. As one progresses and gains new experiences, the idea starts taking shape that there is something higher, a greater presence toward which one is progressing. This feeling becomes stronger as the ego sublimates, and one feels proximity to the Source. This is the second stage: nearness.

Upon further progress, at the twelfth chakra, one arrives at the third stage: identicality. Consciousness is now akin to the new level one arrives at. Lightness in the heart makes the weight of all mental activity lighter. One's thoughts seem lighter, and all interactions have lightness. One feels settled in this stage. The resonance that kept developing with the Center is now complete, and one is akin to the Source. This is the stage where one is at the pinnacle of purity.

MEDITATE AND TRANSCEND

Pinnacle of Purity

At the twelfth chakra, one is purity personified. Purity is the absence of any contradiction. In such a state, thought loses its weight, there is no heaviness of emotions, and there is unity in one's being. One arrives at sameness with the Absolute through the purification of all the chakras and cultivating a lifestyle that nurtures inner hygiene. This includes cleaning the samskaras and correcting the workings of the mind to develop correct thinking, the right understanding, and an honest approach to life. The discernment one develops helps preserve and nurture the purity within.

We originated from purity. The pure streams that caused our being also originated from the purest source, and for that reason, the thought of purity persisted in us through the passage of time. Establishing a relationship of devotion with the Source, the inner zeal of interest, and the guru's guidance help one arrive at this rarefied place of purity.

And in this lap of purity, one rests.

At this stage, the ego is sublimated, and all that is left of it is the finest membrane of identity. Desires bid farewell a long time ago. At the twelfth chakra, the desire to progress spiritually also ends. You are in perfect contentment, where you want nothing and need nothing. And why should you? You are safe in the lap of the Absolute.

Perhaps, though, you already see the problem. Though we have reached the Absolute and identify with it completely, we are not yet one. We have not merged and, so, there is a standoff. You are perfectly content, at peace in the Region of Absolute and lacking motivation to move further, yet the Source is still awaiting you. How are we to resolve this standoff?

To add to the complexity of this situation, the twelfth chakra is also where the Brahmarandhra, through which the soul enters the body, is located. At the moment of conception, the soul arrives and stays close to the expectant mother. The soul circles around the expectant

The Twelfth Chakra: Settledness

mother's stomach; staying outside, the soul gives momentum to the cellular process for fetal development. This process happens in the first trimester of pregnancy. It accelerates the division of the cells, and the first organ that forms in the fetus is the heart. From the heart, the other organs are nourished. Once the fetus's Brahmarandhra is well developed, the soul enters the body. At the time of death, the souls of liberated beings exit the body through the Brahmarandhra. If one has not arrived at the level of liberation, then the soul may leave the body through any of the orifices like the behind, eyes, ears, mouth, or nose.

When you are at the twelfth chakra, the natural urge for the soul will be to leave the body. (Don't worry; no one is dying.) This is where the guru takes over. Like the mother kangaroo carries her joey, the guru carries the abhyasi to the Central Region, the thirteenth chakra. In one of the many innovations in the Heartfulness Way, the guru guides the abhyasi's consciousness beyond the Brahmarandhra and facilitates its entry into the Central Region. This marks one's entry into hallowed grounds of the Center. So much awaits the abhyasi there, in what is the largest region of all.

Nature's Gate: Satyapad

Before the guru can take you from the Region of the Absolute to the Central Region, there is a gate that one needs to pass through. This gate is called the Path of Truth (*Satyapad*). Only those whose *I*, *me*, and *myself* have transformed into *thee*, *thou*, and *thine* can pass through the Path of Truth. It's the litmus test of whether anything in one's character might prevent their plunge into the Center. Most of all, it's a check to ensure the ego is entirely sublimated into humility. This is not a judgment of your inherent worthiness—you are and always were one with the Center—but rather a vital support to ensure you are ready for the voyage ahead into the immensity of the Central Region.

Here are some hints to give you an idea of the people who cross the

Path of Truth. People who are at this level no longer love. Their love is not a verb anymore. They *become* love. They are no longer humble; humility is their real nature. Their hearts are filled with childlike innocence.

Such people are like candles that gently illuminate everything around them and are consumed in the process. To you, their actions may seem like a sacrifice, but to them, it is just how they are. Such people have achieved what they needed to achieve in their lives. Their inner transformation is complete. Love is their only discipline. Like the sun that shines for one and all, like the flower that releases its fragrance for the breeze to carry, such individuals embody love. In the company of such people, we forget our worries and are lifted into a state of bliss. The Path of Truth is wide-open for such a heart, and the guru joyfully carries such a beautiful flower into the celestial golden fields.

> ### SELF-REFLECTION
> *Can you relate to the experience of settledness and surrender? How might you describe the situation in your spiritual journal?*
>
> *Can you imagine what it might feel like to be settled within to the extent that there is no conscious awareness of separation from others?*

PART 8

THE CENTRAL REGION

27.

Entry into the Central Region

So far in the yatra, every experience you've had led to gaining knowledge. When someone says, "I know how to drive a car," it means that person has experience driving it. Our experience accumulates to become knowledge. The experiences in the Heart and Mind Regions helped you gain knowledge of those regions. When you arrive at the Central Region, the ego is sublimated, so the notion of experiencing in the traditional sense disappears. When *you* and *thou* become one, there is only unity of being. In that sense, the experiencer and the experience have almost become one. Do you see the conundrum? Over time when one reaches this stage, the conundrum resolves itself in the depths of one's being.

The finest type of superconsciousness pervades the Central Region, but that is not our goal, either. Much in the way children play with dolls or a doctor's kit, a yogi plays with consciousness. What we have access to is only a symbol of what we hope to obtain. What we seek is the potentiality that is the cause for consciousness and then going beyond it toward ultimate Reality. By ultimate Reality, I refer to the original condition of nothingness. It is such a light state that even purity, simplicity, and peace seem dense and heavy in comparison. It is beyond the reach of senses and perception.

Our swim in the Central Region is the most expansive of all the regions.

To give you an idea of its immensity, Babuji has written that the first seer who entered the Central Region after creation is still swimming toward the Center and has made it halfway. In yogic literature, especially the Upanishads, there are a few mentions of the Center (referred to as *Bhūmā*). For example, the Chandogya Upanishad has this verse: "In which one sees nothing else, hears nothing else, understands nothing else, that is Bhūmā. But that in which one sees something else, hears something else, understand something else is finite. That which is Bhūmā (infinite) alone is immortal, and that which is finite is mortal."[28]

Upon entering the Central Region, the first thing that one experiences are the feelings of universal existence. As one proceeds, one swims through rings of splendor, seven of them. During the swim through these, one goes through various conditions. After all this, one reaches the ocean of infinity, from where the swim to the Center, the thirteenth chakra, begins.

Entering the Central Region

To enable entry into the Central Region, the guru must create the necessary momentum in one's consciousness. The guru gives special meditation sittings over two to three days to develop momentum in the abhyasi. During these sessions, the entire journey up to the twelfth chakra is repeated a couple of times. Every chakra undergoes all the four flowering stages in these two to three days. Repeating the journey through all the chakras is like swinging the sling a few times in the air to create momentum launching the rock. Such intense work rattles the state of contentment and enlivens the restlessness within to become one with the Center. When enough momentum has been created, one crosses the Path of Truth and arcing their way into the Central Region, and the final march begins.

There is an important aspect to observe about one's movement from one chakra to another. In the Heart Region, one moves from a lower chakra to a higher one, as though pushed from one chakra to another. When one enters the Mind Region, movement changes to

Entry into the Central Region

expansion. One doesn't get pushed; instead, the higher chakra pulls one up. For example, we don't move from the seventh chakra to the eighth chakra. The eighth chakra attracts you like a magnet, and in this way expansion continues. Noticing the pushes and pulls is helpful in deepening one's sensitivity.

Regarding the entry to the Central Region, there is a technicality that you may find interesting. When one is at the twelfth chakra, the entry into the Central Region is not a straight entry. The Path of Truth is like a curved window, and one is arced into it, like a soccer ball arcs when it's hit from the corner post and curves into the goal. And with this arc, one enters the Central Region and the final march begins.

※

If you think the Center is far out of reach and wonder if you need to know all this, you do. You belong there. It is the rightful place, and your real inheritance awaits you. We are passing through a special moment in time where Mother Nature has opened a window to offer us a quantum leap in this very life into the Center. The way is open, the method is available, the means are simple, and the field is prepared. What it takes is a heart that wants it all—and you are one of them, even if you don't realize it now. The impulse that drives you within will keep you moving forward. So, cast aside any skepticism you have about not making it. Persevere with enthusiasm, and you will not regret it.

28.

The Thirteenth Chakra: Nothingness

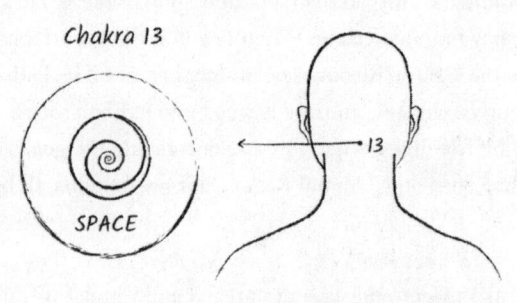

Chakra 13

Chakra in Central Region

Name	Thirteenth Chakra
Prominent Element	Space
Color	Gray
Location	Four finger-widths down from the twelfth chakra
Marquee Quality	Omnipresence, omniscience, omnipotence
Main Feelings	Oneness
Region	Center, *Bhooma*

Entering the Central Region marks the apex of the journey from matter to energy to Absolute. At the time of creation, absolute vibration from the Center gushed out and transformed into energy that further transformed into matter. When you reach the Central Region, your consciousness has evolved from the material level to subtler levels, reestablishing resonance with the Center.

The Thirteenth Chakra: Nothingness

By the time one arrives at this stage, every cell of the body has been purified. All complexities and emotional baggage have been purged from the system, and one is at the highest pitch of purity. Such a transformation results from the unwavering, diligent, devoted commitment to self-transformation.

Up to this point in the yatra, there had always been a polarity that had to be resolved. In the Heart Region, the play of polarity was with emotions: contentment-discontentment, calmness-disturbance, compassion-displeasure, courage-discouragement, and clarity-delusion. In the Mind Region, the polarity was distilled to the soul versus the Source, the lower and higher selves. When one enters the Central Region, the play of polarity ceases. This is the realm of nothingness.

Words fall woefully short of the experience of nothingness. Most descriptions of the Center are limited and use metaphors or negation-based language. However, the description I want to share is more like a travelogue, providing details on the weather and winds of the realm of nothingness. Babuji conducted extensive spiritual research on the Central Region. In this effort, he was guided mainly by Lalaji, and the hierarchy of elevated souls also supported Babuji. Using this body of research and my own experiences, I hope to offer a glimpse into this extraordinary realm.

I pray that someday, you will know it for yourself.

Stages of Ego and the Central Region

By the time you enter the Central Region, your humility and purity create a condition within you where you become like a newborn child, with total innocence. This sentiment is expressed in the Bible: "Truly I tell you, unless you change and become like little children, you will never enter the kingdom of heaven." Like the mother's love protects and cares for the child, in the same way you are now embraced by the Source. Such intimacy between the soul and the Source is because of

MEDITATE AND TRANSCEND

the dissolution of separateness. As the ego is sublimated, the sense of separateness dissolves. Understanding the stages in which the ego sublimates can help one assess where they are in their spiritual journey.

The idea of egoism originates from our identification with the physical body. When we attribute the body's actions to ourselves, our consciousness becomes fixated on the body. Thoughts such as *It's my hard work that made this project successful*, *My creativity produced this work*, and *I am the best at this task* are examples where we perceive the body to be the doer. This is the condition of ego for most people at the beginning.

As we enter into the Mind Region, our perspective shifts from identifying the body as the doer to recognizing something inward or finer. This marks the second stage of egoism. Depending on their beliefs, different people attribute this agency to various entities such as the soul, mind, God, guru, or some higher power. At this stage, the body is no longer considered the sole doer. One attributes their success to the guidance of elders and recognizes a higher power guiding them in their achievements. These feelings reflect the second stage of egoism, where the body's role as the doer is transcended.

As we advance, we reach the third stage of egoism. At this stage, we understand that the work is not being done through the agency of the body or something inward, as felt in the first and second stages. Now, we are on the right path. Neither the body nor the mind is the doer, and we do not feel any other agency doing the work. The work is done automatically, in whatever way it is meant to be. We no longer ponder over questions like: How? By whom? Or through what agency?

As we progress further, we enter the Region of the Absolute, near the tenth chakra. Here, we no longer even feel the work being done. We do not feel it before or after; we know only that it continues automatically as needs demand. Imagine you are sleeping, and a mosquito bites you. You feel an itching sensation, your hand moves to the affected area, and you scratch it, all while remaining asleep. You have no conscious awareness of feeling the itch, and you do not remember

The Thirteenth Chakra: Nothingness

anything about it when you wake up. This is the condition of automatic working, where you do everything circumstances demand, but the actions leave no impression on you. In other words, you carry no burden of doership. As this state matures, the ego is sublimated into identity. This is the fourth and final stage of egoism, and at this stage, you become eligible to enter the Central Region.

The thing I refer to as identity still exists, even in the Central Region. Think of it as the thinnest membrane that separates the soul from the Source. However, this membrane disappears when the Universe dissolves, and everything returns to the Center. During the final dissolution, all the identities of liberated souls merge into one, along with those of others. All individual identities are lost, and the newly formed identity brings forth creation again when the time comes.

Eternal Existence

In the Central Region, the aspirant experiences a profound sense of existence that permeates every aspect of their being. It's like their heart becomes a playground for the entire creation, and they feel the continuum of existence. This feeling arises because the aspirant's consciousness has evolved to such a state that they have transcended beyond consciousness to the potentiality that creates consciousness.

In this elevated state of being, the aspirant's consciousness becomes all-pervasive, and they feel the Universe pulsating to the rhythm of their heart. The experience of eternal existence becomes vividly real, and the aspirant realizes that existence is not just limited to their physical form, but it encompasses everything in the Universe.

This heightened state of existence continues with the realization that existence is eternal and is not bound by time or space. The aspirant becomes aware of the timelessness and infinite nature of existence, where everything is interconnected, and there is no separation between the self and the Universe. Such a high state is a rare achievement, but much more lies ahead.

The Seven Rings of Splendor

When you enter the Central Region, you experience something magnificent that Babuji called the Seven Rings of Splendor. These rings have countless towering waves of power that emanate from the Center, and their beauty is indescribable. To traverse this region, one must ride one wave after another, and it can be challenging for a novice surfer. However, if you are a champion surfer, you go with the flow and find a sweet spot of balance and harmony, feeling entirely weightless (devoid of ego). It is a similar experience to riding the perfect wave. Someone once told me of Laird Hamilton, the legendary surfer, who described riding the big one as being inside a giant cathedral of water, flying and feeling as if time stands still. In the rings of splendor, one rides one big one after another in the infinite ocean.

To ride these waves effortlessly, the secret lies in absolute and total humility. One feels more insignificant than even a speck of dust. This is where the phenomenon of invertendo comes into play. The humbler one is, the higher one rises and the easier it is to ride the waves. Crossing the rings of splendor marks a stage where the swim to the Center begins. This is the final state, the highest level one can achieve in the spiritual anatomy project.

The Final State:
Knowledgelessness and Non-Beingness

In the swim to the Center, the guru and the disciple resonate as one. The guru in front creates a slipstream for the disciple to swim effortlessly and follow. By this time, the state one is in can be described as one of *knowledgelessness*.

To understand this concept, it is crucial to grasp the idea of knowledge and ignorance. Knowledge is like a spotlight that illuminates a specific area while the surrounding areas remain in darkness. For instance, Copernicus's discoveries revealed that the Earth was not the

The Thirteenth Chakra: Nothingness

center of the solar system. This new knowledge removed ignorance. Every time we acquire knowledge, we recognize areas that we were previously ignorant about. Knowledge and ignorance coexist.

The polarity of knowledge and ignorance is resolved in the Central Region. At the final state, there is no "I" to experience, and as a result, there is no knowledge. Such an individual arrives at a condition that could be called *non-beingness*.

Let me explain. In our yatra, as we ascend toward the Absolute, we move from thinking, to feeling, becoming, being, and, lastly, non-being. We start with the mind and *think* of our connection with the Source. Over time thinking shifts to *feeling* the presence of the Source within our hearts and everywhere around us. As we continue to meditate, the feeling leads us on the path of *becoming* more and more in tune with the Source.

To put this in a more familiar context: Let's say you live with your friend for a few weeks. During your stay, you are touched by your friend's kind behavior, warm hospitality, and the joy and happiness his family shares. This inspires you to become like your friend and cultivate a lifestyle that can create such inner wealth. Like that, when we experience the Source within and without and feel the beautiful conditions blossom, we are inspired to change the temporary experience to a permanent one by becoming like the Source. Then a stage comes where the becoming transforms into permanently *being* in osmosis with the Source. While duly discharging all our duties and taking care of our responsibilities, we develop likeness with the Source—secure, poised, infinite, and unperturbed. When we have everything, then we need nothing.

How does this nothingness within express itself in one's behavior? It manifests as complete stillness and poise in one's behavior. When you meet someone in this highly elevated state, your heart will be moved by the absolute naturalness of their being. Even when they do the most mundane things, like passing the salad at the table or picking up a book to read, you can't escape the beauty of their poise and stillness.

MEDITATE AND TRANSCEND

I remember an experience many years ago when I was in Courmettes, France, for a preceptor workshop. Chariji was training a group of us preceptors from Europe and North America, specifically in reading the condition and developing sensitivity. One evening, when I had some time with Chariji, I shared some of my observations with him. Then he asked me a question I wasn't prepared for. He said, "Can you tell me who had the best condition among the people you have studied in this seminar?"

I shared with Chariji my observation about a Danish preceptor, whom I felt was seated in the lap of the Ultimate. Chariji smiled and asked why I thought so. I told him, "When I observe this lady, there is absolute naturalness in her being. Even when she holds her husband's hand, you would not find amorousness in it. There would be simple love flowing. The ease with which she slips into meditation, and the aura of stillness that envelops her even after meditation, there is exquisite subtlety. I notice her absorbency, and I can feel the nothingness that creates such a profound presence."

Chariji winked at me and said, "You are getting there." And then he said, "This is the state of Brahmagati." The word *Brahmagati* expresses the idea of absolute stillness of the original state. This absolute stillness also represents the infinite movement latent in the Center. When such a condition is created in a human being, it is called Brahmagati.*

Witnessing such a high state in someone who blissfully was carrying on with life and its demands is a good reminder that that goal is in reach for all of us. Our keen interest, willingness, and devotion make us worthy of the goal. Philosophy, with words like *nothingness*, *non-beingness*, and *knowledgelessness*, creates cognitive complexity. The concepts can become difficult to grasp, and one starts feeling that this high state may not be for them. When you get such thoughts, remind

---

* *Brahma* is derived from the word *bruha*, meaning "expansion," and *gati* means "state." This is the state of infinite expansion in the Ultimate.

The Thirteenth Chakra: Nothingness

yourself of this story where an everyday householder, with duties and responsibilities, and leading a content and happy life, was also sitting in the lap of infinity. Our focus on creating purity, simplicity, love, and authenticity guides us toward where we need to be. Keep your eyes on the goal and allow the heart to guide you toward the grand destiny.

> ### SPECIAL WILL
>
> There is one aspect of Brahmagati that I would like to explain further. Whoever is in this state, whatever they offer in an affirmation, it shall come to pass. This is called special will. Special will can even affect the workings of nature. This infallibility of will is, in fact, the real interpretation of the characteristic feature of Brahmagati.
>
> Special will admits no doubt or misgiving. The negative ideas are out of the realm of your imagination. Only that which is affirmed, which is "to be," remains in sight. Confidence grows so strong that nothing contrary can ever stand in the way. One does not try to dispel doubts; there is no doubt at all.
>
> Once, a father and son were skiing down the wintry slopes of a steep mountain. Looking down at a patch where fresh powder had fallen the previous night, the father said, "Son, watch out for the rocks and those trees with bent branches." The son, staring intently ahead, said, "What rocks and trees? I see only the trail." Such clarity and certainty are the quintessence of special will.
>
> The special will is used for spiritual work and to fulfill nature's orders. But that doesn't mean you cannot benefit from it. You can take inspiration from such a mindset and avoid harboring thoughts of failure or disappointment. Before starting any work, offer the affirmation that it's completed successfully, and then begin the task in remembrance of the divine.

The promise of human life is the opportunity to make the quantum jump from where we are now into the Center. Life on Earth as a human being is the opportunity to evolve willfully. Right up to the human level, evolution has been automatic. As a human being, you get the chance to make the jump into the Center. I pray that you adopt the highest as your real goal and practice like never before to evolve your consciousness and rightfully claim the spot that awaits you in the highest.

> **SELF-REFLECTION**
>
> *What plans might you put in place to help you evolve your consciousness?*
>
> *Can you imagine living a life in which everything flows without thought or analysis or worry or reaction, and everything that happens is perfect for the circumstance?*

Conclusion

In meditation, we close our eyes and open our hearts. The open heart receives the gift. Appreciating the gift is gratitude, and gratitude creates a condition in our hearts. When we allow the condition to carry us, we soar toward love. That love within creates reverence for the Absolute. As we grow in reverence, the heart attracts waves of grace. As we ride on the waves of grace, submission begins. Submission creates serenity, and in serenity begins surrender. The state of surrender leads us to merger.

Each meditation is a love story. It is the union of the soul with the higher self. It's the journey of the drop becoming one with the ocean.

Let yours be a journey with love overflowing in the heart. Love that drowns you because without drowning in love, there is no rising. With all my heart, I pray you bask in love and cherish oneness on this journey that begins and ends in the deepest recesses of your heart. The way can be narrow and dark. At times it can seem lonely and overwhelming. The ascent can be steep and slippery. But remember what you seek is within you. I know the way and I am here to help you and support you at every step. I hope you soar toward infinity and become one with it. The best gift you can give to the Universe is the gift of your transformed self.

GLOSSARY

Please note that alternative common spellings are given after some words, for example: **samadhi** or **samaadhi**. The phonetic spelling of each Sanskrit word is put in parentheses after the word, for example: **abhyas** or **abhyasa (abhyaas)**.

abhoodhiyat. The spiritual condition of insignificance.

abhyas or **abhyasa (abhyaas).** Practice.

abhyasi. Aspirant; one who practices yoga in order to achieve union with higher Self.

aghori babas. Devotees of Shiva manifested as Bhairava; monists who seek release from the cycle of reincarnation.

Aham Brahmasmi (aham brahmaasmi). I am Brahman/God.

ahuti. Offering. See *pranahuti*.

Ajna Chakra or **Agya Chakra (aajnaa chakra).** The chakra located between the eyebrows; the sixth chakra.

anahat ajapa. Natural vibration of the heart.

Anahata chakra. The heart chakra, first chakra.

Arjuna. Lord Krishna's devotee, and one of the Pandavas (five brothers) to whom Lord Krishna gave the Gita in the epic Mahabharata.

Aum. A sacred syllable; the primordial vibration of space that has been heard by saints and mystics throughout history.

avaran or **avarana**, or **aavaran** or **aavarana.** Layers of grossness; coverings.

Baba. Holy man; guru.

Babuji. Affectionate name for Shri Ram Chandra of Shahjahanpur, the second guru of the Sahaj Marg system, disciple of Lalaji and the founder-president of Shri Ram Chandra Mission, the raja-yoga system of Sahaj Marg.

Glossary

Bhagwad Gita or **Bhagavad Gita**. See *Gita*.

bhoga or **bhogam** or **bhog (bhogaa)**. The process of undergoing the effects of impressions; experience; enjoyment; suffering.

Bhūmā. The Center.

Brahm or **Brahman**. Center, God, Ultimate, higher self.

Brahma Randhra or **Brahmarandhra**. Brahman (higher self) + randhra (aperture). A point or opening near the twelfth chakra.

brahmagati. Divine state, state of Brahman.

Brahmand (brahmaanda) Mandal or **brahmanda desh**. Mental sphere, supramaterial sphere, cosmic region; sphere where everything manifests under a subtle shape before taking place in the material world.

chakra. Center of supervital forces located in different parts of the body; a wheel of energy that creates an energy field like a magnet.

Chariji. Affectionate name for Shri Parthasarathi Rajagopalachari, the third in the line of Masters in Heartfulness.

dheerata. Fortitude.

Gita (Geeta). The Bhagavad Gita, Song of God; divine knowledge given to Arjuna by Lord Krishna in the epic Mahabharata.

guru. One who transmits light, knowledge; a spiritual teacher; literally, one who dispels darkness; a guru dispels the darkness of ignorance through the light of knowledge.

Hanumaan (Hanumaan). Lord Rama's faithful servant in the epic Ramayana.

invertendo. Term coined by Babuji to describe the apparent inversions truth undergoes as it moves through higher levels of abstraction.

karma. Action.

koshas. Five energetic sheaths, or layers, that surround the soul.

Krishna. See *Lord Krishna*.

Lalaji. Affectionate name for Ram Chandra of Fatehgarh, the founder-president of Shri Ram Chandra Mission, the raja-yoga system of Sahaj Marg.

Glossary

layayastha. Merger; "laya" (dissolution) + "avastha" (state); the merging with various stages of consciousness as we move from one chakra to another. The final merger is with the Center.

Lord Krishna. Most recent incarnation of Vishnu; divine personality in the epic Mahabharata.

maha-kal-chakra (maha-kaal-chakra). The wheel of the Supreme.

Maha samadhi (mahaa samaadhi). The final samadhi when saints renounce their body and enter the brighter world.

Manipura. Navel chakra; mani (jewels) + pura (city); the dwelling place of jewels.

Mooladhar. Root chakra; provides the primary support for existence and perpetuates the most fundamental need for survival.

Nasadiya Sukta. Hymn of creation found in the *Rig Veda*, a collection of ancient hymns, the earliest of four Vedas, and one of the most sacred texts in Hinduism.

Para-Brahma. The first wave of creation, through which the currents of absolute vibration began to flow.

Parabrahmand Mandal. The Paracosmic Region.

Pind Pradesh (pinda pradesha) or **Pind Desh (pinda desha).** Material sphere; the Heart Region.

Prabhu. Region of the Absolute. The region covered by tenth, eleventh, and twelfth chakras.

prakriti. The creation.

prana (praana). Life; breath; spiritual energy; life force; souls.

pranahuti (praanaahuti). Process of yogic transmission; the offering of the life force into the aspirant's heart.

Pransya prana. The life of life. Early reference to Transmission found in the Nasadiya Sukta, the Vedic hymn of creation.

Prapanna. A spiritual stage at eighth chakra; also, one who has surrendered.

Prapanna-Prabhu. Spiritual condition experienced as being both the master and one who has surrendered. The condition at the ninth chakra.

Glossary

prapatti. State of loving dependence and a reverential and joyful acceptance of all that comes our way in life.

purusha. See *Para-Brahma*.

Radha (Raadhaa). Lord Krishna's spiritual companion and his beloved.

Raja Yoga. Ancient system or science followed by the great rishis (seers, saints) that helps gently guide the mind toward right thinking and temperance to realize the self or God. Usually used for meditative practices, as distinguished from hatha yoga (yoga of the body).

Sahaj Marg. Natural path, simple path.

Sahasra Dala, Sahasradala, Sahasra Dal Kamal (Sahasra Dala Kamala). Also called SDK, crown chakra, lotus of a thousand petals.

Sayujyata. Merger and beyond. Fourth stage of the flowering of a chakra.

Salokyata. Coexisting in the same world. First stage of the flowering of a chakra.

samadhi or **samaadhi.** Original balance; state in which we stay attached to reality. In Sahaj Marg, the return to the original condition, which reigned in the beginning. The eighth limb of Patanjali's yoga.

Sameepyata. Nearness. The second stage of the flowering of a chakra.

samskaras (samskaaraas). Impressions.

Saranagati. See *prapatti*.

Saraswati. Goddess of knowledge; knowledge point at the eighth chakra.

Saroopyata. Identicality. The third stage of the flowering of a chakra.

Sat-chit-ananda or **Satchidananda (satchidanaanda).** Existence-consciousness-bliss.

satpad or **satyapad.** In Sahaj Marg, the sphere where truth is predominant, a region of light though in a very fine state.

sitting. A session of meditation, usually lasting from twenty minutes to an hour, in which the guru or a Heartfulness trainer meditates with a group or an individual for the purpose of cleaning and transmission.

spiritual anatomy. The subtle energetic system of the human being.

Glossary

subtle bodies. Layers of the human energy field. The four main subtle bodies are Chit (consciousness), Manas (mind), Buddhi (intellect), and Ahankar (ego).

superconsciousness. Higher states of consciousness that are beyond the sensory perception.

Swadhisthana. Swa (self) + adhisthana (dwelling place): dwelling place of the lower self, or sacral chakra.

Trikuti. The point above the nose between the two eyebrows; one of the points of concentration.

Uparati. State of self-withdrawal. Vairagya matures into Uparati.

Vairagya. State of loving detachment. Renunciation.

vikshep or **vikshepa.** Subtle distortions, distraction, mental wandering.

Vishnu. The preserver; one of the Hindu Trinity, the others being Brahma and Shiva.

yatra. A sacred journey to the center within.

yoga. A system of philosophy and practice for uniting the lower self with the higher Self, or God.

HEARTFULNESS RESOURCES

I, and everyone at the Heartfulness Institute, would be honored to support you in your journey to elevated consciousness. Whether you're just learning to meditate or you're a seeker looking to deepen your practice, I hope these resources will be useful to you.

Visit us on our website at https://heartfulness.org.

Visit the book website at https://spiritualanatomy.com.

Download our app: https://www.heartfulnessapp.org.

Follow with us on social: @heartfulness on Facebook, Instagram, and Twitter.

Connect with a trainer or find a Heartfulness Center near you at https://heartfulness.my/heartspots.

NOTES

Chapter 1. Your Inner Journey: The Key to Real Transformation
1. Ganganatha Jha Patanjali and S. Subrahmanya Sastri, *The Yoga-Darshana: Comprising the Sutras of Patanjali with the Bhasya of Vyasa* (Singapore: Asian Humanities Press, 2004), 1.1; *Vyasa*, Yoga Bhashya (1:1).
2. Karen V. Smit and Steven B. Shirey, "Kimberlites: Earth's Diamond Delivery System," *Gems & Gemology* 55, no. 2 (Summer 2019), GIA, https://www.gia.edu/gems-gemology/summer-2019-kimberlites-earths-diamond-delivery-system.
3. Lisa Miller, PhD, *The Awakened Brain: The New Science of Spirituality and Our Quest for an Inspired Life* (New York: Random House, 2021), 8.

Chapter 2. Your True Potential
4. Thomas Gilovich and Victoria Husted Medvec, "The Temporal Pattern to the Experience of Regret," *Journal of Personality and Social Psychology* 67, no. 3 (September 1994): 357–365, https://psycnet.apa.org/buy/1995-05382-001; S. Davidi and T. Gilovich, "The Ideal Road Not Taken: The Self-Discrepancies Involved in People's Most Enduring Regrets," *Emotion* 18, no. 3 (2018): 439–452, https://doi.org/10.1037/emo0000326.
5. Susan Kelley, "Woulda, coulda, shoulda: the haunting regret of failing our ideal selves," *Cornell Chronical*, May 24, 2018, https://news.cornell.edu/stories/2018/05/woulda-coulda-shoulda-haunting-regret-failing-our-ideal-selves.

Chapter 3. The Story of the Soul
6. Sophie Putka, "This Cyclic Model of the Universe Has Cosmologists Rethinking the Big Bang," *Discover*, July 29, 2021, https://www.discovermagazine.com/the-sciences/this-cyclic-model-of-the-universe-has-cosmologists-rethinking-the-big-bang.

Chapter 4. Mapping the Journey to the Center
7. Eckhart Tolle, *A New Earth: Awakening to Your Life's Purpose* (New York: Dutton, 2005), 41.
8. Anurag Shrivastava, Bikesh K. Singh, Dwivedi Krishna, et al., "Effect of Heartfulness Meditation Among Long-Term, Short-Term and Non-meditators on Prefrontal Cortex Activity of Brain Using Machine Learning Classification: A Cross-Sectional Study," *Cureus* 15, no. 2 (February 14, 2023): e34977, doi:10.7759/cureus.34977.

Notes

9. Jayaram Thimmapuram, Robert Pargament, Kedesha Sibliss, et al., "Effect of Heartfulness Meditation on Burnout, Emotional Wellness, and Telomere Length in Health Care Professionals," *Journal of Community Hospital Internal Medicine Perspectives* 7, no. 1 (2017): 21–27, doi:10.1080/20009666.2016.1270806.
10. Kunai Desai, Pratibha Gupta, Priti Parikh, et al., "Impact of Virtual Heartfulness Meditation Program on Stress, Quality of Sleep, and Psychological Wellbeing During the COVID-19 Pandemic: A Mixed-Method Study," *International Journal of Environmental Research and Public Health* 18, no. 21 (October 22, 2021): 11114, doi:10.3390/ijerph182111114.
11. Bhuvnesh Sankar Sylapan, Ajay Kumar Nair, Krishnamurthy Jayanna, et al., "Meditation, Well-Being and Cognition in Heartfulness Meditators—A Pilot Study," *Consciousness and Cognition* 86 (November 2020): 103032, doi:10.1016/j.concog.2020.103032.

Chapter 9. The Elephant and the Chair: Conditioning that Binds Us

12. A. H. Hastorf and H. Cantril, "They Saw a Game; A Case Study," *Journal of Abnormal and Social Psychology* 49 no. 1 (1954): 129–134, https://doi.org/10.1037/h0057880.

Chapter 10. Five Chakras of the Heart Region: The Realm of Opposites

13. Juliana Ukiomogbe, "Where Are Emotions Felt in the Body? This Infographic Will Tell You," infographic, Greatist, September 9, 2020, https://greatist.com/connect/emotional-body-maps-infographic#infographic.
14. Bhagavad Gita, Chapter 2, 2:62–2:63.

Chapter 15. The Third Chakra: Love

15. Luke 23:34 (New International Version).

Chapter 16. The Fourth Chakra: Courage

16. Patel, Kamlesh D., "Confidence, Courage and Self-Awareness" in *The Wisdom Bridge* (p. 194), 2022.

Chapter 18. Freedom from Freedom: The Gift of the Heart

17. Gabriel A. Radvansky, Sabine A. Krawietz, and Andrea K. Tamplin, "Walking Through Doorways Causes Forgetting: Further Explorations," *Quarterly Journal of Experimental Psychology* 64, no. 8 (August 2011): 1632–1645, https://doi.org/10.1080/17470218.2011.571267.
18. Melissa Hughes, "3 Ways Kindness Changes the Brain," Melissa Hughes (website), updated January 8, 2022, https://www.melissahughes.rocks/post/3-ways-kindness-changes-the-brain.

Notes

19. Nigel Mathers, "Compassion and the Science of Kindness: Harvard Davis Lecture 2015," *British Journal of General Practice* 66, no. 648 (July 2016): e525–e527, https://doi.org/10.3399/bjgp16X686041.

Chapter 19. The Mind Region: A Journey to Humility

20. Patel, Kamlesh D., "Confidence, Courage and Self-Awareness" in *The Wisdom Bridge* (p. 191), 2022.

Chapter 20. The Sixth Chakra: Selflessness

21. Matthew 5:8 (NIV).
22. *The Sutta-Nipata: A New Translation from the Pali Canon*, translated by H. Saddhatissa (Oxfordshire, UK: RoutledgeCurzon, 1995), I, 8.

Chapter 22. The Eighth Chakra: Surrender

23. Hellmuth Hecker, "Angulimala: A Murderer's Road to Sainthood," story adaptation, Access to Insight, Barre Center for Buddhist Studies, 2007, https://www.accesstoinsight.org/lib/authors/hecker/wheel312.html.
24. Dacher Keltner and Jonathan Haidt, "Approaching Awe, a Moral, Spiritual, and Aesthetic Emotion," *Cognition and Emotion*, 17 no. 2 (2003): 297–314, https://doi.org/10.1080/02699930302297.

Chapter 23. The Ninth Chakra: Insignificance

25. Dr. Joel Hoomans, "35,000 Decisions: The Great Choices of Strategic Leaders," *The Leading Edge* (blog), Roberts Wesleyan College, March 20, 2015, https://go.roberts.edu/leadingedge/the-great-choices-of-strategic-leaders.

Chapter 25. The Eleventh Chakra: Restlessness

26. Richard S. Westfall, *Never at Rest: A Biography of Isaac Newton* (Cambridge, UK: Cambridge University Press, 1983), chap. 4.
27. Scalora, Suza & Anderson, Micheline & Crete, Abigail & Mistur, Elisabeth & Chapman, Amy & Miller, Lisa. (2022). A Campus-Based Spiritual-Mind-Body Prevention Intervention Against Symptoms of Depression and Trauma; An Open Trial of Awakened Awareness. Mental Health & Prevention. 25. 200229. 10.1016/j.mhp.2022.200229.

Chapter 27. Entry into the Central Region

28. Chandogya Upanishad 7:24:1.

ABOUT THE AUTHOR

DAAJI, also known as KAMLESH D. PATEL, is the fourth and current spiritual guide of the global Heartfulness movement. He has spent the past four decades training people across the globe in Heartfulness meditation. He is the author of numerous books, including the bestselling books, *The Heartfulness Way*, *Designing Destiny* and *The Wisdom Bridge*. He gives keynote addresses at conferences and conducts workshops around the world.

His passion lies in grassroots efforts, especially in taking meditation to the villages of India. Daaji enjoys going on nature walks with his grandchildren in Kanha Shanti Vanam, India, where he lives with his family.

Learn more at www.heartfulness.org.

ABOUT HEARTFULNESS

Heartfulness offers a simple set of meditative practices and lifestyle changes, first developed at the turn of the twentieth century and formalized into teaching through the Shri Ram Chandra Mission in 1945. These practices are a modern form of Yoga designed to promote contentment, inner calm, compassion, courage, and clarity of thought. The Heartfulness practices are fit for people over the age of fifteen from all walks of life, cultures, religious beliefs, and economic situations. More than 5,000 Heartfulness Centers are supported by many thousands of certified volunteer trainers and practitioners in 160 countries. Learn more at www.heartfulness.org.

HarperCollins *Publishers* India

At HarperCollins India, we believe in telling the best stories and finding the widest readership for our books in every format possible. We started publishing in 1992; a great deal has changed since then, but what has remained constant is the passion with which our authors write their books, the love with which readers receive them, and the sheer joy and excitement that we as publishers feel in being a part of the publishing process.

Over the years, we've had the pleasure of publishing some of the finest writing from the subcontinent and around the world, including several award-winning titles and some of the biggest bestsellers in India's publishing history. But nothing has meant more to us than the fact that millions of people have read the books we published, and that somewhere, a book of ours might have made a difference.

As we look to the future, we go back to that one word—a word which has been a driving force for us all these years.

Read.